THE CIVIL WAR DIARY OF
CHARLES A. LEUSCHNER

Charles A. Leuschner, circa 1868.
— Courtesy of Robert Bianchi

THE CIVIL WAR DIARY OF
CHARLES A. LEUSCHNER

Edited by

Charles D. Spurlin

EAKIN PRESS ✚ Fort Worth, Texas
www.EakinPress.com

Copyright © 2000
By Charles D. Spurgeon
Published By Eakin Press
An Imprint of Wild Horse Media Group
P.O. Box 331779
Fort Worth, Texas 76163
1-817-344-7036
www.EakinPress.com
ALL RIGHTS RESERVED
1 2 3 4 5 6 7 8 9
ISBN-10: 1-57168-415-8
ISBN-13: 978-1-57168-415-8

For EarlDeane Tally Holzheuser

Contents

Preface

Three Victoria, Texas, heritage organizations (the Daughters of the American Revolution, the Daughters of the Republic of Texas, and the United Daughters of the Confederacy) utilize appropriately decorated rooms in the Edward Power House, a Texas Landmark, for business meetings. The Confederate room, maintained by the William P. Rogers Chapter of the United Daughters of the Confederacy, has walls adorned with portraits of Robert E. Lee and Stonewall Jackson which peer at the Stars and Bars that stand reverently amidst period furniture the members have lovingly placed to accommodate members and guests. An adjoining storage closet is filled with club records and Confederate memorabilia.

During the summer of 1987, Belva Zirjacks, former president of the local UDC chapter, was rearranging the closet when she came across a small ledger. Curious as to what was in the book, she began to flip through the pages and found that it contained hand-written recipes, poems, and numerous passages written in German. Intrigued by what she saw, Belva began a more detailed analysis of the volume and discovered that it was produced by Charles August Leuschner and within the worn, brown pages was Leuschner's personal day-by-day account of the Atlanta Campaign, the Battle of Franklin, his capture and imprisonment at Camp Douglas, Illinois, and his eventual release and return to Victoria. She attempted, without success, to determine how long the book had been in the closet, who donated it to the chapter, and its age. Belva concluded, and I concur, that the Civil War entry was probably written from notes Leuschner kept during the time the events occurred. The condition of the ledger does not lend itself to having been carried through the hardships the troops encountered in 1864 and 1865. Furthermore, his account is punctuated with personal reflections, such as his comments about William T. Sherman's destruction of Atlanta, that could have only been made after the fact. In the broad spectrum of Civil War historiography, however, it matters little when the journal was produced. What is important is that it exists and, thus, contributes to the body of knowledge on one of the most important episodes in American history.

Charles August Leuschner was born on December 15, 1845, in Torgau, Prussia, to Gottlieb August and Emelie (Heller) Leuschner. He arrived on October 15, 1855, in Galveston, via New Orleans, with his parents and younger brother, August Frederick, after sailing from Hamburg aboard the *Herschel*. The family settled in Victoria where his father worked as a carpenter until his death in 1857. Prior to Leuschner's sixteenth birthday, he enlisted into Company B, Sixth Texas Infantry Regiment. Leuschner participated in every major engagement, except the debacle at Nashville, that the regiment fought. He was at the fall of Arkansas Post, the Confederate triumph at Chickamauga, the heroic stand at Tunnel Hill (Missionary Ridge), the Atlanta Campaign, and at the beginning of the victorious, but tragic, conquest of Franklin. Leuschner's tour included imprisonment in Illinois at Camp Butler and Camp Douglas. Leuschner was considered by his fellow soldiers as one of the bravest, if not the bravest, of the brave. Because he was so well-respected, Leuschner was touted to become a lieutenant, but he rejected the overture on the ground that as a nineteen-year-old he was not ready to become an officer. Leuschner did not have similar misgivings about being elected a sergeant in the company. After the Civil War, he worked as a barber and dabbled in local politics. Leuschner organized a Victoria County German-American Democratic club which was successful in helping to elect selected political candidates. In 1882, he was chosen, perhaps with the support of the political organization he created, to be the county treasurer, a post Leuschner held for over twenty-nine years. He was married twice. On November 8, 1870, Leuschner married a resident of the Inez community, Sophie Elizabeth Bischoff. Eleven children were produced from this union. After his first wife died, on July 12, 1905, he remarried three years later to Sophie Koehler Schorlemmer, a widow who resided in Arneckeville, Texas. There were no children from the second marriage.

Leuschner's reputation among those who knew him was that of a gentleman above reproach. He was described as generous, frank, friendly, sincere, and a man without an enemy. Victor Rose, a noted nineteenth century Texas author, thought enough of Leuschner that he dedicated a poem to him. Leuschner died on January 20, 1912. There was a huge turnout for his funeral. The procession which began at the family residence on Liberty Street extended to over a mile in length and required almost an hour to pass any given point. August Wagner's Silver Cornet Band played funeral dirges as it led the cortege. Included in the procession were two hundred members of the Sons of Hermann and most of the confederate veterans who belonged to Camp William A. Scurry. His body was laid to rest in Victoria's Evergreen Cemetery.

There are many people I am indebted to in bringing this work to fruition. Without Belva Zirjacks' decision to clean and rearrange the storage closet, Leuschner's ledger might have remained unnoticed and, therefore, deprived me of an opportunity to edit it. Joe Pratt, Jr., appeared at a timely manner with the Alexander Hamilton Phillips, Jr., correspondence which provided me valuable information on Arkansas Post. Mary Lee Archer's critique of the initial draft of Leuschner's journal made a rewrite easier. David Bianchi, a descendant of Leuschner, and his wife, Ann, were helpful in providing photographs of Leuschner as well as little known facts on the Leuschner family. Another descendant, Robert Bianchi, was equally generous in sharing with me photographs and other pertinent family items. Much is owed to Patty Navaira for her photographic and cartographic contributions. Special thanks go to Kathy Yaklin and Sandy Summers, two superb secretaries, for enduring the many adversities associated with creating a printed manuscript from handwritten notes. They remained steadfastly good-humored and patient throughout the writing process. Lela Welder Cliburn was an invaluable research source for data on local individuals associated with the Sixth Texas. Finally, there were two individuals who were absolutely indispensable in the completion of the work — EarlDeane Holzheuser and my wife, Pat. Without encouragement from EarlDeane, the enterprise may never have materialized. Pat's assistance was vital in helping to compile the rosters and making research forays with me. During our out of town fact-finding trips, I could always count on her uncovering a valuable tidbit of information that I overlooked.

CHARLES D. SPURLIN
The Victoria College

Prologue

After the fall of Fort Sumter in April 1861, United States President Abraham Lincoln issued a call for volunteers to shoulder arms and save the Union from the secessionists. The Confederate States of America government reacted by beefing up its own military establishment with enlistees from the individual Confederate states. Accordingly, Inspector General Samuel Cooper on June 12, 1861, informed Brigadier General Earl Van Dorn, commander of the Department of Texas, to raise twenty Texas infantry companies. The volunteers were to report to a site selected by the state chief executive and mustered into the service for the duration of the war, "unless sooner discharged." Van Dorn was also told that the men of each company were to elect their own officers, but President Jefferson Davis would appoint the field and staff officers. The respective companies were to consist of a captain, a first lieutenant, two second lieutenants, four sergeants, four corporals, two musicians, and not more than one hundred nor less than sixty-four privates.[1]

A short time later, on June 30, 1861, Confederate Secretary of War Leroy P. Walker instructed Governor Edward Clark of Texas to establish "two camps of instructions at accessible points" where the men could be mustered into service, drilled, and disciplined. The camps were to be under the auspices of the War Department.[2]

In pursuance of Walker's order and at the suggestion of Colonel Henry E. McCulloch, interim commander of the Department of Texas after Van Dorn was reassigned to command the First Division of the Army of the Potomac, Clark chose Victoria as the location of one of the camps and selected Millican as the site for the second military installation.[3]

Meanwhile, Major Alexander M. Haskell and Lieutenant J. H. Dinkins were ordered to Victoria to establish a "depot, muster in and

1

supply the troops, and command them." Haskell, in September 1861, selected Nuner's Mott, four miles north of Victoria as the location of the new camp of instruction. Nuner's Mott, sprinkled with large, lovely live oak trees which afforded the soldiers some relief from the scorching Texas sun, was an ideal site. In honor of the interim commander of the Department of Texas, the military installation was named Camp Henry E. McCulloch. Although Haskell was pleased with Camp McCulloch's location, some of the recruits did not concur. Complaints were expressed that the location was insect infested and unhealthy. Robert R. Gilbert of the Sixth Texas Infantry's Company B in a letter to a Houston newspaper wrote that "the position of the camp is a central one, as you can start from it and go to any part of the world with a furlough." In order to provide adequate medical care for the trainees, the Victoria Male Academy was rented by Haskell from the Corporation of Victoria for fifty dollars a month and served as a hospital facility.[4]

The first of the ten requested companies to arrive at Camp McCulloch and sworn into Confederate service was from Calhoun County. Proudly referring to themselves as the Lavaca Guards, the Calhoun volunteers were under the command of Alexander Hamilton Phillips, Jr., a Port Lavaca lawyer and the son of a prominent Victoria attorney. The unit was mustered into the Confederate army by Haskell on September 27, 1861, and was designated Company A.[5]

Three days later, on September 30, 1861, James A. Rupley's Lone Star Rifles from Victoria County joined the Confederate army and was designated Company B. Rupley was a native Pennsylvanian who settled in Victoria after serving in the Mexican War. Perhaps it was because of his previous military experience that Rupley was elected captain by the Victorians.[6]

The third group to arrive at Camp McCulloch was from Gonzales County and was under the command of Alonzo T. Bass, a former district surveyor and deputy sheriff. The Gonzales men took their Confederate oath on October 3, 1861, and were designated Company C.[7]

Traveling by boat from Matagorda County to Port Lavaca, thence to Victoria by train, Dr. E. A. Peareson's Matagorda Coast Guards were mustered into the service on October 4, 1861, and became Company D.[8]

Almost a month lapsed before the next contingent of men arrived at the camp. Led by John Preston White, a native Virginian and Seguin lawyer who would become an original member of the Texas Court of Appeals, recruits from Guadalupe County reached Victoria and were mustered on October 30, 1861, as Company E.[9]

Company F entered the Confederate army on November 3, 1861. The complement of men were primarily from Bell County and under the charge of Henry E. Bradford, a lawyer and post-Civil War mayor of Victoria and city attorney before he and his wife, Elizabeth Craig, moved to Belton in the early 1880s.[10]

Eleven days after the Bell County volunteers were mustered, the Travis Rifles from Travis County commanded by Rhoads Fisher, the son of Samuel Rhoads Fisher, former secretary of the Texas Navy and a signer of the Texas Declaration of Independence, assembled at Camp McCulloch and enlisted as Company G.[11]

While the first seven companies were being organized in their local communities and preparing to rendezvous at Victoria, Robert R. Garland was appointed by the Confederate government to take command of the newly created Sixth Texas Infantry Regiment which the companies at Camp McCulloch would comprise. Garland was a native of Virginia who entered the regular army on December 30, 1847, as a second lieutenant in the Seventh Infantry Regiment. By the time Virginia seceded in 1861, he had risen to the rank of captain and was stationed at Fort Fillmore, New Mexico. Because Garland's loyalty was greater to Virginia than the Union, he forfeited his commission and entered the Confederate army with his regular army rank. Garland was assigned to duty as Inspector General in the Department of Texas and mustering officer for the cavalry regiments of B. Warren Stone and Middleton T. Johnson. With over thirteen years experience as an infantry officer, he was from the viewpoint of the Confederate officials an ideal person to command one of the new Texas infantry regiments authorized by the War Department. Garland was confirmed Colonel on December 12, 1861 to rank from September 3, 1861.[12]

In addition to Garland, the regiment's original staff and field officers included Lieutenant Colonel Thomas Scott Anderson, an Austin attorney who was a former Texas secretary of state and a delegate to the Secession Convention; Major Haskell; Adjutant Samuel J. Garland, the colonel's nephew; and Quartermaster Udolpho Wolfe. Haskell's tenure as major in the regiment was brief. In December 1861, he was transferred to Van Dorn's command, and A. H. Phillips, Jr., was elevated to his position. Phillips' promotion provoked a controversy in the regiment. His opponents drew up a petition requesting that the promotion be denied on the ground that the captain's military ability was questionable, a point that was contested in a counter petition. Phillips eventually replaced Haskell as major and proved his detractors wrong. During the Battle of Arkansas Post, he performed gallantly despite suffering from diarrhea. [13]

Volunteerism tapered off sharply in Texas toward the end of 1861, causing the required military quotas to go unfulfilled. For example, the Sixth Texas was three companies shy of being at full strength. This shortage of men prompted Governor Francis R. Lubbock to make an impassioned plea to the people of Texas in February 1862 to do their duty and enlist. Lubbock in an eloquent style appealed to "those all over the broad land who believe in the inherent right of self-government . . . to do battle in this war for that great principle." The enemy "who comes with lust in his eye, poverty in his purse, and hell in his heart; who comes a robber and murderer must be stopped," the governor stated, or the result would be subjugation of "our beautiful and sunny South, and our men, women, and children be reduced to the most abject serfdom." Because of the military necessities, Lubbock threatened to draft men if there were not enough volunteers to meet the quotas. He specifically mentioned that the Sixth Texas was deficient of three companies. [14]

Lubbock's exhortation paid dividends for Garland. A sufficient number of volunteers from Calhoun, Lavaca, and Victoria answered the call to form Company H on March 27, 1862. George P. Finley was elected company commander. Samuel H. McAllister, after an unsuccessful attempt to create a company from convicts, put together a Bexar County unit which entered the service as Company K on March 31, 1862. DeWitt County also responded with a company under the command of C. P. Naunheim. The DeWitt County enlistees were mustered at Camp McCulloch on April 11, 1862, as Company I. [15]

When the volunteers entered Confederate service at Victoria, they were variously dressed. Some of the men were wearing homespun clothes, others fancy "store bought" suits, and at least two of the companies were in military attire made by the ladies in their home communities. When the Lavaca Guards reported, the men wore linen jeans with a narrow red stripe, blue flannel frock coats trimmed with red braid, and blue caps with patent leather visors and silver "LG" letters sewed on the front of the crown. The officers were distinguished from the enlisted men by their silver stitched rank. Rivaling the Calhoun County volunteers as the best dressed military organization to assemble at Camp McCulloch was the Travis Rifles who were clad in salt-and-

4

pepper gray uniforms, trimmed in green. Their attire was the handiwork of a group of ladies from the state capital known as the Needle Battalion who were determined that their defenders of liberty were properly dressed. Eventually, despite the claim of William Dunbar of Company D that he was never issued a Confederate uniform during his entire tour of duty, the regiment was homogeneously outfitted with "butternut," light brown, garments made of cloth produced at the State Penitentiary at Huntsville.[16]

Upon arrival at Camp McCulloch, the volunteers were as multiformity armed as they were dressed. Individuals brought with them their personal or family firearms — shotguns, muskets, rifles — in varying degrees of performance capabilities and structural conditions. There was, however, an element of consistency in a few of the companies. The men of Company A were armed primarily with percussion muskets. The Victorians in Company B possessed, for the most part, Minnie Rifles that were purchased at Brownsville by the county and loaned to the Lone Star Rifles after Rupley was bonded and the local soldiers acknowledged that they would keep the weapons in "good order and well taken care of." Before the company left Camp McCulloch in May 1862, the captain was released from his bond when the Confederate government purchased the rifles from the county. Matagorda County Commissioners Court loaned $1,000 to Dr. Peareson to purchase supplies and arms. What type of weapons were bought is not known. Also what is not known is what weapons, if any, that White obtained with part of the $1,000 appropriated by the Guadalupe County Commissioners Court to outfit and to pay transportation expenses to Victoria for the men. The Travis Guards were armed with muskets that were converted from flintlock to percussion by an Austin gunsmith. Prior to leaving Camp McCulloch, the obsolete weapons in Company G were replaced with new Springfield percussion muskets, new belts, and cartridge boxes. Sometime before the engagement at Arkansas Post, the Confederate government provided Enfield rifles to other companies, making Garland's regiment one of the best, if not the best, armed in Arkansas.[17]

Although the Sixth Texas may have been "excellently armed," the lack of funds from the Confederate government caused it to be ill-clad. Soldiers in the regiment complained in letters they wrote home of men being barefoot and the shortage of shirts, pants, and socks on the march to Arkansas. Men who could afford to do so, paid for clothing items from leeching civilians who took financial advantage of the soldiers. In Arkansas, cotton socks were sold for a dollar a pair and home-spun shirts brought from eight to ten dollars a piece. To remedy, or at least to lessen, the clothing hardship, Lieutenant Robert B. Harvey of Company H was placed on detached service to return to Texas and obtain clothes, blankets, and other comforts. Apparently Harvey's efforts were fruitful. Lieutenant Sebron Sneed of Company G wrote his wife that clothing for the company had arrived, and he "never saw a more substantial lot of clothing, quite the kind that is wanted in camp."[18]

Whenever a company became an integral component of the Confederate service at Camp McCulloch, it began a military regimen that involved turning the raw recruits' romantic visions of war to a realistic view of army life. Each company was assigned a specific location at the camp. After the men cleared the area and erected tents, they commenced their martial education in earnest. In the mornings, the men devoted their time to company drill, and in the afternoons, they participated in battalion drill. Garland was a capable garrison commander. He was characterized by William J. Oliphant of Company G as "a perfect martinet and a very fine drill officer." Oliphant further stated that the colonel "kept us hard at work drilling until he converted the regiment into a regular machine which would move on the drill ground with clock-like precision."[19]

Training was briefly interrupted in December 1861 for Companies A, B, D, and G when they were ordered to Matagorda Island. Captain Daniel D. Shea, commanding officer at Saluria, reported a federal vessel in Pass Cavallo. Since his force largely consisted of an artillery battery, and he was concerned that the Yankees would overwhelm his position, Shea sought assistance. Garland was dispatched to Matagorda Island to survey the situation and take appropriate action. After reaching Shea's headquarters and evaluating the Confederate defenses, the colonel instructed Lieutenant Colonel Anderson to take charge of the four companies and proceed to Indianola. Each soldier was to take two days rations, a blanket, and forty bullets. The command left Victoria by rail at 11:00 A.M. after a delay of several hours waiting for railroad cars and reached Port Lavaca at 1:00 P.M. where the men were boarded on a small schooner, the *Corpus Christi,* for Indianola. Due to a strong headwind, the ship's progress was extremely slow. The detachment arrived at Indianola at midnight. Meantime, eighteen men of Captain Edward Beaumont's cavalry company, which was also stationed at Camp McCulloch, reported to Shea. While the other companies remained at Indianola, Garland sent Rupley's Victorians to Saluria "to guard the ferry across the main bayou and to afford any other assistance" necessary. Garland did not send a larger force to Saluria because of the difficulty of acquiring forage and water. Furthermore, the colonel did not think there would be a federal attack. However, should one occur, the reserves at Indianola "were to be notified by signals posted every two miles" between Saluria and Indianola. [20]

The soldiers enjoyed a nine day stay at Indianola while awaiting an enemy assault that never materialized. The climate was more to their liking than Camp McCulloch, and seafood was bountiful. The men literally gorged themselves on fish and oysters during their coastal encampment. [21]

Concern of a federal movement against Shea's position would remain for the entire period of time that the regiment was stationed at Camp McCulloch. On February 6, 1862, Companies A and D under the command of Major A. H. Phillips were sent to Fort Esperanza, near Saluria. The reinforcements reached the fort on February 7 and returned to Camp McCulloch after a few days when the perceived danger passed. [22]

In March 1862, Garland was ordered to break camp and join Van Dorn's Army of the West as soon as his regiment reached the full complement of companies and transportation was available. By the middle of May, the regiment was ready to move eastward. On May 22, the men formed into marching formation and bade farewell to Camp McCulloch. After leaving Victoria, the regiment passed through Hallettsville and reached Eagle Lake by May 30 where the soldiers remained for a week, resting and waiting for further orders. During the march, at a pace of about ten miles a day, the regimental musicians performed as the troops passed through the towns. From Eagle Lake the command, except for the supply wagons and accompanying personnel, traveled by railway through Richmond and Houston until it arrived at Navasota. [23]

During the encampment at Navasota, a member of the regiment stole a revolver that belonged to Captain C. F. Naunheim, commanding officer of Company I. The man was caught when he attempted to sell the pistol on the same day that it was taken. The soldier was tried, convicted, and drummed out of the service, with his head half-shaved and astride a fence rail carried by blacks, as his former comrades lined the street and watched. [24]

After three days at Navasota, the Sixth Texas proceeded to Tyler by way of Rusk. The regiment remained five to seven days at Tyler before resuming its trek to Arkansas. By mid-July, the command crossed the Red River at Texarkana and marched into Arkansas. It passed through Washington, Antwine, Rockport, present-day Malvern, where an outbreak of measles incapacitated many of the soldiers, and Benton before reaching Camp Holmes, ten miles from Pine Bluff. The regiment stayed at Camp Holmes several weeks waiting for the men left at Rockport with the measles. While at Camp Holmes, the Sixth Texas was joined by the Twenty-fourth and the Twenty-fifth Texas Cavalry (dismounted) Regiments.[25]

By the time the Sixth Texas crossed into Arkansas, its regimental flag arrived from Victoria. The standard was produced by Mrs. Richard Owens and her daughters. Garland had originally asked a Victoria ladies association to make the ensign, but because of a shortage of materials, the women were unable to honor the request. Mrs. Owens whose husband operated a local mercantile store assumed the responsibility. She procured the necessary supplies and produced a banner made of red merino, bordered with a white silk fringe. Located in the center was a 28 by 36 inch blue shield which contained twelve silk or satin white stars that circled, six on each side, a large star that represented the state of Texas. Stitched in white silk was "Sixth Texas Infantry Regiment."[26]

East Texas and Arkansas offered unfamiliar terrain to the western Texans. Captain William W. Phillips of Company A noted the absence of flatland when he remarked that "in the last 200 miles we have had about 10 miles of prairie . . . I like the people much better than I do the country, the latter is too broken and sandy, and not enough of prairie." Private Franz Coller of Company H wrote, "Day after day we march in the woods and God knows if we will come out again. I have never seen such a poor region as we see out here in east Texas and Arkansas." Private Benjamin C. Robertson of Company G stated that Arkansas was "the most degraded country I ever saw." Robertson had much the same view of the people. In a letter to his sister, he wrote that "a person cannot form any idea until they travel through the piney wood and rural district [of Arkansas] as I have seen one thousand women I think and I have not seen one that would wear less than a number eight pair of shoes."[27]

In September, Major General T. H. Holmes, commanding officer of the Trans-Mississippi Department, assigned the Sixth Texas and the two dismounted Texas cavalry regiments to Arkansas Post, a community 117 miles below Little Rock and twenty-five miles from the mouth of the Arkansas River. The town was selected as a site for the construction of a Confederate fort that was deemed necessary to help defend the Arkansas River. Responsibility for building the fortification fell to Colonel John W. Dunnington, formerly of the Confederate States Navy.[28]

The Sixth Texas and Twenty-fourth Texas traveled together until they arrived at the Jourdan plantation, eighteen miles from the town, in late afternoon on September 18. As the two regiments made camp, a messenger arrived and informed the Texans that some 2,000 Federals were eight miles from the post and posed a threat to its occupants, Captain L. M. Nutt's independent company of Louisiana cavalry and sailors from the Confederate ram *Pontchartrain* who manned the large artillery pieces. Volunteers were called to make a forced march to the fort. Four hundred men agreed to make the trip. Leaving after dark, the soldiers, instead of following the road, hastened through the fields and traveled over small trails and paths, reaching their destination at sunrise on September 19. To their disgust, they found no federals to fight. Since the enemy chose not to engage the Southerners, the Confederates, itching for action, quickly put into motion a plan which called for Nutt's command to make a demonstration near the Yankee camp, and when the enemy attacked the Louisianians, the reinforcements would ambush the unsuspecting Federals. The Yankees did not take the bait and withdrew from their position. Meanwhile, the remainder of the Sixth Texas and Twenty-fourth Texas leisurely pushed forward, linking-up with their comrades two days later.[29]

Reorganization of the Confederate army in northwestern Arkansas, southwestern Missouri, and the Indian Territory occurred on September 28, 1862. Major General Thomas C. Hindman, commander of the District of Arkansas, was placed in charge of the First Army Corps, Army of the West. The Sixth Texas became part of the First Army Corps' First Brigade. Garland was given command of the brigade and Lieutenant Colonel T. Scott Anderson assumed leadership of the Sixth Texas. Garland's brigade was instructed to provide Dunnington with whatever aid was required in the construction of the fort and to defend "the fortification against any land attack of the enemy."[30]

The Confederates, assisted by slaves, worked through October and into November to complete the fortification. Time was of the essence. Winter rains would soon arrive, raising the water level of the Arkansas River and, therefore, permit the ascendancy of federal gunboats. By mid-November, the Confederates had finished the inner por-

9

tion of the defensive structure. Still to be completed were winter quarters for the soldiers and a network of trenches and rifle pits. Both officers and enlisted men labored the remainder of November and into December to complete log huts, shelters that afforded the soldiers better protection from the inclement weather of winter than tents. By the end of the year, the housing was completed.[31]

As the troops worked toward completion of the fort, an abundance of supplies began to reach the garrison. Shoes, woolen clothes, blankets, and commissary goods were sent from Little Rock to the post. While the goods poured into the fort, the men of the Sixth Texas, most of whom had been waiting for over a year, were paid their enlistment bounty money of fifty dollars. With adequate shelter, shoes for every man, clothing and blankets for warmth, an ample food supply, and, after the bounty payments, money to buy personal luxuries, the soldiers were prepared for an uneventful winter. "This is certainly the most comfortable soldiering I have experienced since I have been in the service," wrote Sebron Sneed of Company G to his wife. There was, unfortunately, a down side to life at the post. Many of the men were plagued with bouts of diarrhea. It was not severe enough to keep them from doing their daily military tasks, but the condition made them feel quite miserable and kept the doctors busy treating the soldiers. Pneumonia also became a problem for the regimental physicians. "The pneumonia here is terrible, a great many die with it," reported William W. Phillips to his father in Victoria.[32]

Rumors of a Federal attack on the Confederate position were persistent at the fort. Whenever scouts sighted Yankee movements, the gossip mill among the Southern soldiers produced an assumption of an eminent assault. Sneed wrote his wife that he did not anticipate a siege but "as we have been deceived in our calculations so often that I scarcely even have an opinion."[33]

While the Confederate garrison at Arkansas Post strengthened its defenses, raids were launched against Federal supply boats as they traveled the Mississippi in the vicinity of the Southern encampment. Occasionally, a Yankee mail ship was captured which served to amuse the Confederates when they read the personal remarks made by the Yankees' loved ones and friends. The attacks on the Federal supply ships were a serious concern to Major General John A. McClernard, a former Illinois Congressman who assumed command of the Federal troops in the region after Major General William T. Sherman's abortive movement against Vicksburg in December 1862. McClernard, impetuous for military action, decided that the 4,900 Confederate defenders at the Post of Arkansas should be seized. The planned attack upon the fort was a cooperative effort between McClernard's force, about 30,000 men, and the commander of the Mississippi Squadron, Acting Rear Admiral David D. Porter.[34]

The Federal advance was detected by Confederate pickets on the morning of January 9, 1863. Upon being informed of the Yankee presence, Brigadier General Thomas J. Churchill, who had assumed command of the Confederate troops at Arkansas Post, ordered the three brigades of the First Corps to be prepared to move against the enemy at a moment's notice. Each soldier was instructed to cook a three day ration supply. Shortly thereafter, the commanding general assigned Garland's brigade to the rifle pits which were located about a mile and half from the fort. Five companies from the Twenty-fourth Texas and the Sixth Texas were detailed as skirmishers. One of the companies selected from the infantry regiment was Phillips' Company A. Except for sporadic picket encounters, and a few harassing shells fired into their position from the Federal gunboats, the Confederate front remained peaceful throughout the evening.[35]

At about 8:00 A.M. on January 10, Porter's gunboats began shelling the Confederate positions in a systematic fashion. By noon, the Confederates, because of the intense cannonading were forced to withdraw from the rifle pits to safer confines, a ditch near the fort. The Sixth Texas assumed a position next to the fort. Garland instructed the troops to strengthen their defenses with brush and any other material that could be found. The work of the men, however, was hampered by a lack of tools. At dusk, the Yankees commenced a three hour bombardment on the fort and the entrenched Confederates. The shelling ceased about 9:30 P.M. and no further military action occurred during the remainder of the night.[36]

The lull abruptly ended at mid-day on January 11. Porter's ships opened the day's activity by bombarding the fort. Not long afterwards, McClernard's soldiers sprang forward from the trees and bushes toward the entrenchments of the Sixth Texas. T. Scott Anderson commanded the left wing of the regiment and Alexander H. Phillips directed the right wing. The Texans repulsed every enemy ground assault, but the defenders at the post did not fare as well. By 3:00 P.M., all the guns inside the fort, except one, had been silenced by the relentless, cannonading of the Yankee gunboats. Despite the loss of the Confederate artillery, fighting continued along the entire defensive line.[37]

11

Fearful that his brigade's left flank was going to be turned by a massed Federal force, Colonel James Deshler called upon Garland for succor. Garland honored the request by dispatching selected companies from the brigade's three regiments. Alexander H. Phillips led the four companies that represented the Sixth Texas. Enemy fire was so intense that the reinforcements were compelled to crawl the entire distance to their destination. Phillips and his men stopped along the way and assisted different commands to repulse Federal assaults. Prior to reaching Deshler's position, two companies of the Sixth Texas were recalled by Garland. Shortly after the reinforcements reached Deshler, about 4:30 P.M., fighting ceased with the capitulation of the Confederate defenders.[38]

Precisely who initiated the surrender is not known. The white flags first appeared in the area held by the Twenty-fourth Texas, commanded by Colonel F. C. Wilkes. Confusion soon reigned among the other Confederate units as to whether the surrender was official. The Yankees took advantage of the circumstances and breeched the Southern defenses. Churchill, as a result, was forced to surrender the remainder of his troops. The Sixth Texas, however, continued to resist until it received specific orders to stop fighting. Since the white flags first appeared in Garland's brigade, Churchill largely blamed the Virginian for the disaster, an opinion that was apparently shared by Confederate civil officials. Consequently, Garland would be relegated to a minor military role throughout the remainder of the Civil War. Whenever vacancies occurred for regimental commands, he was passed over, and the positions filled by officers junior to him. Despite his continued insistence that an inquiry be made as to his conduct at Arkansas Post, his appeals were denied.[39]

The Arkansas Post prisoners were assembled and guards placed around them. Most of the Confederate soldiers had dressed in their least desirable clothing at the outset of the fighting, leaving their blankets, quilts, and extra clothing in the log huts. Although Federal officers assured the Southerners that their private property would be returned to them the next day, the promise was not fulfilled. Without proper winter attire, they were ill-prepared to travel northward to prison camps in the middle of winter.[40]

On January 12, the prisoners, after they were processed, boarded steamboats. Rain began to fall causing the men to seek whatever shelter the vessels offered. The next day the ships left with their human cargoes. As the steamboats made their way toward the Mississippi, the rain gave way to snow. The scantily clothed prisoners suffered terribly from the cold weather. William J. Oliphant wrote that their "faces were struck by the thickly falling snow . . . as though smitten by driving particles of glass, and the icy wind chilled us to the marrow." He added, "Many of the prisoners afterward lost limbs from being frostbitten, and scarce a day passed that we did not leave a lonely grave by the side of the great 'Father of Waters.' "[41]

As the steamboats ascended the Mississippi, they stopped at Memphis for a couple of days before continuing the voyage. From Memphis, the ships went to Cairo, Illinois, then to St. Louis where the enlisted men were separated from their officers. The officers were transferred by train to Camp Chase, a short distance from Columbus, Ohio, while the enlisted personnel were sent to Illinois, by way of Alton, to either Camp Butler, near Springfield, or Camp Douglas at Chicago. The Sixth Texas was assigned to Camp Butler. On the afternoon of January 30, the Texans were ordered off the steamships and crammed into boxcars. After traveling all night, the regiment reached the outskirts of Camp Butler and were marched into the prison.[42]

Prison life at the camps was not too harsh. Franz Coller of Company H remarked that the provisions at Camp Butler "were better than we received in the Confederate states." A member of Company G stated that "the guards treated us very well and we were supplied with good food, the regular army rations, the same as given to the Federal soldiers guarding us." Oliphant wrote that the "barracks were comfortable . . . Stoves were set up for us and we were furnished with plenty of fuel. Clothing and blankets were issued . . . Our food was good and abundant." A Confederate officer at Camp Chase made a similar observation about the food when he stated that "we get plenty to eat — some of the finest cabbage I ever saw are issued to us." Some of the officers were granted paroles and rented rooms at boarding houses in Columbus.[43]

The Confederates were not pressured by their guards to police the prison compound or barracks, nor were they exhorted to practice good personal hygiene. Consequently, sanitary conditions at Camp Butler were poor. Filthy conditions were as prevalent in the hospitals as in the barracks, a factor in the high mortality among the prisoners at the camp. In February 1863, there were 103 deaths reported.[44]

A prisoner could shorten his stay in prison by taking an Oath of Allegiance to the United States and renounce the Confederacy. Oath forms were circulated or posted in the barracks to acquaint the soldiers with the process. The applicants were asked a series of standardized questions, and if the prisoner's responses were deemed sincere by the Federal authorities, he was released to return home or permitted to enlist in the United States army. The former Confederates who joined the Federal army were known as galvanized Yankees and were usually assigned to units on the frontier to protect the settlers against Indian depredations. Most of the men in Company I of the Sixth Texas took the oath. When the regiment was eventually exchanged, the company commander, C. P. Nauheim, resigned his commission because he did not have enough soldiers to constitute a company.[45]

Boredom was a constant problem for the prisoners. To fight their monotonous existence, Confederates bought rubber buttons from the camp sutler and made them into rings. Visitors found the rings to be a novelty and purchased them as souvenirs. The Confederates also merchandised whistles and pipes they whittled from wood. Money raised from the sale of the items was used to purchase tobacco and other articles from the sutler's store. Soldiers who could write wiled away their time by writing letters. The letters, however, could only be one page in length and consist of personal matters. To further occupy their time, the prisoners played cards, chess and marbles, sang songs, read and reread newspapers, and told stories.[46]

By April 1863, arrangements were completed for the Arkansas Post prisoners to be exchanged. The Sixth Texas was the first regiment to leave Camp Butler. On April 7, the enlisted men were marched to the train depot and placed on cars. Meanwhile, the regiment's officers at Camp Chase were released. The officers left the prison compound in a single file and, as local bystanders laughed and poked fun at the Confederates, a Union soldier stripped them of their extra clothing and blankets, leaving the Southern officers with the barest of necessities. After their belongings were confiscated, they boarded passenger cars.[47]

From their respective prisons, the Texans traveled by rail and by water to City Point, Virginia. The route taken by the soldiers from Camp Butler weaved its way through Fort Wayne, Indiana, Cleveland, Ohio, Erie, New York, Harrisburg, Pennsylvania, to Baltimore, Maryland. At Baltimore, they boarded a ship and steamed down the James River. The officers imprisoned at Camp Chase took a somewhat different sojourn. Their train meandered from Columbus through Pennsylvania by way of Pittsburgh and Harrisburg to Philadelphia where they took a ship to Fort Delaware, situated on an island in the middle of the Delaware River some thirty miles below Philadelphia.

The officers remained at the fort for two and a half weeks. On April 29, they steamed from Fort Delaware aboard the *State of Maine* and disembarked on April 30 at City Point and were turned over to Confederate authorities.[48]

During the journey to Virginia, residents crowded the railroad stations to view and to cast scorn upon the prisoners. Periodically, a Southern sympathizer appeared among the local populous and boosted the spirits of the Texans by yelling words of encouragement or waving a Confederate flag. When the officers arrived at Philadelphia, they were met by an unruly throng. Bricks and rocks were thrown at them. Out of concern that the mob might seize the train, the prison cars were taken to the depot where a degree of safety was assured when the station's iron gate was closed to separate the Confederates from the Philadelphians. The prisoners were then hustled aboard the *State of Maine* as soon as feasible.[49]

After disembarking at City Point, the able-bodied enlisted men, who arrived in Virginia before their officers, were transported by train to Petersburg and then marched some two miles to the Model Farm Barracks, a camp used for paroled prisoners. The ill soldiers were placed in Petersburg, Virginia, hospitals. New uniforms and weapons were issued at the Model Farm Barracks to the exchanged soldiers. Since the men's regular officers had not arrived, temporary officers were placed over the Texans.[50]

While the former prisoners were settling down in their new confines, General George Stoneman, commander of a Union cavalry corps, was ordered by General Joseph Hooker, commander of the Army of the Potomac, to disrupt General Robert E. Lee's communications during the Chancellorsville Campaign. A Federal cavalry column destroyed a section of the Virginia Central Railroad from Southanna to Richmond. A second column demolished a portion of the Fredericksburg Railroad and proceeded to within two miles of Richmond. Confederate officials viewed the cavalry advances as a prelude to a possible assault upon Richmond. All available soldiers, including the recently paroled Sixth Texas enlisted men, were hastily positioned around the Confederate capital to repel the Yankees. After Hooker's defeat at Chancellorsville, and the Confederate authorities realized that the city was no longer in danger, the troops were withdrawn.[51]

As Richmond returned to its normal wartime routine, the officers of the Sixth Texas who survived the ordeal of prison were exchanged and assumed command of their respective companies. On May 9, the regiment left the capital by train to join General Braxton Bragg's Army of Tennessee at Tullahoma, Tennessee. After traveling some six days, the troops arrived at Tullahoma and went into encampment.[52]

On May 24, 1863, the Sixth Texas was consolidated with the Tenth Texas Infantry Regiment and the Fifteenth Texas Cavalry (dismounted) Regiment. Colonel Roger Q. Mills, formerly of the Tenth Texas, was given command of the consolidated regiment. Garland as the senior officer would have normally assumed the command, but because he still bore the stigma for the embarrassing Confederate surrender at Arkansas Post, he was bypassed. Under the reorganization, which was prompted by battlefield and prison losses, the senior captain of each consolidated company assumed command of the company. Since the consolidation produced a surplus of officers for a given position, the officers displaced were transferred to the Trans-Mississippi Department.[53]

The consolidated regiment, a component part along with other Lone Star State regiments which comprised the Texas brigade under the command of Churchill, broke camp at Tullahoma on June 2, and marched northward fifteen miles to Wartrace, Tennessee, where it joined Major General Patrick Cleburne's division as a partial replacement of General Bushrod Johnson's Tennessee brigade. A camp rumor which circulated among the Texans suggested that because of their dubious surrender at Arkansas Post, Cleburne was the only divisional commander who would accept the men. Whether there was any truth to the rumor is not known, but the Texans thought so since they became the butt of many verbal jokes by the veteran soldiers in the Army of Tennessee. Comments, such as "We don't want you here if you can't see a Yank without holding up your shirt to him," persisted until the Arkansas Post men demonstrated in battle they were equal to the best soldiers the Confederate army had to offer.[54]

In an effort to keep Bragg from reinforcing the besieged Confederates at Vicksburg, Union General W. S. Rosecrans, on June 23, initiated the Tullahoma Campaign. Fighting erupted in Cleburne's sector near Bell Buckle, Tennessee, five miles from Wartrace, which was held by the Arkansas brigade under the command of General St. John Liddell. The Arkansas troops fought heavy skirmishes on June 24 and June 25. Cleburne on the morning of June 26 ordered the Sixth, Tenth, and Fifteenth Consolidated Regiment to replace elements of Liddell's brigade at Bell Buckle. After assuming its position on the line, the regiment endured picket and skirmish fighting throughout

16

the day. That evening the Texans withdrew to a new location seven miles to the rear. At daybreak on June 27, Cleburne's entire division fell back to Tullahoma.[55]

The retreat was made under the most adverse weather conditions. Heavy rains prevented the men from lighting fires to dry their clothes or to warm the feet of the shoeless soldiers. Many of the men who had shoes lost them in the deep mud of the roads.[56]

Cleburne's division reached Tullahoma, on June 28, and, along with the rest of Bragg's army, formed a defensive line. Two days later elements of the Union army advanced upon the front of the Confederate army as other Yankee units flanked Bragg's entrenchments. When the Confederate commander realized that Rosecrans had out-maneuvered him, which was the norm throughout the campaign, Bragg ordered a retreat across the rain-swollen Elk River. Cleburne's division was assigned the task as rear guard.[57]

After daylight on July 1, Cleburne's division, by way of Bethpage Bridge, crossed the Elk and assumed a defensive alignment. About mid-afternoon the Sixth, Tenth, and Fifteenth Consolidated Regiment recrossed the bridge and marched two miles before forming a line of battle in the enemy's front. As the Yankees closed upon the Texans, Colonel Mills remarked, "Texas cavalry on the right, Texas cavalry on the left, a Texas battery in the center, all supported by Texas Infantry and who dare come against us." Federal intentions, however, did not include a major push against the regiment. Fighting was limited to picket encounters, a charge by the Eleventh Texas Cavalry Regiment, and light cannonading by the Yankees. Within two hours the affair ended, and the Confederates returned to their former encampment. Once the Texans were across the Elk, Bethpage Bridge was destroyed to prevent its usage by the enemy.[58]

Confused to what course of action to take, Bragg decided, without discussing the issue with his corps commanders, to retreat to Chattanooga. Two days, July 3 and July 4, were required for the army to cross the Cumberland Mountains. It reached the Tennessee River on the evening of July 4 and commenced crossing at the mouth of Battle Creek and at Bridgeport, Alabama. Cleburne's division did not, however, descend from the mountains until July 5. The command arrived at the Tennessee River via Jasper where the men rested a couple of days before crossing on pontoons to the south side at Shell Mound. The division proceeded past Chattanooga and encamped at Tyner's Station, nine miles east of the city.[59]

Throughout the remainder of July and the first two weeks of August, in the absence of any significant movement by either side, the Texans performed routine military duties at Tyner's Station. On August 13, some of the Lone Star State volunteers moved six miles further eastward. Meanwhile, Colonel James Deshler was promoted to brigadier general and replaced Churchill as commander of the Texas Brigade. [60]

Federal operations against Bragg were resumed on August 15 when Rosecrans ordered an advance on the Tennessee River. By August 21, Yankee artillery was established on the river bank opposite Chattanooga and began firing into the city. Afterwards, Federal troops arrived at the north bank of the river at Blythe's Ferry. Meanwhile, the brigades in Cleburne's division that were stationed in and around Tyner's Station were moved to Harrison's Landing to guard the fords and ferries in the vicinity. [61]

Soon after the Confederates arrived at Harrison, they enhanced their defensive posture by digging rifle pits and placing artillery at strategic points. Federal artillery fired periodically into the Southerners' positions but did not inflict any damage. During the latter part of August and the first few days of September, the Texans encountered minimal contact with the Yankees as neither side made a significant thrust toward the other. [62]

Cleburne's division on September 6 began to pull-out of its encampment and march to Chattanooga via Tyner's Station where the column halted and rested for a couple of hours. The consolidated regiment reached Chattanooga at about 10:00 P.M. and bedded down for the remainder of the night. By dusk on the next day, the men were on the march again. The Texans were given the point position and led the Army of Tennessee down the LaFayette Road toward Rome, Georgia. Bragg, under the assumption that Rosecrans' army was headed to Rome to cut the railroad communications with Atlanta, wanted to place his force between the enemy and the railroad. [63]

The Texans in the van marched through Rossville, past Rossville Gap, crossed Chickamauga Creek, and bivouacked near Lee & Gordon's Mill. On September 8, Cleburne's troops resumed the trek, and after proceeding fourteen miles, halted at LaFayette. The bulk of the army remained at Lee and Gordon's Mill and southward toward LaFayette. The Texans, after cooking a two day supply of rations, were assigned to help guard Catlett's Gap, one of the three gaps in Pigeon Mountain. [64]

Rosecrans, aware of the Confederate army's withdrawal, concluded, erroneously, the Southerners were in full retreat. He decided to vigorously pursue Bragg's army by dividing his own army and swinging behind Bragg to cut him off from his supplies at Atlanta. During the Yankee maneuvering, General James S. Negley's division of General George H. Thomas' corps proceeded into an exposed position as it went through one of the Lookout Mountain Range passes into McLemore's Cove. Realizing he had an opportunity to envelop and destroy the unprotected Yankee force, Bragg ordered a coordinated attack on September 11 against Negley. Under the plan of attack, General Thomas C. Hindman's division was to open the fight at first light when the enemy could be observed, and Cleburne's division was to advance when Hindman's guns were heard. Between 1:00 A.M. and daylight on September 11, the Texas Brigade, along with General Lucius Polk's brigade, broke camp and marched to Dug Gap to await Hindman's attack. For reasons that remain unclear, Hindman failed to execute Bragg's instructions and did not attack. Meanwhile, Negley and General Absalom Baird's division which had united with Negley at McLemore's Cove realized the danger they faced. At 8:00 A.M., the two Federal divisions began to withdraw from the area through Stevens Gap. About noon, when it became apparent that Hindman was not going to attack, Cleburne moved against the retreating Yankees. His men after crossing the Chickamauga in waist-deep water reached the base of Lookout Mountain at sunset; but, by this time, the two Federal units were out of the grasp of the Confederates.[65]

The Confederate failure to entrap the two divisions blew a golden opportunity to cripple the Federal army. Had the Southerners been successful the bloodshed which followed in the next two and a half months would not have occurred. Following the Yankee retreat, Cleburne's division returned to Pigeon Mountain to guard the gaps.

The Texas Brigade on September 14 was placed in skirmish formation at the mouth of Catlett's Gap opposite a reconnaissance brigade from Thomas' corps. The Federal troops denied the Texans a fight by withdrawing. During the next two days, however, the Yankee brigade attempted to advance, but on both occasions was repulsed. Reinforcements arrived to help Deshler's brigade counter the increased Federal activity. On September 17, the Texans in a picket engagement killed and wounded several enemy soldiers and took a number of prisoners.[66]

By September 19, Bragg and Rosecrans had taken positions on opposite banks of Chickamauga Creek; thus, setting the stage for the bloody Battle of Chickamauga. The clash, which would ultimately be fought along a three mile front, was opened by a small encounter between Confederate cavalry and one of Thomas' divisions. The fighting escalated when Confederate infantry went to the aid of the cavalry.[67]

At about 3:00 P.M., Cleburne's division was ordered to cross the Chickamauga at Thedford's Ford and report to General Lucius Polk who commanded the right wing of the Army of Tennessee. Meanwhile, the fighting subsided and an enlisted man asked the Confederate cavalry commander, General Nathan Bedford Forrest, if they were through for the day. Forrest pointed to a group of rapidly approaching soldiers and responded, "Do you see that large body of infantry marching this way in columns of fours? That is General Pat Cleburne's division; hell will break loose in Georgia in about fifteen minutes."[68]

Deshler's brigade was placed facing the right flank of the line and advanced about 200 yards before being ordered to lie down. The Texans remained prone for only a few minutes before they continued their advance. By the time Deshler's men were in position to move forward, darkness prevailed over the battlefield, making it difficult to separate friend from foe. Darkness was but only one impediment the attackers faced. The Sixth, Tenth, and Fifteenth Consolidated Regiment had to move through dense smoke caused by the burning trees, grass, and rail fences which were set ablaze from artillery fire. Nevertheless, the Texans maintained their steady pace. The entrenched Federals, using the smoke as cover, poured a heavy fusillade into the Confederates. The Texans, undaunted by the adverse conditions, charged, "yelling like demons," through the smoke, fire, over the dead, and the wounded, some of whom had their prostrate bodies burned from the grass fire. Unable to contain Deshler's brigade, the Yankees gave ground. Fighting ceased about 10:00 P.M., and the Texans bivouacked in place on the battlefield. They spent an uneasy night as their physically exhausted bodies lay on the ground. Glowing embers from the fires cast an eerie image over the battlefield as the soldiers stared at the stars wondering what the morrow would bring and listening helplessly to the pleas of help from the Confederate and Yankee wounded.[69]

At first light, Deshler's brigade was placed in reserve, providing the men an opportunity to consume a hastily prepared breakfast, which featured corn meal, and to replenish their canteens with water. At approximately 9:30 A.M. on September 20, the Texas Brigade was ordered to advance as quickly as possible and engage the enemy who had strengthened its line during the night with pine logs. Company G of the consolidated regiment commanded by Captain Rhodes Fisher, was placed in the skirmish position while the remainder of the regiment assembled in battle formation. As the Texans proceeded forward over open ground, the well-protected Yankee artillery fired relentlessly into their ranks. Despite the intense shelling, the brigade maintained its composure and by 10:00 A.M. was ready to make a final charge at the enemy's breastworks. When the Confederates advanced to within 200 yards of the fortifications, the Federal infantry stopped the Texans with a horrendous musket fire. Cleburne ordered Deshler's brigade, which was operating without artillery support, to assume a protective position behind a hillcrest and hold the position as long as possible. The consolidated regiment took heavy casualties as it carried out Cleburne's directive. Captain Robert Harvey, from Victoria and commander of Company H, paid the ultimate price of war when he was killed at the beginning of the fight as he formed his men to return the enemy fire.[70]

By noon, the consolidated regiment was almost out of ammunition. A courier was dispatched by Mills to appraise Deshler of the regiment's precarious situation. Before the message reached the brigade commander, who was to the right of the regiment on his hands and knees peering below the smoke of the battlefield to locate the enemy, a shell hit him in the heart. Mills, because he was the senior officer, assumed command of the brigade. Shortly thereafter, the ammunition supply was exhausted. In anticipation of a Federal charge as soon as the enemy realized the Confederates were out of ammunition, Mills ordered his men to fix bayonets, scavenge the wounded and dead of ammunition, and distribute it so each soldier would have at least one round. The Texans were to hold their fire until the Yankees attacked. Anderson, who became regimental commander when Mills was elevated to brigade commander, shifted four of his companies that were on the extreme left and which had not participated in the small arms exchange to the front of the brigade. The reinforcements kept the enemy behind their barricades until the Confederate cartridge boxes were refilled.[71]

Meanwhile, Federal skirmishers advanced through an opening between the Texas Brigade and the Confederate brigade on the right. Mills dispatched a portion of his command to check the Yankees on his right flank, but the Confederates were unable to hold the Federals and were forced to retreat. Company A of the consolidated regiment was sent to reinforce the withdrawing Confederate skirmishers. The additional troops proved decisive, and the enemy was repulsed. Sporadic firing continued until late in the evening when a major breakthrough

21

was made by the Army of Tennessee and routed the Yankees from the entire battlefield.[72]

Bragg to the astonishment of his staff and field officers did not pursue the defeated, demoralized Federal army. He, therefore, lost another opportunity to destroy his adversary. Instead of fighting the Federal army, Bragg opted to encircle Chattanooga and starve the Yankees into submission. This decision was a mistake, and it would eventually lead to a major disaster for his army.

Cleburne's division marched from Chickamauga on September 21 and was placed at the foot of Missionary Ridge facing Chattanooga on the north end of the Confederate line. In late October, the division was shifted southward along Missionary Ridge. During the investment of Chattanooga, the Sixth, Tenth, and Fifteenth Consolidated Regiment was engaged in picket duty. Meanwhile, the regiment strengthened its defensive posture by erecting breastworks.[73]

In mid-October, Ulysses S. Grant became the commander of the newly-created Military Division of the Mississippi. On October 23, he entered Chattanooga and immediately began to take steps to break out of the Confederate encirclement. Grant reopened the Union supply line to the besieged city and strategically massed troops for an attack upon Bragg's army.

Even though Bragg was aware of Grant's military build-up, he weakened his army by sending General James Longstreet with about fifteen thousand men to seize Knoxville. On November 22, Bragg ordered Cleburne's division to join Longstreet, but, on the following day, while the division was awaiting transportation at Chickamauga Station, which provided service for the Western and Atlantic Railroad, Bragg countermanded the order and instructed Cleburne to place his men in reserve.[74]

At dawn on November 24, Cleburne's troops began to build a line of defense along the top of Missionary Ridge. Around 2:00 P.M., the division was redeployed near the tunnel that passed through Missionary Ridge which was used by the East Tennessee and Georgia Railroad. In his official report, Cleburne referred to his new location as Tunnel Hill. To the immediate front of Tunnel Hill was a detached ridge which jutted out from Missionary Ridge. When Cleburne learned that the enemy was moving to the separated ridge, he ordered the Texas Brigade forward to secure it. The Texans were too late. Union forces had already taken possession of the ridge. The brigade halted on the main ridge opposite the detached ridge and dispatched skirmishers who soon found themselves engaged with the enemy.[75]

About midnight, Cleburne, who thought the undersized Confederate army would retreat across the Chickamauga, received word to prepare for a stand against the enemy. In an effort to strengthen his line, he ordered axes distributed so the men could fell trees for breastworks. The Sixth, Tenth, and Fifteenth Consolidated Regiment commenced to dig entrenchments fortified with logs and rocks, with the few implements they possessed, along the crest of Tunnel Hill.[76]

Company G, commanded by Rhodes Fisher, was placed in a skirmish alignment at the base of the ridge. As the first rays of dawn appeared on the morning of November 25, the Travis County men saw Union skirmishers four hundred yards from their position. The "long blue lines of the enemy, with bayonets gleaming in the sunlight and banners floating in the morning breeze" advanced upon the Texans. As soon as the Union soldiers were in range, Fisher's men opened fire. The two sides remained engaged until about 10:30 A.M. when Company G withdrew to Tunnel Hill. The Union skirmishers fell in with their main line as it moved forward. As the first Yankee line advanced, a second line was formed and pressed toward the Confederate defenses. Meantime, cannonading from the batteries of both sides was intense. At 11:00 A.M., the Union offensive stretched the entire length of the Texas brigade. Incessant Confederate infantry and artillery fire finally stopped the Federals. The accuracy of the Confederate batteries and sharpshooters forced the enemy soldiers to lie prone on the ground for protection. Albert Jernigan, a member of Company G, provided insight of the subsequent events from the perspective of the common soldier in a letter to his parents after the war. He wrote, "Now the enemy is massing his forces against our right, a second, third, fourth and fifth lines come in sight. Blue coats seem to rise up out of the ground. They seem to be without number . . . Like a mighty wave swept on by a furious wind he rushes to the foot of the ridge . . . Now ensues a scene, awfully wild and murderous beyond description. His front rank is mowed down at one full swoop. Their places are filled immediately as if by the spirits of the lifeless bodies at their feet . . . But still they come more, and still more . . . The dead and dying lie heaped upon the ground . . . At length the enemy begins to waver."[77]

Because the Southern artillery was so effective, Union infantry made an attempt to silence the guns. In a counter move, elements of the Sixth, Tenth, and Fifteenth Consolidated Regiment were ordered to charge the Federal troops, a tactic that proved decisive. Both the regimental commander, Mills, and the brigade leader, General J. A. Smith, were wounded in the counterattack. Colonel Hiram B. Granbury of the Seventh Texas Infantry Regiment assumed command of the brigade during the remainder of the fighting at Tunnel Hill. Ultimately, Granbury was promoted to brigadier general and given permanent command of the Texas Brigade.[78]

After being repulsed, the Yankees regrouped and made another assault on the hill. But, as before, they were unable to penetrate the positions of the entrenched Texans. Having been denied their objective, the enemy withdrew to regroup. The Confederates took advantage of the calm to rearrange their forces for the next stage of the battle.[79]

About 1:00 P.M., the engagement resumed as Federal units tried desperately to overpower the Texans' defenses. After an hour and a half of continuous fighting, Cleburne ordered a charge into the Union ranks. Selected to participate in the move were components of the consolidated regiment. The Federal soldiers were surprised by Cleburne's maneuver, and fled the field. Jernigan remarked that "the wildest disorder and confusion ensues, some fly, others surrender, while others, for a brief space continue to fight, but they are soon overcome." Another Texan who took part in the episode wrote that before the order to advance was given he had unbuckled his sword "and as we went over the works left it, grabbed a rock and went in." The Texans chased the retreating Yankees beyond the foot of the hill and several hundred yards across an open field. Federal reinforcements checked the charge, and the Texans fell back to their entrenchments. During the sally, the Sixth, Tenth, and Fifteenth Consolidated Regiment captured four battle flags and presented them to the division commander. Even though the Texas Brigade faced overwhelming odds throughout the battle at Tunnel Hill, the brigade held the sector assigned it. Cleburne in his official report of the engagement praised the unit by referring to it as "this band of heroes."[80]

Cleburne's troops were jubilant over defeating the Yankees and thought that the other Confederate units were just as successful. When they were told that the troops on Missionary Ridge were routed, and the army was retreating, they were appalled. Smiles gave way to scowls. Self-doubt spread through the Confederate army. One soldier asked, "If we can't hold such a line as this against those blasted Federals, where is the line or position between here and the coast of Georgia that we can hold?" Events would prove, there was none.[81]

At 7:45 P.M., corps commander General William J. Hardee began to pull out the defenders on Tunnel Hill. Cleburne's division, with the responsibility of covering the retreat, was the last to retire. Captain Jackson L. Leonard, in command of Company E, deployed four companies as pickets and stationed his men about 150 yards from the ridge. At 11:00 P.M., after the other regiments were safely withdrawn and on their way to Georgia, the remnants of the Sixth, Tenth, and Fifteenth Consolidated Regiment retired.[82]

Except for Cleburne's division, chaos reigned throughout the retiring Confederate army. In describing the retreat, Cleburne wrote, "The dead and a few stragglers lingering here and there under the shadow of the trees for the purpose of being captured, faint-hearted patriots succumbing to the hardships of the war and the imagined hopelessness of the hour." Another eyewitness stated that "everything in confusion-stragglers innumerable hunting their commands . . . Ah the bitter humiliation of this disastrous day." This same individual further stated that he found the army "a howling mob . . . This was my first experience of the demoralization of defeat."[83]

Cleburne's command trudged through the mud and cold during the remainder of the night of November 25 and the following day. By 10:00 P.M. on November 26, the division reached Chickamauga Creek and bivouacked. The next morning at 3:00 A.M., November 27, Cleburne received orders from Bragg to hasten to Ringgold Gap, Georgia, establish a defensive perimeter, and stop the pursuing Federals until the retreating army reached a point of safety. The tired and exhausted heroes of Tunnel Hill were awakened and given marching orders. To reach Ringgold, the men had to wade across the partially frozen Chickamauga. Most of the men took off their pants, shoes, and underclothing; placed the tail of their shirts into their belts which they fastened around their armpits; held their clothes and weapons above their heads; and crossed the creek. After wading the Chickamauga, the troops built fires and dressed. The soldiers who chose to ford the creek fully clothed suffered unduly from the cold on the march.[84]

Rapidly passing through the town of Ringgold, the division was deployed by Cleburne along Taylor's Ridge which was a short distance east of the town and divided by a half mile gap. The Sixth, Tenth, and Fifteenth Consolidated Regiment under the command of Captain Jonathan R. Kennard, who was elevated to regimental commander after Mills was wounded, was placed behind trees at the base of the right or north side of the ridge. Around 8:00 P.M., the Federal troops in columns of four, completely unaware that the Confederates occupied the gap, passed through Ringgold with "banners flying, drums beating, with heads up and tails over the dashboard sort of way, as if they had nothing to do now but march right along through the country." When the unsuspecting Yankees were less than a hundred yards from the concealed Confederates, Cleburne's artillery and infantry opened fire.[85]

The Federal columns collapsed from the intense Confederate fusillade. The men ran for cover "as fast as their legs could carry them." During this initial encounter, Lieutenant Philip E. Peareson commanded vedettes composed from selected members of the consolidated regiment. Meanwhile, Company D, led by Lieutenant Samuel H. Atkins while Peareson performed vedette duty, was deployed as skirmishers. The Yankees after regaining their composure, resumed the advance. Fighting soon afterwards became general along the entire Confederate line. About 11:00 A.M., as the engagement progressively intensified, Company C, commanded by Lieutenant Thomas L. Flynt, and Company L, under Captain L. M. Nutt, were assigned to reenforce the Seventeenth, Eighteenth, Twenty-fourth, and Twenty-fifth Texas Consolidated Cavalry (dismounted) Regiment. The remainder of the Sixth, Tenth, and Fifteenth Consolidated Regiment fixed bayonets, assumed proper position in line, and prepared for a charge. Around 1:00 P.M., after Hardee informed Cleburne that the wagon train was out of danger of being overtaken by the Federals, the consolidated regiment was ordered to withdraw. The Texans moved silently "along the side of the hill" until they came upon railroad tracks which were followed until the Southerners were out of range of the Federals. After the main body of the division left Taylor's Ridge, the skirmishers, shortly after 2:00 P.M., retired. Cleburne's command halted and waited for the Federals about one mile in the rear of Dick's Ridge, but the Yankees broke off the encounter and did not pursue. Later, on the evening of November 27, the division marched three miles to Tunnel Hill, Georgia. Because Cleburne's stand at Taylor's Ridge saved Bragg's army, the Confederate Congress passed a joint resolution expressing its thanks to the general officers and men of the division.[86]

The Texas Brigade remained at Tunnel Hill, seven miles northwest of Dalton, to prevent the Federal army from advancing into Georgia. The assignment was viewed by the Texans as a compliment and recognition of their achievements at Missionary Ridge and Taylor's Ridge. While the Texans remained static, they performed picket and reconnaissance duties and built winter quarters. Some of the troops

26

constructed wooden huts which housed two to six men and were warmed with fireplaces fashioned out of barrels, straw, and mud. To keep the men from having to sleep on the cold, barren ground, bunks were built. Other soldiers, less industrious, dug depressions in the ground and covered them with pine boughs.[87]

After the Chattanooga debacle, Bragg, at his own request, was relieved as commanding general of the Army of Tennessee. Hardee led the army until a new commander was appointed by President Jefferson Davis. On December 27, General Joseph E. Johnston acquired the herculean task of rebuilding the demoralized army. He immediately began to improve the conditions of the troops by providing new clothes and increasing rations. His actions caused morale among the soldiers to increase dramatically.[88]

To maintain discipline in his division and prevent problems that might arise due to idleness, Cleburne established a drill program. He instructed each brigade commander as to what drills were to be used. The brigade commanders then passed the orders down the chain of command until they reached the company level for implementation.[89]

Before daylight on February 22, 1864, the Texas Brigade left its encampment at Tunnel Hill, marched at double time to Dalton, and boarded railroad cars. The unit was part of a Confederate detachment ordered to Alabama to intercept an advancing Federal force that was proceeding from Jackson, Mississippi, to Selma, Alabama, where there was an arms factory. By the time the consolidated regiment reached Montgomery, Alabama, the Union command had ended its drive toward Selma and turned in the direction of Vicksburg. On February 24, the day following the arrival of the Texans at Montgomery, the consolidated regiment received orders to return to Dalton. As the cars rumbled through the towns along the railroad route, the soldiers tied notes that included their names and military units to sticks or rocks, and they threw the missives to the young ladies who stood along the track waving to the troops. Sundry responses were received from the girls, resulting in the development of pen pal relationships that lasted until the end of the war.[90]

Even though the movement of the Confederate troops to Alabama was shrouded in secrecy, the Federal forces opposite Dalton learned of Cleburne's absence and began probing activities to find out if the town was evacuated. Union advances were repulsed in every instance except for Dug Gap, a pass in Rocky Face Ridge, five miles southwest of Dalton. When the Texas Brigade reached Atlanta on the return trek, it was ordered to proceed posthaste to Dalton and attack the Federal brigade holding Dug Gap. Before leaving Atlanta, the ladies of the city cooked a two day ration for the Texans. The brigade arrived at Dalton on February 25, disembarked from the rail cars and marched to the gap, reaching its foot after sunset. Shortly after sunrise the following morning, the Texans attacked the Union soldiers and drove them from Dug Gap. On February 27, the brigade retired to Mill Creek, on the Middle Spring Road, about three miles east of Dalton. While at Mill Creek, Cleburne's command constructed entrenchments and settled down to camp routine.[91]

During the respite, Granbury was promoted brigadier general and took command of the Texas Brigade. Soon thereafter, he reorganized the brigade. Among the changes made, the Tenth Texas, which was displeased as being part of the consolidated regiment, reacquired its separate identity. Six companies from the Sixth Texas and four companies from the Fifteenth Texas were restructured into the Sixth and Fifteenth Consolidated Regiment. Captain Rhodes Fisher of Company G, Sixth Texas, was made the regimental commander. All the men seemed to be satisfied with the realignment. "'Old Pat' (as we called our Major General) gave every man in the brigade a big drink of whiskey and good humor reigned."[92]

A heavy snowfall greeted the men as they were aroused from their sleep before daybreak, on March 22, and ordered to fall in line. They were marched to an open field east of camp where the division was formed into a three-sided square to witness the execution of a deserter. A wagon carrying a Confederate soldier sitting on a coffin entered the square and stopped. The man descended from his perch, and the coffin was placed on the ground. The condemned person's arms were bound, his eyes covered with a cloth, and he resumed his place on the coffin. An armed group of soldiers stood some twenty paces from the individual. Upon the command of the officer in charge, the detail fired a volley into the deserter who lurched forward into the snow, mortally wounded. To put an end to his agony, the firing squad reloaded and shot a second time, killing the prostrate form. This was the only execution for desertion in Cleburne's division during the entire war.[93]

Stunned by the execution, gloom swept the ranks of the battle hardened veterans. However, their spirits were lifted when they returned to camp, and snowball fights occurred spontaneously throughout the division. Cleburne even became involved in the merriment. The Texas Brigade singled out a Mississippi brigade as its "adversary" and threw snowballs laced with rocks and ice. Fighting lasted among the troops in varying degrees until late afternoon when the men heard, "Come up boys and draw you whiskey." Cleburne had thoughtfully ordered that drinks be distributed to the regiments. Frolicking in the snow gave way to men gathering around campfires yelling at the top of their voices and singing songs.[94]

During April, the troops spent most of their time drilling and performing military exercises. Civilians, a few of whom had come from afar, were often spectators at the maneuvers. They were also present when Johnston reviewed the army as it stood crisply on the parade ground in a long gray line.[95]

In the latter part of the month, the Federal army was regrouped and prepared for a major campaign against Johnston's Army of Tennessee. On May 5, the Union force commenced its movement into Georgia.[96] Here Leuschners' journal begins.

Particulars of the 6th Regt. of Texas Infty. in the

Campaign of Georgia Comencing at Dalton in May 1864

It was at first day's of May that the cannons commenced to thunder, but they still was along ways off from us; but Gen. [J. B.] Hood's Corp's[1] all ways had some light skirmish fighting to do, while our corp's (Hardee's)[2] was still laying in camp; but it was not long before we were ordert to cook up 3 or 4 day's rations; and it was the 7 of May that the whole Army was on foot ready for to march or fight. We left our camps that day and marched to the trenches around Dalton, while we were just waiting eagerly for the yankee's to come, to give them the best we had in our shop, but they came not that day. We heard some heavy cannonading on our left wich we afterwart found to be at Hood's corp's.

May 8, 1864

May, Sunday the 8. We left the above mentioned place about 4 o'glock in the evening and were ordert of in double quick. After we had run about 5 miles, we reached the foot of Rocky face Mountain at Duck out Gap [Dug Gap],[3] but our men were so near out of breath that a great many of them fainted trying to keep up to go up the mountain. We hat to run our [illegible] in running double quik; and as soon as we reached the top, the yankey's had strengthend their line; but when they Saw that we had come to reenforce our cavalry, they fell back. We learned from the cavs. that they repulsed them 5 or 6 times. Our cav. they were Kentukians [Kentuckians]. We all gave them credit for doing good fighting, wich is not often the case that Infty. prais the cav. for there were very few cav. that done good fighting excepting [N. B.] forrest[4] and Texas Cav.

30

May 9, 1864

May, monday the 9th. Here we stoped that day at the same place [and] build breast works. We could see the yankey's at the foot of the mountain. There was som heavy going on on the right off us. Here we received New's from Gen. [R. E.] Lee, wich was read to us, that he had whiped the yankey's badly in Va. last saturday.[5]

May 10, 1864

May, Thuesday the 10. We left duck out gap [Dug Gap] at day-light and marched to Ressacca [Resaca] wich is about 16 miles from were we started. The yankey's [had] a great porition of there Army near that place and had kept a large force concealed near duck out gap [Dug Gap]; and as soon as [illegible] gen. found it out, he sent us right straight back to the gap; and we got back there again by sun-down; and we marched over 35 miles that day through the wood's and all. Here our Pioneer's burried some 200 or 300 hundred yankey's.

May 11, 1864

May, Wednesday the 11th. We marched straight back again to-wards Ressacca [Resaca] and stopped 5 miles from there where we build our breastworks. Here we remained until the 13th.

May 13, 1864

Friday May the 13th. We got up at day light, and as soon as a large wagon train had past us, we marched in rear off it. We stopped 1 mile from Ressacca [Resaca] and awaited the yank's. We marched all the time in line of battle untill evening, and we made 3 lines of breast-works that day, and we dit not get to fight behind them after all. We heard some heavy cannonading on our left and heavy volley's of muske-try on our right. There was a call for volunteer's for skirmishers. Me and mike [Michael] shiwits [Schiewitz] and Harvy Cox[6] volunteert and a good many more out off the Regt. and after dark we were relieved. Here we remained all day the 14th May.

May 14, 1864

Saturday the 14th. About 8 o'Glock in the morning our comp. and H comp. was ordert on skirmish, and we thought it as hard a skir-mish as we had ever ben in.[7] At 4 o'glock in the evening we were re-lieved again. Capt. [A. P.] Cunningham[8] acted as brave as any other man could have done.

May 15, 1864

May, Sunday the 15th. We left the above place at two o'glock in the morning and past through Ressacca [Resaca], and a quarter of a mile south of there, we were put in rear of 3 lines of battle. Here was one of the importanced places on our line. Here we remained until 11 o glock that night, and then our forces commenced falling back and marched all night.

May 16, 1864

May, Monday the 16th. After marching untill nearly day, we rested a couple of hour's and drawed ration. Then we marched off and arrived at Calhown [Calhoun], Ga. about 8 o'clock in the morning, and we soon formed a line of battle and awaited the yankey's. We dit not stay long in Town. We were ordert one mile west of Calhown [Calhoun]. Here we remained in line of battle until 3 o'Clock in the evening. All this time there was nothing but skirmish fighting going on in front of our (Cleburn's) [Cleburne] Division.[9] About this time, a Kentucky Brigade charged the yankey's on our left, running them one mile, and captured a many a prisoner and Ambulances; and the ground was laying thick of dead and woundet. Our loss was but slight. Our division then moved to the left and crossed the [Oostanaula] River and here we stopet and build another line of breastwork's. We remained here all night and had for the first time since we left camp, a whole night's rest. When we would be fast asleep, we'd receive order's to march again, and sometimes we dit not get as much as an hour's rest all night; but we were all satisfied, if we only suffert for the good off our country.

May 17, 1864

may the 17, Thuesday. When we got up next morning, the rest off the Army had all gone but our brigade; and we were left there for rear guard to cover the retreat, and about Sunrise a Comp. off Cav. came up to help us get off from the yankey's sight and kept in front untill we had got off far anough and then they came on down. We marched towarts Kingston, & [duplicate statement] as we reached it within 10 miles, we made halt again and showed the enemy a bold front; and when our Cav. came in, they drawed the yankey's on us, but they would not risk a general Engagement. There was heavy scirmishen going on, on both sides, and we had rest all that night.

May 18, 1864

Wednesday, May the 18th. We were roused up at 3 o'clock in the morning and marched of again at 2 o'clock in the evening. We past through Kingston & stopet 2 mile south off there & camped all day.

May 19, 1864

Thursday, May the 19th. We started from the above mentioned Camp about 10 o'glock & made an advance move on the enemy and marched one mile, forward; but we got nothing out off them, only a heavy Artillery duel. About 3 o'clock in the evening, we fell back to a position, wich Gen. Johnson [J. E. Johnston][10] Selected himself, wich was about 2 miles to the rear from where we started. Here we intended to make a stand, but about 12 o'clock that night Gen. Johnson [Johnston] got a dispatch that the yankey's were flanking us on our left, and at one o'clock [we] were in full retreat.

May 20, 1864

Friday, May the 20. We left at one o'clock in the morning and were in full retreat. At 2 o'clock we past through Casville [Cassville] station and after marching 8 miles farther we came to cartersville. Here we rested about 15 minutes; and then after marching 2 miles, we crossed the Etowa [Etowah] River; and our whole Army crosset right there on 3 pontoon Bridge's and one Railroad bridge. We all got a cross in 4 hour's, and we went 3 miles further and camped in the Altoona [Allatoona] Mountains on Punkin Vine [Pumpkinvine] Creek. Here we remained several day's.

May 23, 1864

May, Monday the 23d. We marched off again and went 12 miles in the direction off Atlanta and camp, wich is about 10 miles from Dalas.

May 24, 1864

May, Thuesday the 24. We marched off at 3 o'clock in the morning. After marching 20 miles, we camped 18 miles from Atlanta.

May 25, 1864

May, Wednesday the 25. We marched of from the above mentioned camp at daylight & went back 2 miles on the same road we came yesterday, & then we took another road wich took us a northeast course. We camped 3 or 4 hours; and we were ordert to march again, without a light to shine upon us, not even a star was to be seen; and after marching a distance of a mile, a heavy rain came pouring upon us, wich wasn't so very pleasant to us. Gen. Hood's Corp's was fighting the yankey's at the time. We could plainly hear the cannons Boom and occasionly the small arms.[11] After marching 4 miles we stopet and camp far the balance of that night, but not an ey wast shut. The rain hat then stoped, but who could sleep with wet garments on or cover with a wet blanket. We soon had large fires build, as there was plenty off railes, for we camped in a lane. We did not look for wood any time.

May 26, 1864

May the 26th. After having driet our cloths and blanket's, day comenced dawning and the sun arose in its beauty. A many an ey was turned towarts the sun while some were thinking the morrow (morning: I may not live to appreciade your beauty anymore.) After the sun had reached above the tree's, we heard the well known call blowed on the bugle — fall in. Every man was ready at an instant for the march. After marching 2 miles, we reached the line of battle, and we were kept for reserve; it was the first time, but we soon got tired off it, for we had to march day and night. Our boy's would say they'd rather fight all day and risk their chance getting killed and have there rest off a night. At dark we marched in front in line off battle, & we remain there all night.

May 27, 1864

Battle of New Hope Church. May, Friday the 27. We fortified the place were we were held all last night, while heavy skirmishing was going on in our front. We were in support off two battery's, wich our Regt. was to hold if the yankey's should charge. After having these work's well finished, we heard some right smart fighting going on, and it was the yankey's driving our cav. skirmisher's in; they called for reenforcements. It was then about 4 o'clock in the evening, and the yankey's were just preparing for a big charge, and came all ready forward. It was then that our (Granbury's) Brigade[12] receivd order's to move by the right flank double quick. After we run a mile and a half we just arived when the cav. were running back. We quikly threw out skirmishers and they was not out more than a minute when they were runin and reported the yankey's advancing in full force; and at that same moment we seen yankey's within 15 yards from us, for we could not see them any sooner. The bushes were so thick that it was an impossibility to see further, and at some parts of the line we could not see that far; so when we got the first sight of them, we comencet firing as long as we could see any. The yankey had allready once headed in our rear when one Regiment of Govan's (Arkansas) Brigade[13] came up and run them back, and gen. granbury'[s] Adjuntant Gen. [Joseph T. Hearne] led the charge and got Killed.[14] It was now dark, and we had driven the enemy back when gen. granbury ordert not to fire at the sound of our bugle, that the 3 Regt. of our Brigade was to charge at the sound of the bugle. The 3 Regiments was the 10th Texas, the 7 Tex and the 24 & 25 consolitated [regiments][15]; and as the bugle soundet, these 3 Regiment went forward an run the yankey over 500 yards. They would sometime be so mixt up that they could not tell wich was a rebel or wich was the yankey's; and they would ask what Regiment do you belong to, and sometimes the answer would be the 40th, and our boy's knew that we dit not have no 40th Regt. in our Brigade; and, therefore, they would Kill such. Sometimes the answer would be the 24th; and when they would ask the 24 What, "the 24 Ohio," and they were servet the same. We could not see that affel sceine. It was to dark in front of our line that night, but next morning evry body opent his ey's with astonishment. We have bin in many a battle it is true, but never dit we see such a sight before as it was before our ey's then.[16]

May 28, 1864

Saturday, May 28th. Gen. Johnson [Johnston] called together all general's to look at the battle field, and all gen. remarked that they dit not see such a sight through all the war, & no other but brave men could do the execution.[17] We burried the yankey's & put from 40 to 150 in one grave, one on top off the other. When night came, scrmishing wassn't as heavy as it was all day.

May 29, 1864

Sunday, May the 29th. We left the battlefield at sunup, & Went back to our own (Hardee's) Corp's in the center of the Army. We had ben with gen. Hood's Corp's for the last 3 day's to help him finish his line. After marching 8 miles we reached our (Hardee's) Corp's, & here we were held in reserve again. Major Dixon[18] off gen. Cleburn's [Cleburne's] staff tole us that we would rest all day. If the yankey's would not attack us, we would have to hold ourself's in readines in case that they would break our line, we would have to go & drive them back; but as it happened, the yankey's dit not attack us, & we rested pretty well that day; & at a 11 o'clock off night, we had to rise for our ration had come what was right in our hand for we were all hungry; & as soon as we had got up, we heard heavy cannonading on our right; & before we all had our ration, heavy skirmish firing comenced on the left and in front off us; & at the same instant, the order was given to packup & hold ourself's in readines, to march at a moments warning. We stopt here in this position untill 3 o'clock in the morning when the firing ceased; & it was not long before a courir came & tole us that we could lay down again; but every 10 & 20 minutes the firing would comence again & keep it up for a little wile, & we dit not shut an ey when the sun arose in her glory. [19]

May 30, 1864

Monday, May the 30th/64. Heavy skirmish fighting comenced with the morning dawn as usal, all along the line. About 11 o'clock before noon, we left the above mentioned camp; & marched 2 miles to the right, about 1 mile to the left off gen. Johnson's [Johnston's] Hd. Qtr's., & here we camped that night.

May 31, 1864

Thuesday, May the 31st. Same camp.

June 1, 1864

Wednesday, June the 1st. We left here at 10 o'clock in the morning, & marched 2 miles to the right. We expected an attack here, but they dit not come. At 2 o'clock in the evening, we marched 2 miles further to the right, and at dark we left the road to rest for the night. About 1 o'clock in the night the yankey's comenced shelling us and threw some shell's right among us; & they killed and wounded 8 men out of gen. Laury's [M. P. Lowrey's] Alabamma [Alabama] Brigade; [20] & as soon as it ceased we went to sleep again. Occassionally a miny bullet could be heard flying over us; but we were allready getting used to sleep when bullets were flying about, for the sleep that we lost would make anybody sleepy. Sometime we would sleep while we were marching, though whenever the cannon's would roar we were allway's wide awake.

June 2, 1864

Thursday, June the 2d. We marched about 2 miles to the left on account those men getting Killed yesterday by shell's. We ditn't want to lose any men when we could save them. Here we remained untill 1 o'clock in the evening when we were ordert of to the right in the heavyst kind off a rain. After marching 5 miles in the rain, we stopet & build another line off breastwork's. After dark, we tore down a fence & made large fire's out off the rail's to dry ourself's; & so we rested all night without being disturbed by the yankey's, only now & then a shower off rain would fall upon us; & we could not sleep on account off it. Our line of battle is said to be 15 miles long.

June 3, 1864

Friday, June the 3d. We remained at the above mentioned place. In our front everything was quite. On our left we could occassionaly hear a cannon fire. Heavy rain all day. We had not even the least thing to protect us from the rain, without tent, for tent's were to much expence to haul them these day's. We are very well satisfied if they only haul ration along for us, for we often failed to get that.

June 4, 1864

Saturday, June the 4th. We remaind at the same camp all day, & in the evening we received order's to march of at one o'clock next morning. It rained heavy all day & night.

June 5, 1864

Sunday, June the 5th. We left the above mentioned camp at one o'clock in the morning under a heavy rain, & by 8 o'clock in the morning we had marched 6 miles. We marched in mud up to our knee's; & after we had stopet, we were fixing up the camp just when an order came to march back 2 miles on the same road that we came; & there we formed a line off fight (battle) & build breast work's. [21]

June 6, 1864

Monday, June the 6th. We left the above mentioned place about 8 o'clock in the morning. Another Brigade relieved us, & we marched back two miles to the rear where our division (Cleburn's) [Cleburne's], had breast work's thrown up. We were put in rear off [L. E.] Polk's Brigade, [22] & we build another line off breast work's.

June 7, 1964

Thuesday, June the 7th. Remained at the same camp. Mr. Britton came in from Gonzalas [Gonzales] with a large mail from Texas. I received one letter from home. Our cav. are 4 miles in front off us. Every think seem's like there was no yankey's near.

June 8, 1864

June, Wednesday the 8. At the same above mentioned camp, 8 miles from Marrietta [Marietta].

June 9, 1864

Thursday, June 9th. Camp 8 miles from Marrietta [Marietta].

June 10, 1864

Friday, June the 10th. 8 miles from Marrietta {Marietta]. Our cav. was driven in and scirmishing comenced in our front. We remained here untill the 16th of June, & heavy scirmish fighting going on all this time.

June 12, 1864

The 12th. Our scirmisher's were driven in, & next day we retook our place again & run the yankey's severall hundred yards.

June 13, 1864

Monday, the 13teenth. Heavy cannonading on our right.

June 14, 1864

Thuesday, the 14th. Still heavy cannonading on our line, gen Johnson [Johnston], Leut. gen Hardee, Hood & [L.] Polk & severall major generals rode along the line to see what was going; & when the yankey's Spiet through a Telescope that they were officer, they threw shell's among our gens, & killed Lieut. gen. Polk,[23] wich was much regretted by our soldiers & citizen.

June 16, 1864

Thursday, June the 16t. About dark our cannons comenced their musick, wich made the yankey prepare to receive a charge and; at 10 o'clock we march 5 miles to the rear & formed another line; & next morning the yankey's seen how we had deceivet them. Our extreme right still held the same position.

June 17, 1864

Friday, June the 17th. We marched 1 mile to the left under a heavy cannon fire. We then on the extreme left off our Army. Our comp. was put in front as scirmisher's. The yankey's shelled us all day, & our battery's returned their fire. We heard some heavy volly's off musketry on our right.[24]

June 18, 1864

Saturday, June the 18teenth. Same camp. Our (B) Comp. was relieved from scirmish. We could hear nothing but connading all day on our right. At 11 o'clock that night, we fell back about 2 miles; but the right off Army remained where it was at first. After marching 2 miles, we stopet & the rain came pouring in torrent's; but still we laid down on our blanket's & slept in the rain, for we were entirely worn out & sleepy that the rain dit not keep us awake. In the morning when we got up, some found themself's 4 & 5 inches deep in water where the rain had run together.

June 19, 1864

Sunday, June the 19th. At the last mentioned place. We build breast work's; & before we finished them, we receid an order to fall back 500 yards on a hill wich was a better position. Here we build work's while the yankey were shelling us, & the rain still kept pouring down. We was now 4 miles from Marrietta [Marietta]. This line was called the Kennesa [Kennesaw] Mountain Line.[25]

June 20, 1864

Monday, June the 20th. The same camp. Rain all da. Only once & a while it would stop. Scirmishing in our front.

June 21, 1864

Thuesday, June the 21s. The same camp, 4 miles from Marrietta [Marietta]. Scirmishing in front & no rain. I have not mentioned anything about our los on skirmish fighting. All the time the fighting be going on, we would allway lose men, killed or wounded. There was not a day that past that we couldn'd see from 2 to 10 Killed and wounded from the scirmish line.

June 22, 1864

Wednesday, June the 22nd. In line of battle, 4 miles from Marrietta [Marietta] in the breast work's. Our (Capt. A. P. Cunningham) Company & Company H went on scirmish. In this fight we lost as brave & good a man as ever walked on the face of the earth to my opinion, but still some dit not like him, this was Lieut. Cocke of Company H. The ball enterd in his forehead, & he died instantly with a smile on his face.[26]

June 23, 1864

Thursday, June the 23d. In the fortification 4 miles from Marrietto [Marietta]. Scirmish fighting in front. Heavy cannonading on our right. About 4 o'clock off evening, the left off our scirmisher give way, wich causet the whole line (Ed O Rily)[27] to give back as the yankey's took advantage off this oppornnity; but our scirmisher's were soon encouraged by a few entreating words & charged the yankey's & retook their old position. Here in this Charge we lost in time of 20 minutes 8 men killd & wounetd out of our Brigade, & it was nothing but a little scirmish.

June 24, 1864

Friday, June the 24t. In line off battle 4 miles from Marrietto [Marietta]. Scirmishing in front.

June 25, 1864

Saturday, June the 25. 4 miles from Marrietto [Marietta].

June 26, 1864

Sunday, June the 26th. In line off battle 4 miles from Marrietto [Marietta]. Our company & H Company went out on scirmish. Our men & the yankey's had made an armistice not to fire at each other unles one side or the other would advance, for it would not amount to anything nohow, to get a man Killed now & then. Neather side would gain anything by it. After the armistice was made, our Boy's would meet the yankey's half-ways & exchange Paper's, so we got to read northern Paper's An they read our paper's; & our men would trade tobacca for coffee; & we sent letter's through to be mailed. We could hear heavy cannonading on our right about 8 miles from here.

June 27, 1864

Monday, June 27th. In line of battle 4 miles from Marrietto [Marietta]. There was nothing but scirmish fithing going on in front of our Brigade, but Polk's brigade from our div. & Cheatham's div.[28] had a right smart battle with the yankey. The yankey's charged up to the work's, but were handsomely repulsed with heavy loss. We captured several hundred prissner's.[29]

June 28, 1864

Thuesday, June the 28th. In line of battle 4 miles from Marrietto [Marieta]. Armistice is up again. We cant hardly hear any shooting. About 8 o'clock in the evening our Capt. Cunningham's company & Company H went out on scirmish.

June 29, 1864

Wednesday, June the 29. In line of battle 4 miles from Marrietto [Marietta]. At daylight we were relieved again from scirmish, every thing was quiet in front of our brigade; but we could hear heavy scirmish fighting on our left towarts Laury's [Lowrey's] & Polk's Brigade's; & about 12 o'clock that night we was aroused from a heavy musketry fire & cannonading, & we prepared to receive an attack; but by one a clock all was quiet again.

June 30, 1864

Thursday, June the 30th. Camp 4 miles from Marrietta [Marietta] in line of battle. Every thing was quiet all day.

July 1, 1864

Friday, July the 1st. In line of battle 4 miles from Marrietta [Marietta]. We could hear the yankey Band's plainly play. Our Capt. Cunninghams Company was out on scirmish. The yankey scirmisher's were only 75 yard's from us. They were standing in groups. The armistice was still kep up. We had order's not to fire on them unless they advance, & they had the same.

July 2, 1864

Saturday, July the 2d. In line of battle 4 miles from west Marrietto [Marietta]. We remained here all day; & at dark we received order's to be ready to move at 11 o'clock; & so we departed at the said time & past through Marietto at 12. We were in full retreat. The yankey's were flanking us again.[30]

July 3, 1864

Sunday, July the 3d. We marched all last night & morning untill day light. We halted 8 miles southwest from Marrietta [Marietta]; & as quick as we halted, we build another line of breast work's; & we worked hard all that day to finish them. After working all day our (Capt. A. P. Cunningham's) Company was put out on scirmish that night where we dit not dare to shut an ey; & we were all very sleepy, for we dit not sleep a night before this, and worked hard all day.

July 4, 1864

Monday, July the 4th. 8 miles from Marrietta [Marietta]. Our (Capt A P cunninghams) Company was relieved from scirmish before day light. About 2 o'clock in the evening, the yankey scirmisher's crawled up on our Videtts & fired in to them & wounded 5; & the yankey's kept a coming on. Our scirmisher's fell back to the line a battle & fought for every inch of ground they give up, & they killed a good many yankey's. We soon received orders that 2 Company's move out of each Regt. had to go to reenforce the scirmishers & retake their old position, for they were fortified too; & at 12 a clock that night, we retreated from there. After marching about 7 miles, we stoped about 3 miles from the railroad bridge across the Chattahoogee [Chattahoochee] were some niggers had made fortifications for us.[31] Our (Hardee's Corp's) held a space of ground 10 miles long, & Gen. Hood's & Polk's Corp's are on the flank, either to attack the yankey's or to keep the yankey's from flanking us.

July 5, 1864

Thursday, July 5th. Our brig. lost 15 killd & wounded. In line of battle 2 miles from the railroad bridge over the Chattahoogee [Chattahoochee] Riv. We finished the work's wich the niggers had made. Heavy scirmish fighting in front.[32]

July 6, 1864

Wednesday, July the 6th. In line of battle 2 miles from the railroad bridge. About 10 a clock in the morning, [illegible] division we were relieved from the front & put in rear as reserve. If the yankey's should attack any part of the lines or break through, we would have to retake the work's again.

July 7, 1864

Thursday, July the 7th. Camp in reserve 1 1/2 miles from the railroad bridge. We could hear light cannonading on the left of our Army about 2 miles from here.

July 8, 1864

Friday, July the 8th. Still in reserve. About 10 o'clock, we went to the front about 1 1/2 [miles] from were we camped; & our (6th Texas) Regt. was put out on scirmish, but no yankey was in sight of us. No firing in front of us.

July 9, 1864

Saturday, July the 9th. On picket. About 8 o'clock in the morning, we were relieved & fell back to the main line where we remained untill 9 o'clock in the evening when we received order's to march off. We crossed the Chattahoogee [Chattahoochee] Riv. about 10 o'clock on a pontoon bridge. We marched all night, & stopet 3 miles from Atlanta in the morning at 8 o'clock; & here we camped in order.

July 10, 1864

Sunday, July the 10. We could hear cannonading in the direction of Chattahoogee [Chattahoochee] Riv. It is supposed the yankey's are trying to cross.

July 11, 1864

Monday, July the 11th. Still can hear cannonading at the Riv.

July 12, 1864

Thuesday, July the 12th. Camp 3 miles from Atlanta. We received News from gen. Lee that [Jubal A.] Early's Corps had taken harpors [Harper's] ferry. We could still hear the cannon's. Had rain in the evening.[33]

July 13, 1864

Wednesday, July the 13th! Camp 3 miles from Atlanta. After dinner we received order's to hold ourself's in readines to march at a moments warning.

July 14, 1864

Thursday, July the 14th. Camp 3 miles from Atlanta.

July 15, 1864

Friday, July the 15th. Camp 3 miles from Atlanta.

July 16, 1864

Saturday, July the 16th. Camp 3 miles northwest of Atlanta.

July 17, 1864

Sunday, July the 17th. Camp 3 miles northwest from Atlanta. Gen. Johnson's [Johnston's] departure from the Army was read to us, & gen. Hood supercedent him. Every soldir's head hung low when we heard that our gallant comander had to give up the comand of the Army, for all our hope & Confident was in Gen. Johnson [Johnston]. We dit not ask for any better gen., & I believe that is what whiped us.[34]

July 18, 1864

Monday, July the 18th. We marched away from the last mentioned camp; & after marching 5 miles, we formed a line of battle about 3 miles & a half from Atlanta.

July 19, 1864

Thuesday, July the 19th. In line 3 & 1/2 miles from Atlanta. We build a line of fortifications that day.

July 20, 1864

Wednesday, July the 20th. 3 miles from Atlanta. About 3 o'clock that evening, we moved to the left about 1 mile. We were put in rear of Cheathams div. as reserve while they were charging the yankey's; but they dit not run them back an inch; & our (Cleburne's) division were catching all the cannon balls. One 18 pound parrot gun ball came within 3 feet of me & killed four men & cut 1 man's leg off. I & Mike Shivits [Schiewitz] & 4 more were be spatter with blood & flesh. Gen. Hardee was in sight when this happened; & he have order's imediately for one Brigade of Cheathams division to charge that battery; & if they failed, our (Granbury) brigade would have to take it; & just as the charge was to be made, gen. Hardee received order's from gen. Hood to fall back. We fell back and marched through Atlanta that night, & next morning we arived 2 miles Southeast of there.[35]

July 21, 1864

Thursday, July the 21st. Two miles Southeast of Atlanta. We comenced building breastwork's soon in the morning, but they comenced shelling us so heavy that we could not finish them. Everytime a shell came over, we could hear men groan & call for the litterbearer's. The yankey's used these shrabnel shells that are loaded with little musket's bullet's. When ever they explode, these little bullet's will scatter like hail. In the 17th Texas,[36] one shell killed & woundet 22 out one Company, killing all officers of the company from Capt. down. (F. Blossman wast killed.)[37] The yankey's only charged us once that day, but we handsomely repulsed them. About 10 o'clock that night, we left that place & went way around to get on the yankey's flank. We only left 5 men out of each company to keep up a big [illegible] that night to make the yankey's believe that we were still all there. We marched all night.[38]

July 22, 1864

Battle near Atlanta. Friday, July the 22d. We were still on the march in the morning & marched till dinner when we formed a line & marched in line of battle untill 3 o'clock when we run on the yankey's & took 3 lines of breastworks from them. Captured the yankey picket post. The yankey's was not expecting us, & we got right on them before they could prepare. General McPhearson [J. B. McPherson] (a yankey Lieut. Gen.) came to the front to see what firing had commeced about, & just as he rode up, some of our boy's killed him.[39] After the fight was over, we seen knapsak's piled up as high as a house; & all of our boy's taken all the clothing they wanted; & the rest we destroyed. Nearly every one of us had 3 or 4 daguerotype's from the yankey's.[40] Freind Shivits [Schiewitz] got woundet in this fight by charging the 2d line of breastwork's. Pack Traylor.[41]

July 23, 1864

Saturday, July the 23d. We have thrown the dead yankey's in their own made fortification & covered them up. We buried our dead, each one in a separate grave. We have fortified here again, nearly on the same groun where the yankey's had their work's.[42]

July 24, 1864

Sunday, July the 24th. In line of fortification 5 miles Southeast east of Atlanta. We were hear on the extreme right of the Army. All quiet in front.

July 25, 1864

Monday, July the 25. 5 miles southeast of Atlanta. All quiet in front.

July 26, 1864

Thuesday, July the 26th. 5 miles from Atlanta.

July 27, 1864

Wednesday, July the 27th. We left the battle field in the morning after sunup & moved to the left about 3 miles; & then we stoped at the edge of the City. We took our position 1 mile east of the City on the left of a Fort.[43] The were throughing shell's at us all the time, day & night.

July 28, 1864

Thursday, July the 28th. We are 1 mile east of Atlanta. Scirmish fighting comenced to get pretty heavy. I was out on scirmish with S. Meyer;[44] & at one o'clock our Arillery opened heavy on the yankey's; & the yankey's replied pretty brisk with their battery's wich caused it to be very hot of shells.[45]

July 29, 1864

Friday, July the 29th. 1 miles east of Atlanta. (I wrote a letter home & one to W. F. Shrader & sent it of).

July 30, 1864

Saturday, July the 30th. 1 mile east of Atlanta. Met myer [Meyer] on picket.

August 1, 1864

Sunday, August the 1st. We remained here one mile east of Atlanta untill the [illigible]. All this time there was scirmishing going on & cannonading.

August 3, 1864

Thuesday, August the 3d. We left the last mentioned place & marched throug Atlanta. As we were marching through the City, I thought to myself: who would not fight for a place like this, "A city so fine & a people so kind." [illigible] would want to see this place burned down to ashes. No, never, but were is this beautifull City now? Perhap's it is scatterd all over the world. Yes Gen. Sherman that never showed any mercy to any human being laid it down to ashes down to a levell; & not only the City but also the country he went through. A man could go a hundret miles before he could see a house. These were my thoughts as we marched through Atlanta.[46] We camp one mile South of Atlanta; & in the evening, the firing of musketry got to be pretty heavy on the left of the Army; & we had to hold ourself's in readines; & not long afterwart's the firing of musketry & cannonading comenced on the right like a havy battle was fought; but we afterwart's found out that the yankey's run our scirmisher's in; & they were soon reenforced & retook their proper place what made the firing be so heavy; & they captured some yankey prisoners. We remained here in reserve until the 6th.

August 6, 1864

Saturday, August the 6th. We left the camp 1 mile South of Atlanta in evening under a heavy rain. After marching 6 miles south, we camped. Rained all night.[47]

August 8, 1864

Monday, August the 8th. We moved one mile to the right.

August 9, 1864

Thuesday, August the 9th. We moved back again. Heavy scirmishing going on all this time. We remained here untill the 19th.

August 19, 1864

Friday, August the 19. We left the camp 6 miles south of Atlanta about 10 a glock at night & marched all night around through the would's untill nearly day. We stoped and slept a few minutes.

August 20, 1864

Saturday, August the 20. At daylight we had to get up & march again, & we took position in the front 2 miles North from east point [East Point]. Here we remained untill the 30. In front of our Brigade was no scirmish fighting all this time, but the yankey's was in Sight of us all the time through the ope[illegible].[48]

August 30, 1864

August the 30th. We left last mentioned camp at sunup & marched all day slowly all day, & at night we received orders to march in force march.[49]

August 31, 1864

Next morning the 31st we arived at Jonesborough [Jonesboro]; & about 10 o'clock in the morning, we made an advance move on the yankey's; & we charged them & drove them one mile accross the [illegible]irdle [Flint] River & turned their Right flank. About 8 o'clock that night we marched 2 miles & a half to the right. 1 mile from Jonesboro.[50]

September 1, 1864

September the 1st. We comenenced to build fortification soon in the morning; but when the fawk (dew) had rose, we had to quit. The yankey's was to close & fired at us, & we coud not finish them.[51] Cheatham's div. was on the extreme right of (Hardee's) Corps, & our (Cleburn's) [Cleburne's] div. was in the centre, & [W. H. T.] Walker's div.[52] on the left, & our Brigade was on the left of govan's Arkansas Brigade. In the evening the yankey's charged in front of Govan's Brigade with 8 lines of battle, & we were put so thin that we wasn't one line of battle. The yankey's run gen. Govan's men out of there work's, capturing a great many & Gen. Govan & his staff. After they were through the line, they come right in our rear & that a great many of our men in bask; but we soon tired; & half of us shot to the rear while the other's were shooting to the front; & so we held our position untill dark.[53] Our (Garland's) Regt. was on the extreme right of our Brigade, & we lost the most men. Our Regt. lost here in this fight 7 killed & 39 woundet, but the majority of the woundet will die.[54] Our of a 150 men, our company lost all woundet. Ed. Mehnert, Segt Louis Coutourier [Couturier] them 2 died in the hospital from their wound. Mehnert was shot in the bowles & Sergt. Coutourier [Couturier] in his right arm, nearly in the shoulder.[55] Lieut. [John] Gibson had a slight wound in the leg, but when he was sent to the hospital, two Railroad train's run to gether & killed him & a many other soldier & a good many Ladie's.[56] Jacob Fox got a slight wound & got well.[57]

At night we retreated to the next station about 6 miles, called Love-Joy [Lovejoy's Station]. We formed a line & build more fortification.[58] Gen. Hood was in Atlanta with two Corps & the militia,[59] but when he found that we had to fall back from Jonesboro, He evacuated Atlanta & Joint our (Hardee) Corps. We remained at Love-Joy [Lovejoy's Station] untill the 8th.

September 7, 1864

The 7. We wake up at daylight, & we could not hear a single gun fired. Our Gen. soon sent scout's out to see wether yankey were gone, & they soon come back & reported them gone.[60]

September 8, 1864

September the 8th. We left Love-Joy [Lovejoy's] Station & went up to Jonesboro & went into regular camp again. For the first time in 6 months, fighting had stoped for the present, & the yankey's furlowed a good many of their men. In this camp we remained untill the 18th.

September 19, 1864

September the 19th. We left the above mentioned Camp about one o'clock in the night, & we camped 3 miles from Palmeto [Palmetto] Station the next day, were we made more fortification. We remained here untill the 29th.

September 26, 1864

September the 26. Prasident [Jefferson] Davis resievet the Army, & in the night Gov. [Francis] Lubuck [Lubbock] made a speech.[61]

September 29, 1864

September the 29th. We marched off from camp & past through Palmetto station, & there we left of from the [West Point] railroad & marched northwest. It rained heavy in the evening.[62]

October 3, 1864

October the 3d. We was 15 miles opposide of Marrietta [Marietta].

October 4, 1864

October the 4th. We hear cannon's again. Our troops have posessan of the railroad above Marrietta [Marietta]. We had rain every day since we left Palmetto station.[63]

October 5, 1864

We left the above mentioned place, & marched West.

October 7, 1864

The 7th. We past through a Town called Ceter-Town [Cedartown] & camped west of here that night.

October 9, 1864

October the 9. We had frost & cold whether.

October 17, 1864

Octob. the 17th. Camped on the line of Georgia & Alabama. From here on, we marched on a mountain untill the 25th Called Sand moutain.

October 27, 1864

October the 27th. We marched around Decator [Decatur], a little Town on the Tennessee River, Alabamma [Alabama]. Our Division formed a line 1 mile west of there. Our Army had the Town suroundet on the west side of the River. We could hear a shell fly over us once & awhile.[64]

October 29, 1864

The 29. We were at the same place, & our Regiment went out on picket. We were within 600 yards from town & fired into it all the time. Here we had heavy scirmishfighting with the yankey's; & in the evening, we left at 3 p.m. & camped 8 miles Northwest of there.

October 30, 1864

The 30th. After marching 20 miles, we camped on a River.

October 31, 1864

October the 31. We camped 1 mile west of Tuscumbia, Ala. on the Tenn. River.

November 7, 1864

November the 7th. We moved camp & moved 1 mile further up the River. About two miles Northwest of there, Our Pontoon bridge is laid across the River.

November 15, 1864

November the 15th. We crossed the Tenn. Riv. & camped at Florence, Alabama.[65]

November 21, 1864

November the 21th. We marched of from Florence while the snow came down thick, & we were bound for Tennessee.[66]

November 22, 1864

The 22nd. We had much colder whether. We marched 16 miles that day.

November 23 , 1864

The 23d. We marched 16 miles & camped at Whaynesbarough [Waynesboro], Tennessee.

November 24, 1864

The 24. We marched 17 miles. The whether is a little warmer, but still our hand's & feed were near frozen off.

November 25, 1864

Nov. the 25. We marched 16th miles. Past through a Town called Williamsboro {Williamsport} & camped 4 miles of there.

November 26, 1864

The 26. We marched 28 miles & past through Mount Pleasant. Camped 3 miles of there. Gen. Forrest is close behind the yankey's. They only was a mile from here.[67]

November 27, 1864

Novem. the 27th. Marched around Columbia & camped 2 miles from there. Our cannons have opend once more to reply the yankey's.

November 28, 1864

November the 28th. The yankey's left Town last night. We could hear cannons in the direction of Nashville.[68]

November 29, 1864

November the 29th. Our division (Cleburn's) {Cleburne's} marched through would's & mountain's all day & about evening we arrived at "Springhill" {Spring Hill}, & we attacked the yankey's there & run them a mile & a half. Captured 75 Prisoner & killed a good many.[69]

November 30, 1864

November the 30th. We marched through springhill {Spring Hill}, & after 15 miles, we found the yankey's waiting for us at Franklin. Our army formed a line of battle & marched in line of battle for a mile & a half before we came close enough to charge the yankey's. We charged on the yankey's & run them out of one line of breast work's without firing a gun. Here we captured a good many Prisoner; & then we charged over to the other line of work's wereas part of the yankey's had allready run; but they soon rallied again & Captured me & some five more. After I was in the 4th line of works I seen a lot of yankey, of about 20, & one threw away his gun, & I tole the rest to do the same & so they dit; & then I tole them they were my Prisoner's; & I then sent them to our rear; & after they were gone, I looked around, & I seen a yankey line of battle within 20 yards of me, & some was about to shoot at me; but I soon threw away my gun, & so I was save; but I was prisoner. It was dark before I got out of the fight, and then I marched all night with 700 more of our men with me.[70]

50

December 1, 1864

December the 1st. We arrived at Nashville about 8 a glock in the morning, and nearly starved to death in the evening. We got a few bites of bread wich only made us hungry'er then we were before.

December 2, 1864

December the 2nd. We were put on the car's before daylight & was on the way to Louisville, Kentucky. We past through 3 long Tunels. One was ove a half a mile long. Past the Town Bowlengrean [Bowling Green] where Gen. [Braxton] Bragg once gained a victory.[71] We arived at Louisville about daylight the 3d of December & remained there 4 hours; & after taking all our poket knifes away, we were marched of through Town & crossed the Ohio River at Jeffersonville Indiana & marched 4 miles to "New" Albany & took the car's to Chicago Illinois. We past through hundreds of city's & Towns wich I now forgot the names of and have not put down.

December 5, 1864

December the 5th. We arived at the prison Camp Douglas and were closely searched, and most everthing was taken away from us except one sead of close. Took our money, watches, & alowed us only one blanket, & some men's feet & finger's were allready frost bidden, and some had to have there feet taken off up to there knees. I was one of the hardest winters they had for some time. I have poured water out of a cup and before it would touch the groun it was ice.

December 17, 1864

Saturday december the 17th. The yankey received some good new's and fired 30 shotts out of the cannon.[72]

December 21, 1864

The 21 of December. I got sick with feber.

January 2, 1865

January the 2nd 1865. I got well.

February 15, 1865

February the 15th. I was sick again with Feber. Got well the 27. 2000 prisoner's has allready left for exchange.

April 3, 1865

The 3 of Apprill. The yankey's fired 97 round's of Artillery for the fall of Rickmond [Richmond].[73]

April 15, 1865

Apprill the 15th. We received new's of President [Abraham] Lincoln's assasination last night,[74] & one of our men rejoiset and said the word "thats bully," & a yankey happening to stand behind him comenced abusing him and kicking him about like a brute. After being through with this performan's, the yankey took the Rebell & put him on a 20 feet high horse out of wood[75] & tied from 5 to 10 pound's of iron on each one of his legg's, and done this four hour's every day for nearly two week's; & I could tell many more such cases wich happens every. We got so little to eat that the yankey's own doctor's tole us that some of our men died for the want of something to eat. Some men would go and pick the bones out of the bone barrels & knaw on them; and if a yankey saw it, he would make 2 get down on their four's; and then he put a bone down between, & make them knaw on it and growl and bark like a dog which nearly happened every day. When a yankey's pistol was loadted to long, he'd come in prison; & if he could see a rebel go a little out of his track or hed tell him to do something, and the Rebel would say I am sick, he would tell him go to work or else I'll shoot you d—m rebel; and if he dit not imediately do it, he would get shott wich could be seen done 3 and 4 times a week; and other punishments could be seen by the hundreds a day. And how dit we not suffer for something to eat. Do they thing that all this can be so easely forgotten? No, never. If a man never was rebel, he got to be one of the best in that prison. I can never forgive what I have seen there.

About the 1st of May we received orders that there was 500 men wanted to go on exchange, & I was one of them that got his name down to go.

May 4, 1865

The 4 of may. We left there in the morning. Our hearts beating for Joy. expecting to See our Dixie's land once more, for we still doubted that Gen. Lee had surrendert.[76] When being on the cars from Chicago to cairo [Cairo], we past through the city's Kankekey [Kankakee] & Champaign and a good many other little Town's.

May 5, 1865

May the 5th. We arived at Cairo 10 o'clock A.M. & went on board of the steamboat T. B. G. Kilgour. Left cairo that night.

May 6, 1865

The 6th. We past by Columbus, Kentucky.

May 7, 1865

The 7th. We past Memphis, Tennessee and Helena, Arkansas.

May 8, 1865

The 8th. We past 3 gunboat's.

May 9, 1865

May the 9th. We arived at Vicksburg at daylight and left there at 8 a.m. Past 14 gunboats & past grand gulf, and the mouth of the Riv. Big Black and Baton Rouge.

May 10, 1865

May the 10th. We arrived at New Orleans at daylight & remained on the Boat all day.

May 11, 1865

May the 11th. We was taken off the Boat & taken to a prison & were guarded by negroes, but the here treated us better than the white at camp Douglas. Here we remained untill May the 23d and went back up the Mississippi River again.

May 24, 1865

The 24. We past by Baton Rouge.

May 25, 1865

May the 25th. In the morning we arived at the mouth of the Red River.

May 26, 1865

The 26. We were exchanged and went on our own Boat and started up the Red River May the 27th.

May 28, 1865

28. We past by Allexandria & a good many fortifications.

May 30, 1865

May the 30th. We arived at Shreveport.

June 2, 1865

June the 2d. We past through Lick skilled [Panola County, Texas] right on the line of Texas and Louiseann [Louisiana].[77] We were 7 of us and were walking a past and caring all or our plunder a gun and catridge Box [illegible], for we were told at shreveport that there was Jay hawker's on the road between there and Houston.[78] If we wanted something to eat, we had to beg it from the Citizens. That was all we had to depent on, but we got along first rade as we alway's met up with good & freehearted fellow's, and so we alway's had anough to eat from Shreveport to Houston. We past through Carthage, Texas, past through Linflat [Linn Flat], through Douglas [Douglass], Altow [Alto], Anderson; & after Marching 250 miles, we arrived at Navasota. From there we took the car's to Houston & past through Hempstead & arived at Houston the same day we left Navasota, wich was the 12 of June.

June 15, 1865

June the 15th. We left Houston with the ballance of our Comand, for they just arrived from galveston,[79] & arrived at Alleton [Alleyton] the same evening and marched to Columbus where the Citizens made us a fine supper, for wich we still owe them a many thank's; and from there we started next morning and went home to Victoria where I am now.

I expectat to be happy, and I was for a little while; but it is not so now, my heart has a whegd thrown upon it wich cannot so easily be taken off. It pains me. I may forget it a minute or two, but it will come in my mind again. I try all in the world to be happy and other's that see me think so, but there is something that works in me wich I dare not to explain. Had we gained our independence, I would have bin happy. My heart would have leaped for joy, but now it is not so. When I am in presence of Ladie's, I forget for a little while; but while I am speaking my troubles come into my mind, where at other times I would have Killed myself a laughing. I could not now make a laughing [illegible] if I was to try my hartest.

Epilogue

Following Hood's defeat at Nashville on December 16, 1864, the once valorous Army of Tennessee reverted to disorganized rabble as the vanquished soldiers rushed pell-mell toward Franklin to escape the clutches of the pursuing Federal army. In the desperate flight southward, the wounded men who were left to fend for themselves hobbled on make-shift crutches or were carried by thoughtful comrades. Small arms were discarded along with artillery, wagons, and baggage by the panic-stricken troops. Hood later wrote that he "beheld for the first and only time a Confederate Army abandon the field in confusion."[1]

Elements of General Stephen D. Lee's corps and General James R. Chalmer's cavalry division initially served as a rear guard and prevented the Yankees from overtaking and capturing the entire Confederate army. On December 20, General Nathan B. Forrest's cavalry and selected infantry units, which included the Texas Brigade, under the command of General Edward C. Walthall were assigned as rear guard. During the retreat, the Confederate soldiers suffered from the cold and rain. The men without shoes and blankets had no protection from the bitter north wind and the mud-covered stones that lay in their path. Feet became frostbitten, swollen, bruised, and bloody. Approximately four hundred of Forrest's rear guard were relieved from duty for lack of shoes. Compounding the soldiers' misery were hunger pains induced by short rations.[2]

By December 24, Hood's advance columns reached the Tennessee River near Bainbridge, Alabama. After pontoon bridges were hastily constructed, the disheartened Confederates began crossing into Alabama the day after Christmas. All of the troops, including the rear guard, had crossed the bridges by December 28. The Federal pursuit halted at the Tennessee River, thus bringing to a close Hood's ill-fated Tennessee Campaign.[3]

Freed from enemy harassment, the Army of Tennessee marched leisurely through Tuscumbia, Alabama, and Iuka, Mississippi, reaching the vicinity of Corinth, Mississippi, on January 1, 1865. Nine days later, the troops arrived at Tupelo, Mississippi, where they bivouacked for the better part of January. Before the Texan troops were fully recuperated from their retreat, they were ordered eastward to reinforce Hardee who was operating against Sherman in the Carolinas. On January 25, the Texas Brigade was moved in crowded boxcars and flatcars to Mobile, Alabama. From Mobile, the men were transported on a riverboat up the Tensaw River to Tensaw Landing where they boarded trains to Montgomery, Alabama. While in Montgomery, the soldiers went on a rampage. Their pent-up anger from not being paid for ten months and being denied the simple pleasures of life, such as tobacco, burst loose. Stores were broken into for tobacco and liquor. William E. Stanton of Company A wrote his cousin Mary G. Moody, the eldest daughter of Victoria postmaster James Moody, that "he never seen men go do as our Brigade done." Another Texan at Montgomery stated, "The center of attraction was a kind of free-for-all, route step, go easy, beer-jerking place called the 'Light House,' located a little way down the river. The Arkansas and Texas boys took charge of this outfit, music, dance hall and all, and run it for all there was in sight."[4]

On January 13, 1865, Hood asked to be relieved as commanding general of the Army of Tennessee. The Richmond authorities promptly granted his request and replaced him with General Richard Taylor, commander of the Department of East Louisiana, Mississippi, and Alabama on January 23. To boost the troops' morale, Taylor granted furloughs by lot to non-essential personnel. One of the lucky men was Captain Andrew P. Cunningham of Company B.[5]

Meanwhile, President Davis faced congressional pressure to restore General Joseph Johnston to his old command. Although the Confederate president initially rejected, for political and personal reasons, the unwanted advice, the deteriorating military situation from Georgia to North Carolina and the request by General Robert E. Lee, newly appointed general in chief, he reluctantly ordered Johnston on February 23 to assume command of the Army of Tennessee and the Department of South Carolina, Georgia, and Florida.[6]

After the binge at Montgomery, the Texans boarded trains for Columbus, Georgia. Upon arriving at the Columbus depot, the troops were feasted by the residents of the town. The soldiers repaid the hospitality by a lesser version of the Montgomery performance. The following day the men resumed their train trip eastward. They made a brief stop at Fort Valley, Georgia, sixty miles east of Columbus, and were greeted with hand baskets of food that were prepared by the ladies of the village. The gifts were accepted by the troops with civility. Once the men resumed their train trip, they traveled through Macon to Milledgeville, Georgia, where they made camp before proceeding by foot to South Carolina via Augusta. At Newberry, South Carolina, the Texas Brigade bivouacked several days while foraging parties were sent into the countryside. From Newberry, the Texans marched to Chester, South Carolina, where they boarded trains and traveled to Greensboro, North Carolina. At Greensboro, the men encamped a short time before the brigade again was loaded on a train. The troops traveled through Raleigh to Smithfield, North Carolina, where they disembarked from the cars. Soon after they left the train, the men marched to Bentonville, North Carolina, and rejoined the other Army of Tennessee units which preceded them.[7]

While the Texas Brigade made its way into North Carolina, Johnston decided to attack a Federal corps as it approached Bentonville. By mid-morning on March 19, fighting broke out between the two sides. What was perceived by Johnston before the engagement as an excellent opportunity to crush a Yankee contingent vanished when subordinate officers failed to carry out the general's plan of attack.[8]

Arriving too late to participate in the initial stages of the Battle of Bentonville, the Texas Brigade dug in close to the Mill Creek bridge, the only avenue of retreat to Raleigh for the Confederate army. During the early morning hours before daybreak on March 22, Johnston withdrew his army across the bridge and marched to Smithfield. The march was made in an incessant rain. Despite the misery of wearing wet clothes, the men as they trudged down the Smithfield road "were cheerful as larks, 'Johnson was in command.' "[9]

At the Smithfield encampment, Johnston on April 9 reorganized the Army of Tennessee for the last time. Casualties, desertions, and furloughs had reduced the army to slightly over sixteen thousand effectives. In the restructure, the Texas Brigade was reduced to the First Texas Consolidated Regiment and placed under the command of Lieutenant Colonel William A. Ryan, formerly of the Eighteenth Texas Cavalry Regiment and the highest ranking officer remaining in the brigade. All nine companies of the Sixth Texas were consolidated and designated Company A in the new regiment. The First Texas Consolidated was assigned to D.C. Govan's brigade, John C. Brown's division, William J. Hardee's corps.[10]

Between April 9 and April 26, the Army of Tennessee, in reaction to movements by the Federal army, shifted to various locations in North Carolina. One day after it was reorganized, the army left Smithfield for Raleigh. On April 12, after two days of marching, it arrived at Raleigh where the troops remained for only one day before being ordered to break camp and depart for Chapel Hill, North Carolina. Johnston's army continued on to New Salem, North Carolina, where it bivouacked until April 23. By April 26, the Confederate army was relocated ten miles in the direction of Greensboro.[11]

While the men were in motion toward Raleigh, word reached the army that Robert E. Lee had surrendered his forces in Virginia. Johnston quickly realized that further continuation of the war would lead to the destruction of his undersized army and lives would be lost needlessly. He, therefore, wrote to Sherman on April 14 asking for a temporary suspension of hostilities while a peace agreement was arranged. Sherman consented to the request. Subsequently, a meeting was held between the two commanders, on April 17, at Durham Station, North Carolina, and an armistice was agreed to the following day. Included under the terms of the covenant, known as the "Memorandum, or Basis of Agreement," Johnston's forces were to be disbanded; soldiers could return home with their arms which they would deposit in the state arsenals; the people were guaranteed their political rights; and the Confederates would be granted a general amnesty.[12]

Andrew Johnson who became president when Abraham Lincoln died after being shot by John Wilkes Booth rejected the compact. Sherman was instructed to give Johnston forty-eight hours to surrender and if the Confederate general did not comply, hostilities were to be resumed. When Johnston was given the message, he requested another meeting. The two commanding generals met again on April 26 and a formal surrender was made. The Confederate enlisted men, under the terms agreed upon, were to place all arms, with some exceptions, and public property at Greensboro. Officers could, however, keep their sidearms. Furthermore, the vanquished soldiers were to be given paroles when they pledged never to take up arms against the United States government again. Also, both officers and enlisted men could keep their private horses and baggage. Finally, as the Southerners returned home, they were not to be molested by United States authorities; the Texas and Arkansas troops were to be provided with water transportation from Mobile or New Orleans; and, wherever possible, land transportation was to be loaned to the homeward bound former Confederate soldiers.[13]

When the meetings between Johnston and Sherman began, trepidation among the Confederate soldiers over the prospect of unfavorable surrender terms led to mass desertions. Johnston estimated that between April 19 and April 24 approximately eight thousand men, many taking with them artillery horses and baggage train mules, left the Army of Tennessee. Hardee, without placing a figure on the number of deserters, acknowledged the exodus from his corps.[14]

In the twilight days of the Army of Tennessee, discipline crumbled. Officers found that fewer and fewer of the units responded to orders. William E. Stanton of Company A, Sixth Texas, wrote his cousin Mary Moody in Victoria, Texas, that the Texas Brigade "behaved shamefully all the way around from Tupelo, Miss. to Raleigh, N.C." and "there was not an officer that could do anything with them." Major J. W. Green of the army engineers informed Johnston that he was only able to maintain control at Catawa Bridge and Hughey's Ferry "by promising each man a mule." Governor Zebulon B. Vance of North Carolina complained to Johnston that he witnessed the plundering of a train carrying blankets and leather "as officers of nearly all grades were standing quietly around."[15]

On May 2, paroles were issued to what remained of the Army of Tennessee. Out of the nine hundred men who served with the Sixth Texas, only sixty-five were present at the surrender in North Carolina. Regimental attrition during the three and a half years of service, however, was not due entirely to battlefield deaths. Although the unit was involved in some of the most fierce fighting of the Civil War, only sixty men, or 6.6%, were killed in action. The Battle of Missionary Ridge, or Tunnel Hill as the Texans referred to the engagement, extracted the heaviest toll. There were 157 members of the Sixth Texas who were wounded in the battle. The figure does not incorporate, however, the twenty-seven soldiers who were wounded two or more times. In a few instances, the wounds were so severe that the infantryman was granted a disability discharge or was assigned light duty at rear echelons other than the Army of Tennessee. Ninety men (young adults in the cases of the four discharged for being under age) were given non-combat disability discharges. Pneumonia and other diseases counted for 157 deaths, almost three times greater than combat deaths. An interesting feature of death by natural causes was that eighty-three died while prisoners of war. Seventy-five of the volunteers were captured in campaigns after the regiment was exchanged in 1863 and were not repatriated before the war ended. A sizeable number, 152, took an oath of allegiance while in prisoner of war camps pledging not to take up arms against the United States government. The bulk of the men who took the oath were Europeans who migrated to Texas in the decade that preceded the war and the Northern born volunteers. With a few exceptions, all the men of DeWitt County's Company I, comprised predominately of immigrant Germans, took the oath. Of the 157 who switched allegiance, nine volunteered for frontier service with the United States army. Another 116 were reassigned to units in the Trans-Mississippi Department. Included in this latter group were those who escaped capture at Arkansas Post, and officers who lost their commands when the Sixth, Tenth, and Fifteenth Consolidated Texas Regiment was formed in 1863 after the exchange at City Point. Other factors that contributed to the depletion of the Sixth Texas were detached service, desertion, escapees from Camp Butler who never returned to duty, and furloughs after the Tennessee Campaign.[16]

There is little doubt that the men who fought with the Sixth Texas covered themselves with glory. Their descendants have every right to be proud of their forefathers. Unfortunately, the western theatre has not received the historical analysis as Lee's activities have in the east. Perhaps, future historians will adjust the emphasis, and, if so, the Sixth Texas, along with the other Texas regiments in the Army of Tennessee, will receive the accolades they deserve. Rest in Peace, ye warriors of the Sixth Texas Infantry Regiment.

SIXTH TEXAS INFANTRY REGIMENT

FIELD AND STAFF

ROBERT R. GARLAND, Colonel, 38 (5'10", gray eyes, gray hair, fair complexion, born in Virginia; assumed command of the Second Brigade on August 22, 1862; taken prisoner at Arkansas Post, Arkansas, on January 11, 1863)

THOMAS SCOTT ANDERSON, Lieutenant Colonel, 34 (6'0", hazel eyes, brown hair, dark complexion; taken prisoner at Arkansas Post, Arkansas, on January 11, 1863; served in Trans-Mississippi Department from ?)

A. M. HASKELL, Major (Transferred to Earl Van Dorn's command on December 2, 1861)

SAMUEL J. GARLAND, Adjutant, 21 (5'9"; taken prisoner at Arkansas Post, Arkansas, on January 11, 1863; died at St. Louis, Missouri, on February 2, 1863)

UDOLPHO WOLFE, Quartermaster, 26 (5'8", blue eyes, brown hair, light complexion; taken prisoner at Arkansas Post, Arkansas, on January 11, 1863; transferred to Trans-Mississippi Department on May 6, 1863)

JOHN E. GAREY, Assistant Quartermaster

JAMES K. P. CAMPBELL, Assistant Chief of Staff

A. JONES, Surgeon (Transferred to the Third Texas Cavalry Battalion on ?, 1862)

JOHN H. LYONS, Surgeon (Served in Trans-Mississippi Department from ?)

DAVID McKNIGHT, Surgeon

S. E. GOSS, Assistant Surgeon (Died at ? on November 23, 1862)

J. PURVIS JENKINS, Assistant Surgeon (Assigned to the Sixth and Fifteenth Consolidated Texas Regiment on March 23, 1864; present at final surrender at Greensboro, North Carolina, on April 26, 1865)

R. A. SMITH, Assistant Surgeon (Assigned to the Sixth and Fifteenth Consolidated Texas Regiment on March 5, 1864)

GEORGE W. TRIBBLE, Assistant Surgeon (Assigned to the Sixth and Fifteenth Consolidated Texas Regiment on May 5, 1864; taken prisoner at Franklin, Tennessee, on December 17, 1864)

B. H. HARRIS, Chaplain (Served in Trans-Mississippi Department from ?; resigned on October 28, 1864)

R. McCOY, Chaplain (Resigned on November 30, 1864)

COMPANY A — LAVACA GUARDS — Composed of personnel recruited primarily in Calhoun County, Texas. Mustered into Confederate service on September 27, 1861.

OFFICERS

A. H. PHILLIPS, Jr., Captain, 30 (Promoted major on March 3, 1862; taken prisoner at Arkansas Post, Arkansas, on January 11, 1863; died at Montgomery, Alabama, on June 4, 1863)

R. E. SUTTON, First Lieutenant (Promoted captain on March 3, 1862; resigned on November 28, 1862)

WILLIAM W. PHILLIPS, Second Lieutenant, 28 (Promoted first lieutenant on March 3, 1862; promoted captain on November 28, 1862; taken prisoner at Arkansas Post, Arkansas, on January

61

11, 1863; died at Camp Chase, Ohio, on February 12, 1863)

SIMON K. LONGNECKER, Third Lieutenant, 25 (5'9", gray eyes, dark hair, fair complexion; promoted second lieutenant on March 3, 1862; promoted first lieutenant on November 28, 1862; taken prisoner at Arkansas Post, Arkansas, on January 11, 1863; promoted captain on May 23, 1863)

NON-COMMISSIONED OFFICERS

L. C. DAVIS, First Sergeant, 29 (5'9", blue eyes, brown hair, born in New York; returned to ranks on ?, 1862; taken prisoner at Arkansas Post, Arkansas, on January 11, 1863; took oath of allegiance to the U.S.A. at ? on March ?, 1863)

CHARLES SEAMAN, Second Sergeant, 37 (5'7¼", gray eyes, dark hair, dark complexion, born in New York; reduced to ranks on April 11, 1862; transferred to Company H on April 11, 1862)

GILBERT D. WATTERS, Third Sergeant, 21 (5'8", gray eyes, dark hair, florid complexion; taken prisoner at Arkansas Post, Arkansas, on January 11, 1863; taken prisoner near Atlanta, Georgia, on July 21, 1864)

WILLIAM MARTIN, Fourth Sergeant, 39 (Resigned on January 20, 1862; received a ? discharge on January 4, 1863)

F. E. BLOSSMAN, First Corporal, 19 (Reduced to ranks on January 29, 1862; taken prisoner at Arkansas Post, Arkansas, on January 11, 1863; WIA at Chickamauga, Georgia, on September 20, 1863; KIA near Atlanta, Georgia, on July 21, 1864)

D. F. BREEDEN, Second Corporal, 29 (6'½", dark eyes, black hair, dark complexion; promoted fifth sergeant on January 24, 1862; promoted junior second lieutenant on April 3, 1862; taken prisoner at Arkansas Post, Arkansas, on January 11, 1863; died at Camp Chase, Ohio, on March 5, 1863)

PHILIP KLEAS, Third Corporal, 22 (Promoted first corporal on January 24, 1862; promoted fourth sergeant on April 14, 1862; taken prisoner at Arkansas Post, Arkansas, on January 11, 1863; present at final surrender at Greensboro, North Carolina, on April 26, 1865)

H. DIAL, Fourth Corporal, 28 (Returned to ranks on December 21, 1861; dropped from roll as deserter on February 20, 1862)

CHARLES BRIMINGHAM, Musician, 41 (5'8", blue eyes, light hair, fair complexion; received a disability discharge on April 8, 1862)

CHRISTIAN FINK, Musician, 29 (Born in Prussia; taken prisoner at Arkansas Post, Arkansas, on January 11, 1863; took oath of allegiance to the U.S.A. at Camp Butler, Illinois, on February 18, 1863)

JAMES MAXWELL, Musician, 36 (Reduced to ranks on December 14, 1862; served with the Fourth Texas Artillery Battalion from ?, 1863)

PRIVATES

ALLISON, S. GEORGE, 30 (5'2", gray eyes, light hair, fair complexion, born in New York, occupation a carpenter; received a disability discharge on November 12, 1862)

BARBER, D. A., 17 or 21 (Taken prisoner at Arkansas Post, Arkansas, on January 11, 1863; died at Camp Butler, Illinois, on April 10, 1863)

BARTON, S. H., 21 (Promoted fifth sergeant on November 8, 1861; promoted fourth sergeant on ?, 1862; promoted third sergeant on ?; taken prisoner at Arkansas Post, Arkansas, on January 11, 1863; transferred to ? on December ?, 1863)

BENDON, J. W. H., 31 (5'5", hazel eyes, black hair, born in the West Indies; promoted regimental sergeant major on November ?, 1861; taken prisoner at Arkansas Post, Arkansas, on January 11, 1863; took oath of allegiance to the U.S.A. at Camp Butler, Illinois, on March ?, 1863)

BENEDICT, GEORGE B., 20 (5'10", hazel eyes, auburn hair, fresh complexion; taken prisoner at Arkansas Post, Arkansas, on January 11, 1863; taken prisoner at Missionary Ridge, Tennessee, on November 25, 1863; took oath of allegiance to the U.S.A. at Rock Island Barracks, Illinois, on ?)

BOSWORTH, J. H., 17 (Taken prisoner at Arkansas Post, Arkansas, on January 11, 1863; died at St. Louis, Missouri, on March 8, 1863)

BRADFORD, SAMUEL, 35 (5'7", blue eyes, black hair, born in Pennsylvania; taken prisoner at Arkansas Post, Arkansas, on January 11, 1863; took oath of allegiance to the U.S.A. at ? on ?)

BRITTON, GEORGE W., 18 (Died at Arkansas Post, Arkansas, on October 22, 1862)

BURLEY, SYLVESTER, 25 (Transferred to Company F on April 11, 1862)

BUTTS, JOHN W., 18 or 19 (Taken prisoner at Arkansas Post, Arkansas, on January 11, 1863; died at Camp Butler, Illinois, on February 28, 1863)

CANTWELL, WILLIAM J., 24 (Taken prisoner at Arkansas Post, Arkansas, on January 11, 1863; WIA at Chickamauga, Georgia, on September 20, 1863; taken prisoner at Missionary Ridge, Tennessee, on November 25, 1863; enlisted into the U.S. Army on October 14, 1864)

CARLYLE, WILLIAM T., 27 (5'8", gray eyes, gray hair, dark complexion; promoted quartermaster sergeant of the regiment on November 6, 1861; taken prisoner at Arkansas Post, Arkansas, on January 11, 1863; promoted second lieutenant on March 9, 1864; transferred to field and staff of Hiram Granbury's Brigade as acting assistant quartermaster on ?; taken prisoner at ? on ?)

CARPENTER, JEFF, 16 (Taken prisoner at Arkansas Post, Arkansas, on January 11, 1863; died at Atlanta, Georgia, on March 1, 1864)

CARPENTER, W. (Name only appears on an Arkansas Post POW list with remarks: name canceled, no such man in company)

CASEY, JOHN, 26 (Taken prisoner at Arkansas Post, Arkansas, on January 11, 1863; KIA at Missionary Ridge, Tennessee, on November 25, 1863)

CHERRY, R. W., 21 (5'8", blue eyes, red hair, fair complexion; taken prisoner at Arkansas Post, Arkansas, on January 11, 1863; taken prisoner near Atlanta, Georgia, on July 22, 1864)

COLEMAN, THOMAS, 24 (Promoted third corporal on April 14, 1862; returned to ranks on ?, 1862; taken prisoner at Arkansas Post, Arkansas, on January 11, 1863; WIA at Missionary Ridge, Tennessee, on November 25, 1863; taken prisoner near Columbia, Tennessee, on December 22, 1864; enlisted into the U.S. Army on April 22, 1865)

COUPER, WILLIAM C., 19 (5'6", brown eyes, dark hair, born in Scotland; taken prisoner at Arkansas Post, Arkansas, on January 11, 1863; took oath of allegiance to the U.S.A. at ? on March ?, 1863)

COX, JOHN, 25 (Transferred to Company H on April 11, 1862)

DEBROH, ISHAM, 26 (Promoted second corporal on April 14, 1862; promoted first corporal on ?, 1862; taken prisoner at Arkansas Post, Arkansas, on January 11, 1863; KIA at Missionary Ridge, Tennessee, on November 25, 1863)

DEBROH, J. M., 19 (Taken prisoner at Arkansas Post, Arkansas, on January 11, 1863; WIA at Chickamauga, Georgia, on September 20, 1863; died of wounds at ? on ?)

DRAKE, JAMES A., 33 (5'8", dark eyes, dark hair, dark complexion, born in New York, occupation a bookkeeper; received a disability discharge on April 16, 1862)

EBNER, FREDERICK, 23 (Taken prisoner at Arkansas Post, Arkansas, on January 11, 1863; POW? at Jonesboro, Georgia, on August 31, 1864)

FINCH, R., 30 (5'7", blue eyes, dark hair, light complexion, born in Carroll County, Tennessee; transferred from Company C on ?; MIA at Arkansas Post, Arkansas, on ?; served in Trans-Mississippi Department from ?)

FOWLER, A. W., 16 (5'8", gray eyes, light hair, fair complexion; taken prisoner at Arkansas Post, Arkansas, on January 11, 1863; WIA at Jonesboro, Georgia, on September 1, 1864)

GISLER, JACOB, 22 (Transferred to Company H on April 11, 1862)

GOODALL, JOHN, 35 (5'10", blue eyes, brown hair, born in England; taken prisoner at Arkansas Post, Arkansas, on January 11, 1863; took oath of allegiance to the U.S.A. at Camp Butler, Illinois, on March ?, 1863)

HAMPIL, CHARLES, 18 (Taken prisoner at Arkansas Post, Arkansas, on January 11, 1863; WIA at Chickamauga, Georgia, on September 20, 1863; cited for gallantry at Chickamauga, Georgia)

HANNA, ALBERT, 19 (Taken prisoner at Arkansas Post, Arkansas, on January 11, 1863)

HARLESS, J. H., 21 (Died near Rockport, Arkansas, on August 5, 1862)

HARLESS, WILLIAM D., 21 (Promoted fourth corporal on ?, 1862; promoted third corporal on ?, 1862; taken prisoner at Arkansas Post, Arkansas, on January 11, 1863; died at Camp Butler, Illinois, on April 8, 1863)

HARMES, CASPER, 18 (5'4", gray eyes, brown hair, fair complexion; taken prisoner at Arkansas Post, Arkansas, on January 11, 1863; taken prisoner near Atlanta, Georgia, on July 22, 1864)

HARRELL, JOHN E., 24 (6'0", gray eyes, dark hair, dark complexion; promoted second corporal on January 24, 1862; promoted fifth sergeant on April 14, 1862; promoted first sergeant on ?,

1862; promoted second lieutenant on January 6, 1863; taken prisoner at Arkansas Post, Arkansas, on January 11, 1863; promoted first lieutenant on October 19, 1863)

HARRIS, HENRY H., 17 (5'6", gray eyes, dark hair, fair complexion, occupation a farmer, born in Kentucky; received a disability discharge on December 9, 1862)

HAYNES, C. C., 18 (Promoted fourth corporal on September ?, 1862; taken prisoner at Arkansas Post, Arkansas, on January 11, 1863; promoted third corporal on July ?, 1863; promoted second corporal on September ?, 1863; promoted junior second lieutenant on March 9, 1864; WIA at ? on June 16, 1864; present at final surrender at Greensboro, North Carolina, on April 26, 1865)

HAYNES, JAMES H., 24 (Died in Lavaca County, Texas, on January 23, 1862)

HAZLE, WILLIAM (Deserted near Fairfax County, Virginia, on June 14, 1863; took oath of allegiance to the U.S.A. at ? on ?)

HENRY, J. R., 21 (Promoted fourth corporal on April 14, 1862; promoted second corporal on September ?, 1862; taken prisoner at Arkansas Post, Arkansas, on January 11, 1863; died at Camp Butler, Illinois, on April 7, 1863)

HOGAN, JOHN W., 18 (5'10", black eyes, light hair, fair complexion; taken prisoner at Arkansas Post, Arkansas, on January 11, 1863; WIA at Chickamauga, Georgia, on September 20, 1863; promoted first corporal on April 1, 1864; taken prisoner near Atlanta, Georgia, on July 21, 1864)

HOLLAND, J. F., 21 (Taken prisoner at Arkansas Post, Arkansas, on January 11, 1863; took oath of allegiance to the U.S.A. at Camp Butler, Illinois, on ?)

HOLLAND, T. J., 25 (Died near Pine Bluff, Arkansas, on September 1, 1862)

HOLT, JAMES, 19 (Taken prisoner at Arkansas Post, Arkansas, on January 11, 1863; died at ? on August 2, 1863)

HOLT, THOMAS (Taken prisoner at Arkansas Post, Arkansas, on January 11, 1863; taken prisoner at Missionary Ridge, Tennessee, on November 25, 1863; enlisted into the U.S. Army on October 17, 1864)

HORNBURG, HENRY, 24 (Taken prisoner at Arkansas Post, Arkansas, on January 11, 1863; died at Camp Butler, Illinois, on March 7, 1863)

JOHNSON, GEORGE, 29 (Transferred to Company H on April 11, 1862)

JOHNSON, JAMES P., 21 (Died at Arkansas Post, Arkansas, on December 15, 1862)

JOHNSON, M. R., 24 (Taken prisoner at Arkansas Post, Arkansas, on January 11, 1863)

KELL, GEORGE, 30 (6'0", blue eyes, sandy hair, light complexion; taken prisoner at Arkansas Post, Arkansas, on January 11, 1863; taken prisoner at Chickamauga, Georgia, on September 20, 1863; took oath of allegiance to the U.S.A. at ? on January 22, 1865)

KNOPP, JOHN, 19 (5'8", gray eyes, dark hair, fresh complexion; taken prisoner at Arkansas Post, Arkansas, on January 11, 1863; WIA at Chickamauga, Georgia, on September 20, 1863; taken prisoner at Missionary Ridge, Tennessee, on November 25, 1863)

KNOPP, PETER, 21 (5'8", gray eyes, light hair, light complexion, born in Germany, occupation a farmer; served in Trans-Mississippi Department from ?)

KUHLENTHAL, ED., 23 (Transferred to Company H on April 11, 1862)

LANDELL, ED. H., 28 (Taken prisoner at Arkansas Post, Arkansas, on January 11, 1863; WIA at ? on ?)

LEWIS, JOSIAH, 17 (Taken prisoner at Arkansas Post, Arkansas, on January 11, 1863; died at Camp Butler, Illinois, on February 17, 1863)

LINDSAY, JOHN, 20

LINDSAY, THOMAS (Served in Trans-Mississippi Department from ?)

LONDON, MAX H., 23 (Transferred to brigade hospital as a steward on March 6, 1862)

LOWTHER, N. B., 32 (6'0"; taken prisoner at Arkansas Post, Arkansas, on January 11, 1863; died at St. Louis, Missouri, on February 10, 1863)

MAHAN, JOHN, 22 (Taken prisoner at Arkansas Post, Arkansas, on January 11, 1863; escaped while in transit on the Mississippi River on ?)

MARTIN, AUGUSTUS, 22 (Taken prisoner at Arkansas Post, Arkansas, on January 11, 1863; WIA at Missionary Ridge, Tennessee, on November 25, 1863)

MARTIN, ROBERT, 18 (Taken prisoner at Arkansas Post, Arkansas, on January 11, 1863; WIA at Chickamauga, Georgia, on September 20, 1863)

MARTIN, SEBASTIAN, 35 (Taken prisoner at Arkansas Post, Arkansas, on January 11, 1863; died at LaGrange, Georgia, on December 8, 1863)

MAXWELL, WILLIAM W., 27 (Died at Washington, Arkansas, on August 5, 1862)

McDONALD, LEWIS, 18 (Died at Arkansas Post, Arkansas, on November 25, 1862)

McDONALD, WILLIAM R., 17 (6'0"; taken prisoner at Arkansas Post, Arkansas, on January 11, 1863; died at St. Louis, Missouri, on March 29, 1863)

McNAMARA, WILLIAM, 26 (6'1", blue eyes, brown hair, born in Ireland; transferred to Company H on April 11, 1862)

MILLER, JOHN, 24 (Taken prisoner at Arkansas Post, Arkansas, on January 11, 1863; took oath of allegiance to the U.S.A. at ? on ?)

MOORE, BEDE, 35 (Taken prisoner at Arkansas Post, Arkansas, on January 11, 1863; died at Camp Butler, Illinois, on March 7, 1863)

NEWPORT, JAMES A., 25 (Transferred to Company H on April 11, 1862)

NICHOLS, JOHN, 18 (Taken prisoner at Arkansas Post, Arkansas, on January 11, 1863)

NIMMO, JOSEPH W., 26 or 27 (5'5", blue eyes, fair hair, light complexion, born in Homby County, Mississippi, occupation a painter; transferred to Company H on April 14, 1862)

PEARCE, JAMES H., 32 (Received a disability discharge on August 7, 1862)

POSTON, WILLIAM, 37 (5'9½", dark eyes, dark hair, light complexion, born in Cleveland County, North Carolina, occupation a farmer; promoted third corporal on January 24, 1862; promoted first corporal on ?, 1862; promoted fifth sergeant on July ?, 1862; transferred to Company A, Twelfth Texas Infantry Regiment on ?)

POWER, JOHN, 25 (Promoted fourth corporal on January 24, 1862; transferred to Company H on April 11, 1862)

RAGLAND, JAMES, 28 (6'0", dark eyes, dark hair, dark complexion, born in Alabama; received a disability discharge on February 18, 1862)

RANDALL, OLIVER P., 23 (Taken prisoner at Arkansas Post, Arkansas, on January 11, 1863; WIA at Jonesboro, Georgia, on September 1, 1864; promoted corporal on ?; present at final surrender at Greensboro, North Carolina, on April 26, 1865)

RILEY, GEORGE J., 23 (Died at White Sulphur Springs, Arkansas, on September 27, 1862)

RILEY, T. W., 28 (5'8½", blue eyes, light hair, light complexion, born in Perry County, Missouri; transferred to Company A, Twelfth Texas Infantry Regiment on ?)

ROSE, GEORGE W., 21 (Taken prisoner at Arkansas Post, Arkansas, on January 11, 1863)

ROSE, JOHN, 22 (Taken prisoner at Arkansas Post, Arkansas, on January 11, 1863; died at Camp Butler, Illinois, on March 3, 1863)

SAMUELS, B., 22 (Served in Trans-Mississippi Department from ?)

SEERY, PETER, 24 (5'5½", hazel eyes, dark hair, red complexion; taken prisoner at Arkansas Post, Arkansas, on January 11, 1863; WIA at Chickamauga, Georgia, on September 20, 1863; taken prisoner near Nashville, Tennessee, on December 15, 1864)

SIMS, HENRY H., 21 or 26 (Transferred to Company H on April 11, 1862)

SMITH, E. R., 17 (Taken prisoner at Arkansas Post, Arkansas, on January 11, 1863; promoted second corporal on April 1, 1864; POW? near Atlanta, Georgia, on July 22, 1864)

SNIDER, WILLIAM, 22 or 23 (Taken prisoner at Arkansas Post, Arkansas, on January 11, 1863; WIA at Missionary Ridge, Tennessee, on September 20, 1863; WIA near Atlanta, Georgia, on July 21, 1864)

SQUYRES, LEMUEL, 16 (Received a ? discharge on November 30, 1861)

STANTON, WILLIAM E., 18 (Taken prisoner at Arkansas Post, Arkansas, on January 11, 1863; WIA at Chickamauga, Georgia, on September 20, 1863; present at final surrender at Greensboro, North Carolina, on April 26, 1865)

STAPP, CHRISTOPHER, 18 (Taken prisoner at Arkansas Post, Arkansas, on January 11, 1863; WIA at Jonesboro, Georgia, on September 1, 1864)

STEHR, AUGUST, 21 (5'7", gray eyes, brown hair, born in Germany; transferred to Company B on May 1, 1862)

SURLAN, FREDERICK, 38 (Taken prisoner at Arkansas Post, Arkansas, on January 11, 1863; died at Camp Butler, Illinois, on February 20, 1863)

TAYLOR, ADOLPHUS, 18 (Taken prisoner at Arkansas Post, Arkansas, on January 11, 1863; WIA near Atlanta, Georgia, on July 21 or 22, 1864; WIA at Franklin, Tennessee, on November 30, 1864)

THRELKELD, J. B., 20 (Taken prisoner at Arkansas Post, Arkansas, on January 11, 1863; WIA at Franklin, Tennessee, on November 30, 1864)

TRABER, JOSEPH, 25 (5'7", blue eyes, brown hair, fair complexion, born in Texas; received a disability discharge on May 15, 1862)

WALKER, E. H., 21 (Taken prisoner at Arkansas Post, Arkansas, on January 11, 1863; died at Petersburg, Virginia, on July 8, 1863)

WATERS, WILLIAM D. (Transferred from Company B on May 1, 1862)

WETHERELL, JAMES E., 26 (Promoted fourth corporal on December 21, 1861; returned to ranks on January 1, 1862; transferred to Company H on April 11, 1862)

WHELAN, CHARLES, 29 (Taken prisoner at Arkansas Post, Arkansas ,on January 11, 1863; present at final surrender at Greensboro, North Carolina, on April 26, 1865)

WILLIAMS, SAMUEL, 20 (5'7¼", dark eyes, red hair, florid complexion, born in New York, occupation a laborer; received a disability discharge on May 19, 1862)

WILSON, E. T., 22 (Taken prisoner at Arkansas Post, Arkansas, on January 11, 1863; WIA at Missionary Ridge, Tennessee, on November 25, 1863; WIA at New Hope Church, Georgia, on May 27, 1864)

WILSON, J. W., 20 (Taken prisoner at Arkansas Post, Arkansas, on January 11, 1863)

COMPANY B — LONE STAR RIFLES — Composed of personnel recruited primarily in Victoria County, Texas. Mustered into Confederate service on September 30, 1861.

OFFICERS

JAMES A. RUPLEY, Captain, 33 (Resigned on October 21, 1862)

L. SILVERSTINE, First Lieutenant, 41 (Resigned on June 7 or 8, 1862)

A. P. CUNNINGHAM, Second Lieutenant, 22 (5'5", blue eyes, light hair, fair complexion; promoted first lieutenant on June 8, 1862; promoted captain on October 21, 1862; taken prisoner at Arkansas Post, Arkansas, on January 11, 1863; displaced temporarily on May 24, 1863)

HERMAN ZAHN, Third Lieutenant, 31 (Promoted junior second lieutenant on ?, 1861; promoted second lieutenant on June 8, 1862; resigned on September 20, 1862)

NON-COMMISSIONED OFFICERS

P. G. BIEDERMANN, First Sergeant, 26 (6'2", gray eyes, brown hair, fair complexion; promoted junior second lieutenant on July 1, 1862; promoted second lieutenant on September 20, 1862; promoted first lieutenant on October 21, 1862; taken prisoner at Arkansas Post, Arkansas, on January 11, 1863; displaced temporarily on May 24, 1863; transferred to Trans-Mississippi Department on ?; died at ?, Texas, on ?, 1863)

R. WOELFFEL, Second Sergeant, 24 (5'7", blue eyes, flaxen hair, born in Prussia; returned to ranks on July 1, 1862; taken prisoner at Arkansas Post, Arkansas, on January 11, 1863; took oath of allegiance to the U.S.A. at Camp Butler, Illinois, on March ?, 1863)

H. E. SCHRAEDER, Third Sergeant, 22 (5'8", blue eyes, light hair, born in Germany; promoted second sergeant on July 1, 1862; taken prisoner at Arkansas Post, Arkansas, on January 11, 1863; took oath of allegiance to the U.S.A. at Camp Butler, Illinois, on March ?, 1863)

WILLIAM H. CARTER, Fourth Sergeant, 28 (6'1", blue eyes, auburn hair, fair complexion; promoted third sergeant on July 1, 1862; taken prisoner at Arkansas Post, Arkansas, on January 11, 1863; promoted junior second lieutenant on March 9, 1864; taken prisoner near Franklin, Tennessee, on December 17, 1864)

JOHN McCARTY, First Corporal, 26 (Promoted fifth sergeant on January 20, 1862; promoted fourth sergeant on July 1, 1862; returned to ranks on October 22, 1862; WIA at Arkansas Post, Arkansas, on January 11, 1863; taken prisoner at Arkansas Post, Arkansas, on January 11, 1863; died of wounds at St. Louis, Missouri, on February 1, 1863)

ERNEST MARKS, Second Corporal, 24 (Promoted first corporal on ?, 1862; promoted first sergeant on July 1, 1862; promoted junior second lieutenant on October 22 or 23, 1862; promoted second lieutenant on November 9, 1862; displaced temporarily on May 24, 1863; transferred to Trans-Mississippi Department on ?; promoted first lieutenant on September ?, 1863)

A. KLEIN, Third Corporal, 32 (5'6", gray eyes, brown hair, born in Germany; promoted second corporal on ?, 1862; promoted first sergeant on July 1, 1862; taken prisoner at Arkansas Post, Arkansas, on January 11, 1863; took oath of allegiance to the U.S.A. at Camp Butler, Illinois, on March 10, 1863)

VICTOR PELA, Fourth Corporal, 25, (Promoted first corporal on July 1, 1862; taken prisoner at Arkansas Post, Arkansas, on January 11, 1863; WIA at Chickamauga, Georgia, on September 20, 1863)

A. B. JONES, Drummer, 30 (Reduced to ranks on ?, 1862; deserted on June 26, 1862)

F. SCHUBERT, Bugler, 19 (5'3", blue eyes, light hair, born in Germany; taken prisoner at Arkansas Post, Arkansas, on January 11, 1863; took oath of allegiance to the U.S.A. at Camp Butler, Illinois, on ?)

AUGUST WAGNER, Bugler, 21 (5'10", gray eyes, brown hair, born in Germany; promoted to chief musician and transferred to field and staff on July 1, 1862; taken prisoner at Arkansas Post, Arkansas, on January 11, 1863; took oath of allegiance to the U.S.A. at Camp Butler, Illinois, on March ?, 1863)

PRIVATES

ADCOCK, ALEXANDER, 33 (Taken prisoner at Arkansas Post, Arkansas, on January 11, 1863)

ADCOCK, JAMES, 23 (5'7", blue eyes, dark hair, light complexion, born in Monroe County, Alabama; taken prisoner at Arkansas Post, Arkansas, on January 11, 1863; received a disability discharge on August 8, 1863)

ADCOCK, LEWIS, 20 (Taken prisoner at Arkansas Post, Arkansas, on January 11, 1863; WIA near Atlanta, Georgia, on July 21, 1864; present at final surrender at Greensboro, North Carolina, on April 26, 1865)

ALBERT, J.

ALEXANDER, L., 17 (5'6", blue eyes, light hair, born in Germany; taken prisoner at Arkansas Post, Arkansas, on January 11, 1863; took oath of allegiance to the U.S.A. at Camp Butler, Illinois, on March ?, 1863)

ALEXANDER, S., 27 (5'8", brown eyes, red hair, born in Germany; taken prisoner at Arkansas Post, Arkansas, on January 11, 1863; took oath of allegiance to the U.S.A. at Camp Butler, Illinois, on March ?, 1863)

AUSTER, J., 41 (Received a ? discharge on January 5, 1863)

BECK, F., (Received a ? discharge on July 4, 1862)

BECK, L., 19 (5'8", brown eyes, brown hair, born in Germany; taken prisoner at Arkansas Post, Arkansas, on January 11, 1863; took oath of allegiance to the U.S.A. at Camp Butler, Illinois, on March ?, 1863)

BROWN, STANLEY, 18 (5'8", gray eyes, brown hair, born in Washington, D.C.; taken prisoner at Arkansas Post, Arkansas, on January 11, 1863)

CLARK, H., 27 (MIA at Arkansas Post, Arkansas, on ?, 1863)

CONNERY, JAMES, 23 (5'9", brown eyes, brown hair, born in Ireland; promoted fourth sergeant on October 22, 1862; taken prisoner at Arkansas Post, Arkansas, on January 11, 1863; took oath of allegiance to the U.S.A. at Camp Butler, Illinois, on March ?, 1863)

COUTURIER, LOUIS, 34 (Taken prisoner at Arkansas Post, Arkansas, on January 11, 1863; promoted second sergeant on March 1, 1864; WIA at Jonesboro, Georgia, on August 31, 1864; died of wounds at ?, Georgia, on ?, 1864)

CURRAN, T., 30 (Taken prisoner at Arkansas Post, Arkansas, on January 11, 1863; took oath of allegiance to the U.S.A. at Camp Butler, Illinois, on ?, 1863)

DAVIDSBURG, D., 22 (Taken prisoner at Arkansas Post, Arkansas, on January 11, 1863; took oath of allegiance to the U.S.A. at Camp Butler, Illinois, on ?, 1863)

DAVIDSBURG, D. H., 25 (Taken prisoner at Arkansas Post, Arkansas, on January 11, 1863; took oath of allegiance to the U.S.A. at Camp Butler, Illinois, on ?, 1863)

DIETZ, JOHN, 23 (6'0", blue eyes, brown hair, born in Germany; taken prisoner at Arkansas Post, Arkansas, on January 11, 1863; took oath of allegiance to the U.S.A. at Camp Butler, Illinois, on March ?, 1863)

ERNST, JOSEPH, 18 (Taken prisoner at Arkansas Post, Arkansas, on January 11, 1863; transferred to the brigade band on ?, 1864; present at final surrender at Greensboro, North Carolina, on April 26, 1865)

FIEDLER, WILLIAM, 34 (Born in Germany; taken prisoner at Arkansas Post, Arkansas, on January 11, 1863; took oath of allegiance to the U.S.A. at Camp Butler, Illinois, on March 19, 1863)

FOX, JACOB, 18 (Taken prisoner at Arkansas Post, Arkansas, on January 11, 1863; WIA near Atlanta, Georgia, on July 21, 1864; WIA at Jonesboro, Georgia, on September 1, 1864; WIA at Franklin, Tennessee, on November 30, 1864)

FRANZ, H., 23 (5'7", blue eyes, black hair, born in Germany; taken prisoner at Arkansas Post, Arkansas, on January 11, 1863; took oath of allegiance to the U.S.A. at Camp Butler, Illinois, on March 11, 1863)

GABEL, JOSEPH, 18 (5'8", blue eyes, light hair, born in Germany; taken prisoner at Arkansas Post, Arkansas, on January 11, 1863; took oath of allegiance to the U.S.A. at Camp Butler, Illinois, on March ?, 1863)

GENSCH, F., 23 (KIA at Arkansas Post, Arkansas, on January 11, 1863)

GIBSON, JOHN, 26 (5'10", hazel eyes, black hair, dark complexion; promoted junior second lieutenant on November 10 or 14, 1862; taken prisoner at Arkansas Post, Arkansas, on January 11, 1863; promoted second lieutenant on September ?, 1863; WIA at Missionary Ridge, Tennessee, on November 25, 1863; WIA at Jonesboro, Georgia, on September 1, 1864; killed in a train wreck at ? on September 2, 1864)

GILBERT, R., 36 (5'10¾", blue eyes, light hair, light complexion, born in Essex County, New York, occupation a teacher; received a disability discharge on May 13 or June 7, 1862)

HAHN, JOHN, 49 (Taken prisoner at Arkansas Post, Arkansas, on January 11, 1863; present at final surrender at Greensboro, North Carolina, on April 26, 1865)

HANNE, J. F., 25 (5'6", gray eyes, black hair, born in Germany; promoted fourth corporal on December 13, 1862; taken prisoner at Arkansas Post, Arkansas, on January 11, 1863; took oath of allegiance to the U.S.A. at Camp Butler, Illinois, on March ?, 1863)

HANS, J., 20 (5'6", brown eyes, black hair, born in Germany; taken prisoner at Arkansas Post, Arkansas, on January 11, 1863; took oath of allegiance to the U.S.A. at Camp Butler, Illinois, on March ?, 1863)

HECK, CHRISTIAN, 25 (Promoted fourth corporal on July 1, 1862; promoted third corporal on October 22, 1862; returned to ranks on December 15, 1862; served in Trans-Mississippi Department from ?)

HERMANNS, H. (Taken prisoner at Arkansas Post, Arkansas, on January 11, 1863; took oath of allegiance to the U.S.A. at Camp Butler, Illinois, on ?, 1863)

HILF, CHARLES, 25 (Promoted fourth corporal on January 20, 1862; promoted second corporal on July 1, 1862; promoted first sergeant on October 22, 1862; taken prisoner at Arkansas Post, Arkansas, on January 11, 1863; took oath of allegiance to the U.S.A. at Camp Butler, Illinois, on ?, 1863)

HILLER, A., 19 (5'9", blue eyes, light hair, dark complexion, born in Germany; taken prisoner at Arkansas Post, Arkansas, on January 11, 1863; took oath of allegiance to the U.S.A. at Camp Butler, Illinois, on ?, 1863)

HOENES, P., 18 (5'6", gray eyes, dark hair, dark complexion, born in France, occupation a blacksmith; MIA at Arkansas Post, Arkansas, on ?; transferred to Company A, Twelfth Texas Infantry Regiment on ?)

HOFFMAN, SEBASTIAN

HOMAN, A., 23 (Taken prisoner at Arkansas Post, Arkansas, on January 11, 1863; took oath of allegiance to the U.S.A. at Camp Butler, Illinois, on ?)

KAISER, B., 25 (5'5", gray eyes, sandy hair, born in Germany; taken prisoner at Arkansas Post, Arkansas, on January 11, 1863; took oath of allegiance to the U.S.A. at Camp Butler, Illinois, on March ?, 1863)

KERN, JACOB, 20 (WIA at Arkansas Post, Arkansas, on January 11, 1863; taken prisoner at Arkansas Post, Arkansas, on January 11, 1863)

KOLLE, F., 25 (5'4", brown eyes, black hair, born in Germany; taken prisoner at Arkansas Post, Arkansas, on January 11, 1863; took oath of allegiance to the U.S.A. at Camp Butler, Illinois, on March ?, 1863)

KROSCHEL, L., 20 (5'6", gray eyes, brown hair, born in Germany; taken prisoner at Arkansas Post,

Arkansas, on January 11, 1863; took oath of allegiance to the U.S.A. at Camp Butler, Illinois, on March ?, 1863)

LANGNER, O. (Taken prisoner at Arkansas Post, Arkansas, on January 11, 1863; took oath of allegiance to the U.S.A. at Camp Butler, Illinois, on March ?, 1863)

LEUSCHNER, CHARLES A., 18 (Taken prisoner at Arkansas Post, Arkansas, on January 11, 1863; promoted first sergeant on ?; taken prisoner at Franklin, Tennessee, on November 30, 1864; correct age at time of enlistment was 15)

LEVY, S., (Taken prisoner at Arkansas Post, Arkansas, on January 11, 1863; took oath of allegiance to the U.S.A. at Camp Butler, Illinois on ?, 1863)

LEWIS, G. S., (POW records state that he was taken prisoner near Atlanta, Georgia, on July 22, 1864)

LEWIS, JOHN M., 27 or 29 (Taken prisoner at Arkansas Post, Arkansas, on January 11, 1863; KIA at Missionary Ridge, Tennessee, on November 25, 1863)

LOBMAN, SAMUEL

MEHNERT, EDWARD (Taken prisoner at Arkansas Post, Arkansas, on January 11, 1863; WIA at ? on ?, 1864; WIA at Jonesboro, Georgia, on August 31, 1864; died of wounds at ? on ?, 1864)

MEYER, SEBASTIAN, 19 (Taken prisoner at Arkansas Post, Arkansas, on January 11, 1863; taken prisoner near Nashville, Tennessee, on December 17, 1864)

MITCHELL, J. S., 35 (Deserted on February 19, 1862)

NETTER, J., 28 (Taken prisoner at Arkansas Post, Arkansas, on January 11, 1863)

PIEKERT, JOSEPH, 30 (Taken prisoner at Arkansas Post, Arkansas, on January 11, 1863)

PILGRIM, J., 18 (5'6", black eyes, black hair, born in Germany; taken prisoner at Arkansas Post, Arkansas, on January 11, 1863; took oath of allegiance to the U.S.A. at Camp Butler, Illinois, on March 7, 1863)

PONTON, A. J., 25 (MIA at Arkansas Post, Arkansas, on ?)

RIDER, WILLIAM, 26 (Taken prisoner at Arkansas Post, Arkansas, on January 11, 1863; took oath of allegiance to the U.S.A. at Camp Butler, Illinois, on ?, 1863)

RIEGER, BENJAMIN (Taken prisoner at Arkansas Post, Arkansas, on January 11, 1863; KIA at Chickamauga, Georgia, on September 20, 1863)

ROBINSON, WILLIAM, 36 (Deserted on January 8, 1862)

SANDERS, J., 28 (Taken prisoner at Arkansas Post, Arkansas, on January 11, 1863; died at Camp Butler, Illinois, on ?, 1863)

SASSE, F., 30 (5'5", blue eyes, brown hair, born in Prussia; taken prisoner at Arkansas Post, Arkansas, on January 11, 1863; took oath of allegiance to the U.S.A. at Camp Butler, Illinois, on March ?, 1863)

SCHIEWITZ, MICHAEL, 18 (Taken prisoner at Arkansas Post, Arkansas, on January 11, 1863; WIA near Atlanta, Georgia, on July 21, 1864)

SCHOTT, SEBASTIAN, 20 (Taken prisoner at Arkansas Post, Arkansas, on January 11, 1863)

SCHUCHERT, LUDWIG, 36 (Taken prisoner at Arkansas Post, Arkansas, on January 11, 1863; WIA at Taylor's Ridge, Georgia, on November 27, 1863)

SCHUPPE, A., 28 (5'5", blue eyes, brown hair, born in Germany; promoted third corporal on July 1, 1862; promoted second corporal on October 22, 1862; taken prisoner at Arkansas Post, Arkansas, on January 11, 1863; took oath of allegiance to the U.S.A. at Camp Butler, Illinois, on ?, 1863)

SILVERSTINE, S., 44 (5'3½", dark eyes, dark hair, dark complexion, born in Prussia, occupation a laborer; received a disability discharge on April 16, 1862)

SINNER, S., 20 (5'6", black eyes, brown hair, fair complexion, born in France, occupation a laborer; received a disability discharge on April 16, 1862)

SPAITH, D., 34 (Died at White Sulfur Springs, Arkansas, on September 29, 1862)

SPENCER, J. A., 26 (Promoted fourth corporal on October 22, 1862; promoted third corporal on December ?, 1862; taken prisoner at Arkansas Post, Arkansas, on January 11, 1863; died at Camp Butler, Illinois, on March 5, 1863)

SPENCER, WILLIAM H., 24 (Died at Victoria, Texas, on March 20, 1862)

STEHR, AUGUST, 21 (5'7", gray eyes, brown hair, born in Germany; transferred from Company A on May 1, 1862; promoted musician on August 4, 1862; taken prisoner at Arkansas Post, Arkansas, on January 11, 1863; took oath of allegiance to the U.S.A. at Camp Butler, Illinois, on March ?, 1863)

STEINMETZ, L., 17 or 18 (5'5", gray eyes, brown hair, born in Germany; promoted musician on December 1, 1862; taken prisoner at Arkansas Post, Arkansas, on January 11, 1863; took oath of allegiance to the U.S.A. at Camp Butler, Illinois, on March ?, 1863)

STEWART, JAMES, 24 (Taken prisoner at Arkansas Post, Arkansas, on January 11, 1863; present at final surrender at Greensboro, North Carolina, on April 26, 1865)

STRAUSS, FRANK 23 (Served in Trans-Mississippi Department from ?)

UPSTETT, F., 22 (Taken prisoner at Arkansas Post, Arkansas, on January 11, 1863; took oath of allegiance to the U.S.A. at Camp Butler, Illinois, on ?, 1863)

VERMILLION, R. A., 24 (Taken prisoner at Arkansas Post, Arkansas, on January 11, 1863; deserted on January 15, 1864)

VOIGHT, A., 24 (KIA at Arkansas Post, Arkansas, on January 11, 1863)

VOIT, J., 26 (Served in Trans-Mississippi Department from ?)

WALTER, C., 26 (5'5", brown eyes, black hair, born in Germany; taken prisoner at Arkansas Post, Arkansas, on January 11, 1863; took oath of allegiance to the U.S.A. at Camp Butler, Illinois, on March ?, 1863)

WATERS, WILLIAM D., (Transferred to Company A on May 1, 1862)

WEISS, O., 30 (5'8", gray eyes, brown hair, born in Germany; taken prisoner at Arkansas Post, Arkansas, on January 11, 1863; took oath of allegiance to the U.S.A. at Camp Butler, Illinois, on March ?, 1863)

WERTHEIMER, W., 24 (Taken prisoner at Arkansas Post, Arkansas, on January 11, 1863; took oath of allegiance to the U.S.A. at Camp Butler, Illinois, on ?, 1863)

WESTLY, J. H. (WIA at ? on ?)

WHELLIN, EDWARD, 33 (Taken prisoner at Arkansas Post, Arkansas, on January 11, 1863)

WILBURN, T. L. (Taken prisoner at Arkansas Post, Arkansas, on January 11, 1863)

WURZ, A. N. (Taken prisoner at Arkansas Post, Arkansas, on January 11, 1863; took oath of allegiance to the U.S.A. at Camp Butler, Illinois, on ?, 1863)

WURZ, J., 15 (5'6", blue eyes, light hair; taken prisoner at Arkansas Post, Arkansas, on January 11, 1863; took oath of allegiance to the U.S.A. at Camp Butler, Illinois, on May 8, 1863)

ZMUDA, M., 30 (Taken prisoner at Arkansas Post, Arkansas, on January 11, 1863; took oath of allegiance to the U.S.A. at Camp Butler, Illinois, on ?, 1863)

COMPANY C — Composed of personnel recruited primarily in Gonzales County, Texas. Mustered into Confederate service on October 3, 1861.

OFFICERS
ALONZO T. BASS, Captain (Resigned on October 22, 1862)

ELI A. McCORKLE, First Lieutenant, 40 (Promoted captain on October 21, 1862; taken prisoner at Arkansas Post, Arkansas, on January 11, 1863; displaced temporarily on May 24, 1863; transferred to Trans-Mississippi Department on ?)

THOMAS L. FLYNT, Second Lieutenant, 25 (5'4", gray eyes, dark hair, light complexion; promoted first lieutenant on October 21, 1862; taken prisoner at Arkansas Post, Arkansas, on January 11, 1863; resigned on ?)

JAMES L. SUTON, Third Lieutenant (Resigned on October 21, 1862)

NON-COMMISSIONED OFFICERS
JAMES L. BRANCH, First Sergeant, 23 (5'8", gray eyes, dark hair, dark complexion; promoted second lieutenant on November 14, 1862; taken prisoner at Arkansas Post, Arkansas, on January 11, 1863; displaced temporarily on May 24, 1863; transferred to Trans-Mississippi Department on ?)

JOHN CONWAY, Second Sergeant, 20 (Resigned and returned to ranks on November 10, 1862; taken prisoner at Arkansas Post, Arkansas, on January 11, 1863; taken prisoner at Franklin, Tennessee, on November 30, 1864)

JOHN J. McVEA, Third Sergeant, 28 (Resigned and returned to ranks on December 11, 1862; taken prisoner at Arkansas Post, Arkansas, on January 11, 1863; WIA at Missionary Ridge, Tennessee, on November 25, 1863; promoted second lieutenant on July 1, 1864; KIA near Atlanta,

Georgia, on July 22, 1864; POW records state that he died at Camp Butler, Illinois, on April 1, 1863)

THOMAS C. SHARP, Fourth Sergeant, 23 (Resigned and returned to ranks on November 10, 1862; WIA at Arkansas Post, Arkansas, on January 11, 1863; taken prisoner at Arkansas Post, Arkansas, on January 11, 1863; died of wounds at Memphis, Tennessee, on January 16, 1863)

JAMES A. BARNETT, Fifth Sergeant, 34 (6'3", gray eyes, dark hair, dark complexion; promoted second lieutenant on November 9 or 10, 1862; displaced temporarily on May 24, 1863; transferred to Trans-Mississippi Department on ?)

DAVID MURPHY, First Corporal, 37 (Resigned and returned to ranks on November 10, 1862; taken prisoner at Arkansas Post, Arkansas, on January 11, 1863; died at Camp Butler, Illinois, on April 4, 1863)

LUDY C. ALSUP, Second Corporal, 20 (Resigned and returned to ranks on November 10, 1862; taken prisoner at Arkansas Post, Arkansas, on January 11, 1863)

JAMES W. BRYAN, Third Corporal, 29 (Served in Trans-Mississippi Department from ?)

JOHN H. TUMLISON, Fourth Corporal, 21, (Promoted fifth sergeant on November 11, 1862; taken prisoner at Arkansas Post, Arkansas, on January 11, 1863; WIA at Chickamauga, Georgia, on September 20, 1863)

GEORGE HENRIQUES, Musician, 27 (Turned over to civil authorities on December 8, 1861)

PRIVATES

ALSUP, R. J., 22 (Taken prisoner at Arkansas Post, Arkansas, on January 11, 1863; died at Petersburg, Virginia, on May 28, 1863)

ALSUP, WILLIAM R., 18 (Taken prisoner at Arkansas Post, Arkansas, on January 11, 1863; WIA at Jonesboro, Georgia, on September 1, 1864)

ANDERSON, A. R. (Died at Arkansas Post, Arkansas, on October 22, 1862)

BAKER, A., 58 (Received a disability discharge on March 9, 1862)

BAKER, J., 37 (Taken prisoner at Arkansas Post, Arkansas, on January 11, 1863; present at final surrender at Greensboro, North Carolina, on April 26, 1865)

BAKER, J. L. (Dropped from roll as deserter on August 10, 1862)

BAKER, THOMAS, 47 (5'9", black eyes, black hair, born in England; taken prisoner at Arkansas Post, Arkansas, on January 11, 1863; took oath of allegiance to the U.S.A. at Camp Butler, Illinois, on ?, 1863)

BARNETT, J. P., 28 (Promoted fourth sergeant on November 11, 1862; taken prisoner at Arkansas Post, Arkansas, on January 11, 1863; WIA at New Hope Church, Georgia, on May 27, 1864; present at final surrender at Greensboro, North Carolina, on April 26, 1865)

BATLING, HENRY, 22 (Taken prisoner at Arkansas Post, Arkansas, on January 11, 1863; WIA at Chickamauga, Georgia, on September 20, 1863)

BELLINGER, W. R., 26 (Promoted first sergeant on November 11, 1862; taken prisoner at Arkansas Post, Arkansas, on January 11, 1863; WIA at New Hope Church, Georgia, on May 27, 1864)

BENHAM, LEE (Died at Arkansas Post, Arkansas, on November 10, 1862)

BLOOMBERG, J., 16 (5'4", blue eyes, black hair, born in Prussia; taken prisoner at Arkansas Post, Arkansas, on January 11, 1863; took oath of allegiance to the U.S.A. at Camp Butler, Illinois, on ?, 1863)

BOTTS, H. C., 28 (Taken prisoner at Arkansas Post, Arkansas, on January 11, 1863; died at Petersburg, Virginia, on ?, 1863)

BOWERMAN, WILLIAM, 21 (Taken prisoner at Arkansas Post, Arkansas, on January 11, 1863)

BRITTON, C., 34 (Taken prisoner at Arkansas Post, Arkansas, on January 11, 1863; taken prisoner near Atlanta, Georgia, on July 22, 1864)

BURNS, W., 35 (Taken prisoner at Arkansas Post, Arkansas, on January 11, 1863; WIA at New Hope Church, Georgia, on May 27, 1864; WIA near Atlanta, Georgia, on July 21, 1864; taken prisoner at Franklin, Tennessee, on November 30, 1864)

CLARK, F. B., 16 (Taken prisoner at Arkansas Post, Arkansas, on January 11, 1863; WIA near New Hope Church, Georgia, on May 27, 1864; died of wounds at ? on ?)

CONNALLY, C., 43 (Served in Trans-Mississippi Department from December 14, 1862)

CROSS, S. F., 24 (Served in Trans-Mississippi Department from ?)

CROZIER, W. A., 19 (Taken prisoner at Arkansas Post, Arkansas, on January 11, 1863; KIA at Franklin, Tennessee, on November 30, 1864)

CUMMINGS, J. F., 19 (WIA at Arkansas Post, Arkansas, on ?; taken prisoner at Arkansas Post, Arkansas, on January 11, 1863; served in Trans-Mississippi Department from ?)

DAY, J. R., 24 (Received a disability discharge on December 26, 1862)

DEITCH, SOLOMON, 19 (5'4", hazel eyes, brown hair, dark complexion; taken prisoner at Arkansas Post, Arkansas, on January 11, 1863; WIA near Atlanta, Georgia, on July 22, 1864; taken prisoner at Franklin, Tennessee, on November 30, 1864; took oath of allegiance to the U.S.A. at ? on ?)

DEROZIER, ALEX, 25 (Taken prisoner at Arkansas Post, Arkansas, on January 11, 1863; WIA at ? on ?, 1865)

DICK, T. A., 46 (5'7", dark eyes, dark hair, dark complexion, born in Tennessee; received a disability discharge on June 4, 1862)

DUNLOP, COLIN, 25 (Taken prisoner at Arkansas Post, Arkansas, on January 11, 1863)

FINCH, R., 30 (5'7", blue eyes, dark hair, light complexion, born in Carroll County, Tennessee; served in Trans-Mississippi Department from ?, 1863)

FRANK, B., 28 (Received a disability discharge on ?, 1862)

GIPSON, SAMUEL, 21 (Taken prisoner at Arkansas Post, Arkansas, on January 11, 1863; present at final surrender at Greensboro, North Carolina, on April 26, 1865)

HAHN, A. B., 17 (Taken prisoner at Arkansas Post, Arkansas, on January 11, 1863; WIA near Marietta, Georgia, on June 21, 1864; died at ? on ?)

HALFIN, ELI, 25 (5'8", brown eyes, brown hair, fair complexion; taken prisoner at Arkansas Post, Arkansas, on January 11, 1863; taken prisoner near Nashville, Tennessee, on December 16, 1864)

HALIBURTON, M., 19 (Taken prisoner at Arkansas Post, Arkansas, on January 11, 1863)

HARRISON, CHARLES, 16 (Received a disability discharge on September 1, 1862)

HENSON, W. H., 18 (Taken prisoner at Arkansas Post, Arkansas, on January 11, 1863; died at Camp Butler, Illinois, on ?, 1863)

HILLIARD, G. W. (Died at Arkansas Post, Arkansas, on December 20, 1862)

HURLEY, W., 25 (5'10", hazel eyes, dark hair, florid complexion, born in New Jersey; taken prisoner at Arkansas Post, Arkansas, on January 11, 1863; WIA at New Hope Church, Georgia, on May 27, 1864; WIA near Atlanta, Georgia, on July 22, 1864; received a disability discharge on November 10, 1864)

JONES, A. W., 17 (Taken prisoner at Arkansas Post, Arkansas, on January 11, 1863; WIA at Spring Hill, Tennessee, on November 29, 1864)

KELLEY, W., 25 (5'9", gray eyes, brown hair, born in Germany; taken prisoner at Arkansas Post, Arkansas, on January 11, 1863; took oath of allegiance to the U.S.A. at Camp Butler, Illinois, on February 4, 1863)

LEWIS, HARVEY, 18 (Died at Victoria, Texas, on May 7, 1862)

LIGHT, M. L., 25 (Taken prisoner at Arkansas Post, Arkansas, on January 11, 1863; WIA near Atlanta, Georgia, on July 22, 1864; present at final surrender at Greensboro, North Carolina, on April 26, 1865)

LIGHT, V. D., 22 (Taken prisoner at Arkansas Post, Arkansas, on January 11, 1863)

LIGHT, W. R., 28 (Died at Washington, Arkansas, on August 4, 1862)

MALONE, J.

MARTIN, T. J., 19 (Promoted third sergeant on December 13, 1862; taken prisoner at Arkansas Post, Arkansas, on January 11, 1863; WIA at New Hope Church, Georgia, on May 27, 1864; WIA at Franklin, Tennessee, on November 30, 1864; taken prisoner at Franklin, Tennessee, on December 17, 1864)

McCAUGHAN, JOHN D., 27 (Taken prisoner at Arkansas Post, Arkansas, on January 11, 1863; WIA at New Hope Church, Georgia, on May 27, 1864; promoted second lieutenant on July 26, 1864; WIA at Jonesboro, Georgia, on August 31, 1864)

McDONALD, D., 36 (Served in Trans-Mississippi Department from ?)

McGINNIS, PATRICK, 38 (5'7", black eyes, dark hair, dark complexion, born in Ireland, occupation a planter; taken prisoner at Arkansas Post, Arkansas, on January 11, 1863; transferred to Engineer Corps on ?, 1863)

McVEA, J. A., 26 (Taken prisoner at Arkansas Post, Arkansas, on January 11, 1863; transferred to Engineer Corps on August 9, 1863)

McVEA, J. G., 19 (Taken prisoner at Arkansas Post, Arkansas, on January 11, 1863; died at Camp Butler, Illinois, on April 1, 1863)

McVEA, MARTIN, 17 (Taken prisoner at Arkansas Post, Arkansas, on January 11, 1863; WIA near Atlanta, Georgia, on July 21, 1864; WIA at ? on January 27, 1865; died at Milledgeville, Georgia, on February 9, 1865)

NATIONS, L. B., 18 (Taken prisoner at Arkansas Post, Arkansas, on January 11, 1863; WIA at Jonesboro, Georgia, on September 1, 1864; WIA at Franklin, Tennessee, on November 30, 1864)

NATIONS, W. A., 46 (Taken prisoner at Arkansas Post, Arkansas, on January 11, 1863; died at Camp Butler, Illinois, on February 7, 1863)

NATIONS, W. C. (Taken prisoner at Arkansas Post, Arkansas, on January 11, 1863; served in Trans-Mississippi Department from ?)

NORFLEET, J. M., 16 (Promoted fourth corporal on November 11, 1862; taken prisoner at Arkansas Post, Arkansas, on January 11, 1863; KIA at Chickamauga, Georgia, on September 20, 1863; POW records show that he died at Camp Butler, Illinois, on March 24, 1863)

O'NEILL, DAVID, 27 (Transferred to William T. Mechling's Texas Battery on ?)

RAMSAY, J., 48 (Taken prisoner at Arkansas Post, Arkansas, on January 11, 1863; present at final surrender at Greensboro, North Carolina, on April 26, 1865)

RAMSAY, T. O., 16 (Taken prisoner at Arkansas Post, Arkansas, on January 11, 1863; taken prisoner near Jonesboro, Georgia, on September 1, 1864; died at Milledgeville, Georgia, on February 20, 1865)

REESE, CHARLES, 19 (5'8", gray eyes, dark hair, fair complexion; taken prisoner at Arkansas Post, Arkansas, on January 11, 1863; WIA near Atlanta, Georgia, on July 21, 1864; taken prisoner at Jonesboro, Georgia, on September 6, 1864)

ROEBUCK, R., 30 (Taken prisoner at Arkansas Post, Arkansas, on January 11, 1863; WIA near Atlanta, Georgia, on July 22, 1864)

SHEFSKY, H., 36 (Transferred to Company I on August 1, 1862)

SHOEMAKER, DAVID, 20 (Taken prisoner at Arkansas Post, Arkansas, on January 11, 1863; WIA near Marietta, Georgia, on June 21, 1864; present at final surrender at Greensboro, North Carolina, on April 26, 1865)

STEINER, L.

STEVENSON, JOHN, 40 (Taken prisoner at Arkansas Post, Arkansas, on January 11, 1863; WIA at Franklin, Tennessee, on November 30, 1864; taken prisoner at Franklin, Tennessee, on December 18, 1864)

STROOPE, ISSAC P., 16 (5'11" or 6'0", blue or gray eyes, light hair, light complexion, born in Texas or Arkansas; received a disability discharge on November 29, 1862)

STROOPE, JOHN P., 19 (Taken prisoner at Arkansas Post, Arkansas, on January 11, 1863; WIA at New Hope Church, Georgia, on May 27, 1864; WIA at Jonesboro, Georgia, on September 1, 1864)

STROOPE, S. C., 22 (Died at Arkansas Post, Arkansas, on November 12, 1862)

TAYLOR, DANIEL, 19 (Taken prisoner at Arkansas Post, Arkansas, on January 11, 1863; WIA at Franklin, Tennessee, on November 30, 1864; present at final surrender at Greensboro, North Carolina, on April 26, 1865)

TAYLOR, T. R., 18 (Promoted second sergeant on November 11, 1862; taken prisoner at Arkansas Post, Arkansas, on January 11, 1863; present at final surrender at Greensboro, North Carolina, on April 26, 1865)

THETFORD, T. C., 26 (5'6", gray eyes, dark hair, fair complexion, born in Mississippi; promoted second corporal on November 11, 1862; taken prisoner at Arkansas Post, Arkansas, on January 11, 1863; WIA at New Hope Church, Georgia, on May 27, 1864; received a disability discharge on January 31, 1865)

TUMLISON, J. L., 19 (Promoted first corporal on November 11, 1862; taken prisoner at Arkansas Post, Arkansas, on January 11, 1863; died at Camp Butler, Illinois, on February 24, 1863)

TURNER, JOHN, 32 (6'0", blue eyes, dark hair, dark complexion, born in Tennessee; received a disability discharge on April 16, 1862)

TYLER, WILLIAM G., 18 (Taken prisoner at Arkansas Post, Arkansas, on January 11, 1863)

WALLACE, E. W., 23 or 24 (5'4" or 5'8", blue eyes, red hair, fair complexion, born in Mississippi; received a disability discharge on June 4, 1862)

WILSON, W., 30 (Received a disability discharge on February 6, 1862)

WOLFE, J. A., 30 (Taken prisoner at Arkansas Post, Arkansas, on January 11, 1863; took oath of allegiance to the U.S.A. at St. Louis, Missouri, on March 11, 1863)

WOOTEN, J. F. M., 29 (Taken prisoner at Arkansas Post, Arkansas, on January 11, 1863; took oath of allegiance to the U.S.A. at St. Louis, Missouri, on March 11, 1863)

WOOTEN, S. M., 27 (Taken prisoner at Arkansas Post, Arkansas, on January 11, 1863; took oath of allegiance to the U.S.A. at St. Louis, Missouri, on March 11, 1863)

COMPANY D — MATAGORDA GUARDS — Composed of personnel recruited primarily in Matagorda County, Texas. Mustered into Confederate service on October 4, 1861.

OFFICERS

E. A. PEARESON, Captain, 46 (Resigned on May 13 or 20, 1862)

JAMES SELKIRK, First Lieutenant, 37 (5'10½", gray eyes, light hair, dark complexion; promoted captain on May 13 or 20, 1862; taken prisoner at Arkansas Post, Arkansas, on January 11, 1863; displaced temporarily on May 24, 1863; WIA at Franklin, Tennessee, on November 30, 1864)

STEWART GREENBERRY, Second Lieutenant, 33 (6'0", blue eyes, brown hair, dark complexion; promoted first lieutenant on May 13 or 20, 1862; taken prisoner at Arkansas Post, Arkansas, on January 11, 1863; displaced temporarily on May 24, 1863; transferred to Trans-Mississippi Department on ?)

PHILIP E. PEARESON, Third Lieutenant, 20 (5'7" or 5'8", gray eyes, dark hair, fair or dark complexion; promoted second lieutenant on May 13 or 20, 1862; taken prisoner at Arkansas Post, Arkansas, on January 11, 1863; taken prisoner at Franklin, Tennessee, on November 30, 1864)

NON-COMMISSIONED OFFICERS

GEORGE S. LEWIS, First Sergeant, 25 (Taken prisoner at Arkansas Post, Arkansas, on January 11, 1863; returned to ranks on October 1, 1863; WIA at Missionary Ridge, Tennessee, on November 25, 1863; taken prisoner near Atlanta, Georgia, on July 22, 1864)

JOHN F. DALE, Second Sergeant, 26 (6'0", gray eyes, light hair, fair complexion; taken prisoner at Arkansas Post, Arkansas, on January 11, 1863; promoted junior second lieutenant on May 14, 1863; displaced temporarily on May 24, 1863; transferred to Trans-Mississippi Department on ?; died at ? on January 1, 1864)

WILLIAM H. GIBSON, Third Sergeant, 22 (Returned to ranks on October 17, 1862; died at Arkansas Post, Arkansas on ?, 1862)

DAVID CULVER, Fourth Sergeant, 35 (Taken prisoner at Arkansas Post, Arkansas, on January 11, 1863; promoted second lieutenant on March 1, 1864)

RICHARD FLOOD, First Corporal, 32 (Returned to ranks on ?, 1861; taken prisoner at Arkansas Post, Arkansas, on January 11, 1863; transferred to Engineer Corps on August 2, 1863)

JAMES STERRY, Second Corporal, 32 (5'11", gray eyes, black hair, dark complexion; resigned on October 17, 1862; taken prisoner at Arkansas Post, Arkansas, on January 11, 1863; taken prisoner at ? on October ?, 1864)

JOHN RAIMAN, Third Corporal, 34 (Taken prisoner at Arkansas Post, Arkansas, on January 11, 1863; WIA at Missionary Ridge, Tennessee, on November 25, 1863; WIA at Jonesboro, Georgia, on September 1, 1864)

BERNARD FREDERICK, Fifer, 22 (Taken prisoner at Arkansas Post, Arkansas, on January 11, 1863; took oath of allegiance to the U.S.A. at City Point, Virginia, on April 15, 1863)

WILLIAM HOLMES, Drummer, 25 (5'6", blue eyes, brown hair, dark complexion, born in Denmark, occupation a sailor; received a disability discharge on December 6, 1862)

CHARLES BRANDIS, Clerk, 36 (5'5", brown eyes, dark hair, dark complexion, born in France; received a disability discharge on June 27, 1862)

PRIVATES

BALLINGER, GREEN (WIA near Atlanta, Georgia, on July 22, 1864; taken prisoner near Atlanta, Georgia, on July 22, 1864; died at Marietta, Georgia, on August 26, 1864)

BATES, THOMAS F., 35 (Absent on surgeon's certificate of disability since May 20, 1862)

BAXTER, WILLIAM, 23 (Taken prisoner at Arkansas Post, Arkansas, on January 11, 1863; died at Camp Butler, Illinois, on February 10, 1863)

BENSON, ISAAC, 32 (Died at Arkansas Post, Arkansas, on November 4, 1862)

BERNARD, LOUIS, 21 (Received a disability discharge on ?, 1862)

BRIDGES, JOHN, 18 (Taken prisoner at Arkansas Post, Arkansas, on January 11, 1863; promoted second corporal on March 1, 1864; KIA near Atlanta, Georgia, on July 22, 1864)

BROWN, JOHN, 22 (Deserted at Victoria, Texas, on November 14, 1861)

BROWN, LEWIS, 18 (Taken prisoner at Arkansas Post, Arkansas, on January 11, 1863; transferred to regimental band on ?, 1863; transferred to brigade band on March 12, 1864)

BROWN, WILLIAM, 23 (Taken prisoner at Arkansas Post, Arkansas, on January 11, 1863; transferred to C.S. Navy on April 11, 1864)

BRUCE, ARTHUR C., 24 (Taken prisoner at Arkansas Post, Arkansas, on January 11, 1863; promoted fourth sergeant on March 1, 1864; promoted ensign on May 25, 1864; promoted first lieutenant on August 16, 1864)

BRYANT, WOLFRED, 23 (5'0", gray eyes, dark hair, fair complexion, born in Banger, Maine; received a disability discharge on May 20, 1862)

CHEESMAN, ARTHUR, 18 (Promoted fifth sergeant on May 14, 1862; resigned and returned to ranks on October 17, 1862; taken prisoner at Arkansas Post, Arkansas, on January 11, 1863; died at Camp Butler, Illinois, on April 13, 1863)

CLOUDER, GEORGE, 21 (Taken prisoner at Arkansas Post, Arkansas, on January 11, 1863; WIA near Atlanta, Georgia, on July 21, 1864; died of wounds at ? on ?)

COVENEY, JOHN, 23 (Taken prisoner at Arkansas Post, Arkansas, on January 11, 1863; took oath of allegiance to the U.S.A. at Camp Butler, Illinois, on ?, 1863)

CRILL, JOSEPH, 18 (Transferred to Company I on August 1, 1862)

DAVIS, THOMAS, 24 (Taken prisoner at Arkansas Post, Arkansas, on January 11, 1863; died at Camp Butler, Illinois, on February 12, 1863)

DEMONET, JOHN, 19 (Taken prisoner at Arkansas Post, Arkansas, on January 11, 1863; KIA at Missionary Ridge, Tennessee, on November 25, 1863)

DIETRICH, SEBASTIAN, 35 (5'2½", blue eyes, dark hair, light complexion, born in Europe; received a disability discharge on July 4, 1862)

DRESSY, ALEXANDER, 45 (Taken prisoner at Arkansas Post, Arkansas, on January 11, 1863; died east of Natchez, Mississippi, on June ?)

DUFFY, AUGUSTUS, 23 (Taken prisoner at Arkansas Post, Arkansas, on January 11, 1863)

DUNBAR, ADAM, 44 (Taken prisoner at Arkansas Post, Arkansas, on January 11, 1863; WIA near Atlanta, Georgia, on July 21, 1864)

DUNBAR, WILLIAM, 21 (Taken prisoner at Arkansas Post, Arkansas, on January 11, 1863; taken prisoner near Atlanta, Georgia, on July 22, 1864; present at final surrender at Greensboro, North Carolina, on April 26, 1865)

DYSON, ROBERT, 23 (Taken prisoner at Arkansas Post, Arkansas, on January 11, 1863; died at Richmond, Virginia, on May ?, 1863)

EDGAR, EDWARD, 18 (Taken prisoner at Arkansas Post, Arkansas, on January 11, 1863; present at final surrender at Greensboro, North Carolina, on April 26, 1865)

EIDELBACH, JOHN, 21 (Taken prisoner at Arkansas Post, Arkansas, on January 11, 1863; WIA at Missionary Ridge, Tennessee, on November 25, 1863; present at final surrender at Greensboro, North Carolina, on April 26, 1865)

FUNK, MARTIN, 21 (Taken prisoner at Arkansas Post, Arkansas, on January 11, 1863; WIA near Atlanta, Georgia, on July 22, 1864; present at final surrender at Greensboro, North Carolina, on April 26, 1865)

GOLDEN, W. M., 32 (Taken prisoner at Arkansas Post, Arkansas, on January 11, 1863; promoted third corporal on March 1, 1864; present at final surrender at Greensboro, North Carolina, on April 26, 1865)

GUTHRIE, C. S. (WIA at Missionary Ridge, Tennessee, on November 25, 1863)

GUTHRIE, CHARLES, 21 (Taken prisoner at Arkansas Post, Arkansas, on January 11, 1863; died at Camp Butler, Illinois, on April 2, 1863)

HASBROOK, ROBERT, 24 (Served in Trans-Mississippi Department from ?)

HILL, JOHN, 25 (Taken prisoner at Arkansas Post, Arkansas, on January 11, 1863; died at Petersburg, Virginia, on April ?, 1863)

HILL, THOMAS, 19 (Taken prisoner at Arkansas Post, Arkansas, on January 11, 1863; died at Camp Butler, Illinois, on February 10, 1863)

HINES, MORRIS, 18 (Taken prisoner at Arkansas Post, Arkansas, on January 11, 1863; WIA at Missionary Ridge, Tennessee, on November 25, 1863; taken prisoner at Franklin, Tennessee, on November 30, 1864)

HOLT, JOHN F., 23 (Promoted second sergeant on May 14, 1862; taken prisoner at Arkansas Post, Arkansas, on January 11, 1863; promoted ordnance sergeant on May 24, 1863; promoted junior second lieutenant on March 9, 1864; WIA at Jonesboro, Georgia, on September 1, 1864)

HUNT, WHEELER D., 38 (5'6", dark eyes, brown hair, dark complexion, born in Connecticut, occupation a laborer; received a disability discharge on May 20, 1862)

INGLEHART, EDWARD, 26 (Taken prisoner at Arkansas Post, Arkansas, on January 11, 1863; WIA at Missionary Ridge, Tennessee, on November 25, 1863; WIA at New Hope Church, Georgia, on May 27, 1864; WIA near Atlanta, Georgia, on July 22, 1864)

JAMES, SIDNEY, 26 (Taken prisoner at Arkansas Post, Arkansas, on January 11, 1863; KIA at Missionary Ridge, Tennessee, on November 25, 1863)

JONES, HENRY, 30 (Taken prisoner at Arkansas Post, Arkansas, on January 11, 1863; served in Trans-Mississippi Department from ?)

KELLER, FREDERICK, 23 (Taken prisoner at Arkansas Post, Arkansas, on January 11, 1863; transferred to Engineer Corps on August 2, 1863)

KIMBALL, THOMAS, 37 (Taken prisoner at Arkansas Post, Arkansas, on January 11, 1863; KIA at Missionary Ridge, Tennessee, on November 25, 1863)

KUYKENDALL, ROBERT, 23 (Taken prisoner at Arkansas Post, Arkansas, on January 11, 1863; died at Camp Butler, Illinois, on April 20, 1863)

LEHMAN, SAMUEL, 36 (5'3", black eyes, black hair, dark complexion, born in Switzerland, occupation a laborer; received a disability discharge on June 4, 1862)

LEWIS, D. (Taken prisoner at Arkansas Post, Arkansas, on January 11, 1863; died at Camp Butler, Illinois, on February 20, 1863)

LUDWIG, CONRAD, 21 (Taken prisoner at Arkansas Post, Arkansas, on January 11, 1863; WIA at Spring Hill, Tennessee, on November 29, 1864)

MAIHAIVIER, ANTONIO, 23 (Promoted fifth sergeant on December 14, 1862; taken prisoner at Arkansas Post, Arkansas, on January 11, 1863; WIA at Missionary Ridge, Tennessee, on November 25, 1863; promoted third sergeant on March 1, 1864; WIA near Marietta, Georgia, on July 4, 1864; KIA at Franklin, Tennessee, on November 30, 1864)

McCUE, THOMAS, (Taken prisoner at Arkansas Post, Arkansas, on January 11, 1863; present at final surrender at Greensboro, North Carolina, on April 26, 1865)

McLEOD, DANIEL, 27 (Taken prisoner at Arkansas Post, Arkansas, on January 11, 1863; transferred to C.S. Navy on April 12, 1864)

McNABB, JOHN, 23 (Served in Trans-Mississippi Department from ?)

MEYERS, JACOB (5'2", gray eyes, light hair, fair complexion, born in Germany, occupation a laborer; received a disability discharge on May 20, 1862)

MYLIUS, HERMAN, 23 or 24 (Absent on surgeon's certificate of disability since May 20, 1862)

NOLTE, JOSEPH, 40 (Taken prisoner at Arkansas Post, Arkansas, on January 11, 1863; served in Trans-Mississippi Department from ?)

NYE, THOMAS C., 18 (5'10½", gray eyes, dark hair, fresh complexion; taken prisoner at Arkansas Post, Arkansas, on January 11, 1863; WIA at Chickamauga, Georgia, on September 20, 1863; taken prisoner at Missionary Ridge, Tennessee, on November 25, 1863)

NYE, WILLIAM, 28 (6'0", gray eyes, dark hair, light complexion, born in Texas, occupation a farmer; received a disability discharge on November 15, 1862)

OLLENDOFF, JOHN G., 22 or 23 (Taken prisoner at Arkansas Post, Arkansas, on January 11, 1863; WIA near Atlanta, Georgia, on July 22, 1864)

PAIRON, JOHN, 33 (Taken prisoner at Arkansas Post, Arkansas, on January 11, 1863; promoted first corporal on March 1, 1864; WIA at Franklin, Tennessee, on November 30, 1864)

PEDEN, LEWIS (Taken prisoner at Arkansas Post, Arkansas, on January 11, 1863)

PHILLIPS, JOHN, 24 (Taken prisoner at Arkansas Post, Arkansas, on January 11, 1863; promoted

fifth sergeant on March 1, 1864; WIA at Jonesboro, Georgia, on August 31, 1864; present at
final surrender at Greensboro, North Carolina, on April 26, 1865)

PLAGGE, RICHARD, 18 (Taken prisoner at Arkansas Post, Arkansas, on January 11, 1863)

PRICE, JOHN, 18 (Taken prisoner at Arkansas Post, Arkansas, on January 11, 1863; died at Camp
Butler, Illinois, on March 31, 1863)

QUEDANS, BARNEY, 24 (Taken prisoner at Arkansas Post, Arkansas, on January 11, 1863; died
at Atlanta, Georgia, on October 20, 1863)

RIERDEN, LAWRENCE (WIA at Arkansas Post, Arkansas, on January 11, 1863; died of wounds at
Arkansas Post, Arkansas, on January 20, 1863)

RODGERS, MARTIN, 22 (Taken prisoner at Arkansas Post, Arkansas, on January 11, 1863; took
oath of allegiance to the U.S.A. at Camp Butler, Illinois, on ?, 1863)

SALZEGER, GODFRIED, 26 (Taken prisoner at Arkansas Post, Arkansas, on January 11, 1863;
WIA at Taylor's Ridge, Georgia, on November 27, 1863; present at final surrender at Greensboro, North Carolina, on April 26, 1865)

SAVARY, WILEY P., 13 (4'8", brown eyes, auburn hair, light complexion, born in Port Lavaca,
Texas; taken prisoner at Arkansas Post, Arkansas, on January 11, 1863; received a discharge for
being a minor on May 2, 1863)

SAVERY, HARVEY T., 42 (Taken prisoner at Arkansas Post, Arkansas, on January 11, 1863; served
in Trans-Mississippi Department from ?)

SCHUBERT, JOHN, 32 (Deserted at Victoria, Texas, on November 12, 1861)

SCHWERBURGER, WENDELIN, 35 (Taken prisoner at Arkansas Post, Arkansas, on January 11,
1863; taken prisoner at Missionary Ridge, Tennessee, on November 25, 1863; enlisted into the
U.S. Navy on May 23, 1864)

SERRILL, RICHARD O., 38 (Taken prisoner at Arkansas Post, Arkansas, on January 11, 1863;
taken prisoner near Franklin, Tennessee, on December 17, 1864)

SHAFER, HENRY, 18 (Taken prisoner at Arkansas Post, Arkansas, on January 11, 1863; WIA at
Missionary Ridge, Tennessee, on November 25, 1863; present at final surrender at Greensboro,
North Carolina, on April 26, 1865)

SHEPPARD, W. D., 30 (Taken prisoner at Arkansas Post, Arkansas, on January 11, 1863)

SHORTRIDGE, JOHN H., 28 (Hazel eyes, black hair, fair complexion, born in Alabama, occupation a chicken raiser; promoted fifth sergeant on December 28, 1861; received a disability discharge on May 20, 1862)

SMITH, FRANCIS, 28 (5'10", blue eyes, light hair, fair complexion, born in Sweden, occupation a
sailor; WIA at Arkansas Post, Arkansas, on January 11, 1863; taken prisoner at Arkansas Post,
Arkansas, on January 11, 1863; present at final surrender at Greensboro, North Carolina, on
April 26, 1865)

SMITH, HENRY, 19 (Taken prisoner at Arkansas Post, Arkansas, on January 11, 1863; died
aboard the steamer *John J. Roe* on January ?, 1863)

SMITH, JOHN, 32 (Taken prisoner at Arkansas Post, Arkansas, on January 11, 1863; KIA near Atlanta, Georgia, on July 22, 1864)

SMITH, THOMAS (Taken prisoner at Arkansas Post, Arkansas, on January 11, 1863; took oath of
allegiance to the U.S.A. at Camp Butler, Illinois, on ?, 1863)

SOPER, PETER (Taken prisoner at Arkansas Post, Arkansas, on January 11, 1863; transferred to the
C.S. Navy on April 12, 1864)

STERLING, RUDOLPHUS, 28 (Died at Arkansas Post, Arkansas, on October 12, 1862)

STERLING, WILLIAM, 24 (5'5", dark eyes, brown hair, dark complexion, born in Matagorda,
Texas, occupation a sailor; received a disability discharge on June 10, 1862)

STEWART, JOHN A., 22 (Taken prisoner at Arkansas Post, Arkansas, on January 11, 1863; died at
Petersburg, Virginia, on May 30, 1863)

STEWART, SCOTT, 18 (Taken prisoner at Arkansas Post, Arkansas, on January 11, 1863; WIA at
Missionary Ridge, Tennessee, on November 25, 1863; WIA near Atlanta, Georgia, on July 22,
1864; present at final surrender at Greensboro, North Carolina, on April 26, 1865)

STICKLES, PETER D., 25 (5'8", blue eyes, red hair, born in New York; taken prisoner at Arkansas
Post, Arkansas, on January 11, 1863; took oath of allegiance to the U.S.A. at Camp Butler, Illinois, on March ?, 1863)

Van BREMER, SAMUEL, 52 (5'11", blue eyes, brown hair, dark complexion, born in New York;

received a disability discharge on December 16, 1862)

VOGG, CHARLES, 27 (Promoted second corporal on October 17, 1862; taken prisoner at Arkansas Post, Arkansas, on January 11, 1863; died at Cassville, Georgia, on March 19, 1864)

WADSWORTH, WILLIAM, 19 (Promoted third sergeant on October ?, 1862; returned to ranks on December 14, 1862; served in Trans-Mississippi Department from ?)

WALDMAN, CHARLES, 18 (Promoted fifth sergeant on October 17, 1862; promoted third sergeant on December 14, 1862; taken prisoner at Arkansas Post, Arkansas, on January 11, 1863; WIA at Chickamauga, Georgia, on September 20, 1863; promoted first sergeant on March 1, 1864; KIA at Spring Hill, Tennessee, on November 29, 1864)

WATROUS, F. A., 23 (Taken prisoner at Arkansas Post, Arkansas, on January 11, 1863; KIA at Missionary Ridge, Tennessee, on November 25, 1863)

WILKINSON, GID, 15 (Taken prisoner at Arkansas Post, Arkansas, on January 11, 1863; WIA at Franklin, Tennessee, on November 30, 1864; present at final surrender at Greensboro, North Carolina, on April 26, 1865)

WOODMAN, WILLIAM, 24 (Died near Tyler, Texas, on July ?, 1862)

YEAMANS, ERASTUS, 24 (Taken prisoner at Arkansas Post, Arkansas, on January 11, 1863; WIA near Atlanta, Georgia, on August 15, 1864; taken prisoner at West Point, Georgia, on April 16, 1865)

ZIPPRIAN, CHRISTIAN, 18 (Taken prisoner at Arkansas Post, Arkansas, on January 11, 1863; WIA at Missionary Ridge, Tennessee, on November 25, 1863; WIA near Atlanta, Georgia, on August 15, 1864; present at final surrender at Greensboro, North Carolina, on April 26, 1865)

ZIPPRIAN, JOHN, 24 (Promoted first corporal on October 17, 1862; taken prisoner at Arkansas Post, Arkansas, on January 11, 1863; WIA at Franklin, Tennessee, on November 30, 1864)

COMPANY E — Composed of personnel recruited primarily in Guadalupe County, Texas. Mustered into Confederate service on October 30, 1861.

OFFICERS

JOHN P. WHITE, Captain, 29 (6'1½", gray eyes, dark hair, dark complexion; taken prisoner at Arkansas Post, Arkansas, on January 11, 1863; displaced temporarily on May 24, 1863; transferred to Trans-Mississippi Department on ?)

HOUSTON TOM, First Lieutenant, 30 (6'0", gray eyes, dark hair, dark complexion; taken prisoner at Arkansas Post, Arkansas, on January 11, 1863; displaced temporarily on May 24, 1863; transferred to Trans-Mississippi Department on ?)

WILLIAM L. MALONE, Second Lieutenant, 26 (Taken prisoner at Arkansas Post, Arkansas, on January 11, 1863; died at Camp Chase, Ohio, on March 11, 1863)

DARIUS MARSH, Second Lieutenant, 28 (5'8", blue eyes, sandy hair, sandy complexion; transferred from Company G on May 24, 1863; promoted first lieutenant on February 29, 1864; died at ? on May 30, 1864)

WILLIAM MEDLIN, Junior Second Lieutenant, 26 (5'11", gray eyes, light hair, fair complexion; taken prisoner at Arkansas Post, Arkansas, on January 11, 1863; promoted second lieutenant on March ?, 1863; displaced temporarily on May 24, 1863; transferred to Trans-Mississippi Department on ?)

NON-COMMISSIONED OFFICERS

JOSEPH WILSON, First Sergeant, 28 (Served in Trans-Mississippi Department from ?)

HENRY T. NOEL, Second Sergeant, 21 (5'8", blue eyes, brown hair, born in Kentucky; resigned and returned to ranks on November 5, 1861; taken prisoner at Arkansas Post, Arkansas, on January 11, 1863; took oath of allegiance to the U.S.A. at Camp Butler, Illinois, on March 10, 1863)

WILLIAM G. HUBERT, Third Sergeant, 29 (Resigned on November 5, 1861; promoted commissary sergeant on March 9, 1862; resigned on May 22, 1862; served in Trans-Mississippi Department from ?)

JAMES H. COMBS, Fourth Sergeant, 20 (Promoted third sergeant on November 6, 1861; returned to ranks on October 1, 1862; served in Trans-Mississippi Department from ?)

MARTIN V. McANELLY, First Corporal, 26 (5'4" or 5'5", hazel eyes, red or sandy hair, light or sandy complexion; resigned and returned to ranks on December 11, 1862; taken prisoner at Arkansas Post, Arkansas, on January 11, 1863; WIA at Chickamauga, Georgia, on September 24, 1863; taken prisoner near ?, Georgia, on May ?, 1864; took oath of allegiance to the U.S.A. at ? on May ?, 1864)

JAMES A. ROBERTSON, Second Corporal, 36 (5'10", blue eyes, light hair, fair complexion; resigned and returned to ranks on November 5, 1861; served in Trans-Mississippi Department from ?; received a disability discharge on March 23, 1863)

ALEXANDER OCHLETREE, Third Corporal, 30 (Resigned and returned to ranks on November 5, 1861; taken prisoner at Arkansas Post, Arkansas, on January 11, 1863; KIA at Chickamauga, Georgia, on September 20, 1863)

JOSHUA ROSE, Drummer, 15 (Taken prisoner at Arkansas Post, Arkansas, on January 11, 1863; transferred to regimental band on August 1, 1863; discharged as a minor on November 12, 1863)

HENRY C. NEILL, Fifer, 16 (Resigned on January 31, 1862; taken prisoner at Arkansas Post, Arkansas, on January 11, 1863; present at final surrender at Greensboro, North Carolina, on April 26, 1865)

PRIVATES

ALEXANDER, ALFRED A., 21 (Taken prisoner at Arkansas Post, Arkansas, on January 11, 1863; promoted fourth sergeant on March 1, 1864; WIA near Atlanta, Georgia, on July 20, 1864; died of wounds at ? on ?)

ANDERSON, HENRY M., 18 (5'9", dark eyes, dark hair, dark complexion, born in Mississippi, occupation a laborer; received a disability discharge on May 19, 1862)

BARNES, S. M. (5'8", blue eyes, light hair)

BARRY, JOHN (5'9", dark eyes, brown hair, born in Ireland; taken prisoner at Arkansas Post, Arkansas, on January 11, 1863; took oath of allegiance to the U.S.A. at Camp Butler, Illinois, on February 4, 1863)

BOHSLE, JOHN, 23 (5'5", blue eyes, light hair, born in France; taken prisoner at Arkansas Post, Arkansas, on January 11, 1863)

BOLLINI, CHARLES, 36 (Taken prisoner at Arkansas Post, Arkansas, on January 11, 1863; died at Camp Butler, Illinois, on February 6, 1863)

BROOK, JOHN R., 30 or 32 (Taken prisoner at Arkansas Post, Arkansas, on January 11, 1863; died at Camp Butler, Illinois, on March 28, 1863)

BROTHERS, THOMAS J., 16 (Received a disability discharge on September 1, 1862)

BULGER, PHILIP, 18 (5'10", gray eyes, sandy hair, born in Pennsylvania; taken prisoner at Arkansas Post, Arkansas, on January 11, 1863; took oath of allegiance to the U.S.A. at ? on February 27, 1863)

BULGER, SAMUEL B., 22 (5'11", gray eyes, sandy hair, born in Pennsylvania; taken prisoner at Arkansas Post, Arkansas, on January 11, 1863; took oath of allegiance to the U.S.A. at ? on February 27, 1863)

CAMPBELL, ALEXANDER, 30 (5'10", black eyes, dark hair, dark complexion, born in Tennessee; received a disability discharge on May 19, 1862)

CLEMENSEN, HENRY, 22 (Promoted musician on February 1, 1862; taken prisoner at Arkansas Post, Arkansas, on January 11, 1863; transferred to regimental band on August 1, 1863; transferred to brigade band on March 12, 1864; present at final surrender at Greensboro, North Carolina, on April 26, 1865)

COCKRUM, ANDREW J., 22 (Promoted first corporal on ?; taken prisoner at Arkansas Post, Arkansas, on January 11, 1863; served in Trans-Mississippi Department from ?)

COCKS, HARDY D., 17 (Taken prisoner at Arkansas Post, Arkansas, on January 11, 1863; WIA at Chickamauga, Georgia, on September 20, 1863)

COCREHAM, SYLVESTER K. (Transferred from Fifteenth Texas Cavalry Regiment on December 1, 1862; taken prisoner at Arkansas Post, Arkansas, on January 11, 1863; KIA at Chickamauga, Georgia, on September 20, 1863)

COGSWELL, WILLIAM T., 26 (Taken prisoner at Arkansas Post, Arkansas, on January 11, 1863; escaped from Memphis, Tennessee, on January 20, 1863)

COWEY, CHARLES W., 26 (Taken prisoner at Arkansas Post, Arkansas, on January 11, 1863)

CRENSHAW, HENRY L., 25 (Promoted fifth sergeant on ?, 1862; promoted second sergeant on October 1, 1862; promoted first sergeant on December 11, 1862; taken prisoner at Arkansas Post, Arkansas, on January 11, 1863; died at ?, Georgia, on December 6, 1863)

CRENSHAW, NICHOLAS, 16 (Received a disability discharge on September 3, 1862)

DONEGAN, JOHN R., 19 (Taken prisoner at Arkansas Post, Arkansas, on January 11, 1863; WIA at Chickamauga, Georgia, on September 20, 1863; cited for gallantry at Chickamauga, Georgia; WIA at Franklin, Tennessee, on November 30, 1864)

DUCROIS, ELI, 25 (Received a disability discharge on ?)

ECKOLS, DAVID W., 25 or 26 (Taken prisoner at Arkansas Post, Arkansas, on January 11, 1863; POW? near Atlanta, Georgia, on July 21, 1864)

ECKOLS, J. F. (Taken prisoner at Arkansas Post, Arkansas, on January 11, 1863; died at Camp Butler, Illinois, on February 4, 1863)

ECKOLS, THOMAS J., 20 (Taken prisoner at Arkansas Post, Arkansas, on January 11, 1863; WIA at Chickamauga, Georgia, on September 20, 1863; taken prisoner at Macon, Georgia, on April 20 or 21, 1865)

GLOSSON, W. M., 18 (Promoted fourth corporal on ?, 1862; died at Arkansas Post, Arkansas, on December 18, 1862)

HAMLIN, VINCENT B., 23 (6'0", hazel eyes, black hair, dark complexion; promoted second sergeant on November 6, 1861; resigned and returned to ranks on October 1, 1862; taken prisoner at Arkansas Post, Arkansas, on January 11, 1863; taken prisoner at Villa Rica, Georgia, on July 13, 1864)

HIGGINS, WILLIAM (Taken prisoner at LaGrange, Tennessee, on December 12, 1862)

HOKE, BURLIN A., 28 (Taken prisoner at Arkansas Post, Arkansas, on January 11, 1863; WIA at Chickamauga, Georgia, on September 20, 1863; KIA at Jonesboro, Georgia, on September 1, 1864)

INGRAM, ROBERT, 17 (Discharged on account of minority on February 18, 1862)

KARNES, JOHN, 35 (Taken prisoner at Arkansas Post, Arkansas, on January 11, 1863; WIA at New Hope Church, Georgia, on May 27, 1864)

KERN, JOHN, 28 (5'6", blue eyes, black hair, born in Germany; taken prisoner at Arkansas Post, Arkansas, on January 11, 1863; took oath of allegiance to the U.S.A. at ? on March 3, 1863)

KINCAID, JAMES M., 19

LANCASTER, JAMES A. L., 21 (Taken prisoner at Arkansas Post, Arkansas, on January 11, 1863; died at Petersburg, Virginia, on May 23, 1863)

LOPEZ, ISAAC, 32 (Taken prisoner at Arkansas Post, Arkansas, on January 11, 1863; died at Petersburg, Virginia, on ?)

MADDOX, AMOS H., 23 (6'0", blue eyes, auburn hair, fair complexion, born in Marion, Alabama, occupation a farmer; received a disability discharge on June 27, 1862)

MADDOX, LEVI, 25 (Taken prisoner at Arkansas Post, Arkansas, on January 11, 1863; WIA at Chickamauga, Georgia, on September 20, 1863; WIA at Missionary Ridge, Tennessee, on November 25, 1863; taken prisoner at Taylor's Ridge, Georgia, on November 27, 1863; died at Rock Island Barracks, Illinois, on February 4, 1864)

MATHEWS, SAMUEL R., 19 (Promoted fourth corporal on November 5, 1861; resigned and returned to ranks on ?, 1862; taken prisoner at Arkansas Post, Arkansas, on January 11, 1863; promoted third corporal on April 6, 1864; present at final surrender at Greensboro, North Carolina, on April 26, 1865)

MAYFIELD, JOHN W., 26 (6'1", gray eyes, dark hair, dark complexion; taken prisoner at Arkansas Post, Arkansas, on January 11, 1863; deserted near Jonesboro, Georgia, on September 14, 1864; enlisted into Company D, Sixth Regiment U.S. Volunteers on March 24, 1865)

MAYFIELD, LUKE, 23 (Received a disability discharge on September 3, 1862)

McGUFFEY, WILLIAM J., 28 (Taken prisoner at Arkansas Post, Arkansas, on January 11, 1863; served in Trans-Mississippi Department from ?)

McKINNEY, FREDERICK A., 20 (Promoted fifth sergeant on October 1, 1862; taken prisoner at Arkansas Post, Arkansas, on January 11, 1863; WIA at Missionary Ridge, Tennessee, on November 25, 1863; WIA at Jonesboro, Georgia, on August 31, 1864)

McLELLAND, ANDREW, 19 (Deserted on October 30 or 31, 1861)

MILLER, JAMES, 22 (Promoted second corporal on November 6, 1861; promoted fourth sergeant on

October 1, 1862; taken prisoner at Arkansas Post, Arkansas, on January 11, 1863; promoted first sergeant on March 1, 1864; KIA at Franklin, Tennessee, on November 30, 1864)

MILLER, JOHN R., 15 or 22 (Died at Victoria, Texas, on ?, 1862)

MOLTZ, MICHAEL, 22 (5'6", gray or blue eyes, chestnut or brown hair, dark or fair complexion, born in Prussia, occupation a farmer; served in Trans-Mississippi Department from ?; transferred to Company A, Twelfth Texas Infantry Regiment on ?; took oath of allegiance to the U.S.A. at ? on January 18, 1864)

MOLTZ, PETER, 21 (Taken prisoner at Arkansas Post, Arkansas, on January 11, 1863; present at final surrender at Greensboro, North Carolina, on April 26, 1865)

MOLTZ, WILLIAM, 15 (5'10", hazel eyes, brown hair, dark complexion; taken prisoner at Arkansas Post, Arkansas, on January 11, 1863; WIA at ? on June 16, 1864; WIA at Jonesboro, Georgia, on September 1, 1864)

MOORE, MARK, 33 (Deserted on June 26, 1862)

MORSE, JOHN, 22 (Served in Trans-Mississippi Department from ?)

NANCE, LEWIS H., 18 (Promoted fourth corporal on ?; taken prisoner at Arkansas Post, Arkansas, on January 11, 1863; returned to ranks on November 4, 1863; present at final surrender at Greensboro, North Carolina, on April 26, 1865)

NEWTON, LEMUEL F., 17 (Promoted second corporal on October 1, 1862; taken prisoner at Arkansas Post, Arkansas, on January 11, 1863; WIA at Chickamauga, Georgia, on September 20, 1863; WIA at Jonesboro, Georgia, on September 1, 1864)

OWEN, WILLIAM H., 20 (Taken prisoner at Arkansas Post, Arkansas, on January 11, 1863; WIA at Chickamauga, Georgia, on September 20, 1863)

PARK, JOHN H., 18 (Promoted third sergeant on October 1, 1862; taken prisoner at Arkansas Post, Arkansas, on January 11, 1863; died at Petersburg, Virginia, on April 24, 1863)

RATCLIFF, SAMUEL, 32 or 35 (Taken prisoner at Arkansas Post, Arkansas, on January 11, 1863; died at ? on August 31, 1863)

REA, EDWARD G., 29 (Taken prisoner at Arkansas Post, Arkansas, on January 11, 1863; WIA at Chickamauga, Georgia, on September 20, 1863; WIA at Jonesboro, Georgia, on September 1, 1864)

ROBINSON, CALVIN F., 18 (Taken prisoner at Arkansas Post, Arkansas, on January 11, 1863; KIA at Missionary Ridge, Tennessee, on November 25, 1863)

ROCHELLE, J. W. (Present at final surrender at Greensboro, North Carolina, on April 26, 1865)

ROEMMELL, HENRY, 19 (Taken prisoner at Arkansas Post, Arkansas, on January 11, 1863; WIA near Atlanta, Georgia, on July 22, 1864)

ROSE, ASA S., 35 (5'7", black eyes, dark hair, light complexion, born in New York, occupation a carriage maker; received a disability discharge on March 17, 1862)

SANDERS, ADAMS, 17 (5'8", blue eyes, black hair, fair complexion, born in Withe County, Virginia, occupation a farmer; promoted third corporal on October 1, 1862; taken prisoner at Arkansas Post, Arkansas, on January 11, 1863; WIA at Chickamauga, Georgia, on September 20, 1863; promoted second sergeant on March 1, 1864; WIA at Jonesboro, Georgia, on September 1, 1864; present at final surrender at Greensboro, North Carolina, on April 26, 1865)

SANDERS, STEWART (Taken prisoner at Arkansas Post, Arkansas, on January 11, 1863; died at St. Louis, Missouri, on February 18, 1863)

SIMMONS, MARTIN, 28 (Taken prisoner at Arkansas Post, Arkansas, on January 11, 1863; died at Petersburg, Virginia, on May 13, 1863)

SMITH, ALBERT G., 21 (Served in Trans-Mississippi Department from ?)

SMITH, DANIEL F., 18 (5'3", blue eyes, light hair, fair complexion, born in Fayette County, Alabama, occupation a farmer; taken prisoner at Arkansas Post, Arkansas, on January 11, 1863; served in Trans-Mississippi Department from ?)

SMITH, JAMES I., 19 (Taken prisoner at Arkansas Post, Arkansas, on January 11, 1863; died at St. Louis, Missouri, on February 10, 1863)

SMITH, LEWIS, 20 (Taken prisoner at Arkansas Post, Arkansas, on January 11, 1863; died at Camp Butler, Illinois, on February 12, 1863)

SMITH, WILLIAM, 17 (Taken prisoner at Arkansas Post, Arkansas, on January 11, 1863; died at Camp Butler, Illinois, on February 23, 1863)

SNELL, WILLIAM W., 22 (Promoted third corporal on November 6, 1861; resigned and returned to ranks on September 12, 1862; taken prisoner at Arkansas Post, Arkansas, on January 11, 1863; deserted on August 18, 1863)

STANLEY, E. J., 30 (Transferred to Company D, Third Texas Cavalry Battalion on March 15, 1862)

SUCHART, FRITZ, 18 (Taken prisoner at Arkansas Post, Arkansas, on January 11, 1863; WIA near Atlanta, Georgia, on July 20, 1864)

SULLIVAN, SEABURN J., 24 (Taken prisoner at Arkansas Post, Arkansas, on January 11, 1863; WIA at Franklin, Tennessee, on November 30, 1864)

SWANN, THOMAS H., 22 (Taken prisoner at Arkansas Post, Arkansas, on January 11, 1863; died at Camp Butler, Illinois, on April 11, 1863)

THOMPSON, EDWARD, 18 (Promoted fourth sergeant on November 6, 1861; resigned and returned to ranks on October 1, 1862; taken prisoner at Arkansas Post, Arkansas, on January 11, 1863; WIA at Chickamauga, Georgia, on September 20, 1863; promoted junior second lieutenant on March 9, 1864; KIA at Franklin, Tennessee, on November 30, 1864)

TINER, WILLIAM W., 18 (Died at Victoria, Texas, on February 25, 1862)

VICKERS, WILLIAM R., 19 (Promoted third sergeant on December 11, 1862; taken prisoner at Arkansas Post, Arkansas, on January 11, 1863; WIA at Chickamauga, Georgia, on September 20, 1863; present at final surrender at Greensboro, North Carolina, on April 26, 1865)

WAGNER, JOHN M., 33 (Taken prisoner at Arkansas Post, Arkansas, on January 11, 1863; took oath of allegiance to the U.S.A. at Camp Butler, Illinois, on ?, 1863)

WAKEFIELD, JOHN J., 22 (Taken prisoner at Arkansas Post, Arkansas, on January 11, 1863; KIA at Franklin, Tennessee, on November 30, 1864)

WALLACE, JOHN R., 22 (Taken prisoner at Arkansas Post, Arkansas, on January 11, 1863; died at Camp Butler, Illinois, on March 4, 1863)

WHITE, ABRAHAM M., 20 (6'1", blue eyes, light hair, fair complexion, born in Fayette County, Arkansas, occupation a farmer; served in Trans-Mississippi Department from ?)

WHITE, JAMES A., 25 (Taken prisoner at Arkansas Post, Arkansas, on January 11, 1863; died in Fayette County, Alabama, on September 20 1864)

WHITE, JEPTHA N., 22 or 25 (Taken prisoner at Arkansas Post, Arkansas, on January 11, 1863; KIA at Chickamauga, Georgia, on September 20, 1863)

WILLIAMS, ANDREW, 40 (Deserted on November 9, 1861)

WILLIAMS, GEORGE W., 17 (Died at White Sulfur Springs, Arkansas, on October 20, 1862)

YOUNG, HENRY C. (Deserted on August 18, 1863)

ZORN, PETER, 17 (5'4", gray eyes, brown hair, born in Louisiana; taken prisoner at Arkansas Post, Arkansas, on January 11, 1863; took oath of allegiance to the U.S.A. at Camp Butler, Illinois, on March 15, 1863)

COMPANY F — Composed of personnel recruited primarily in Bell County, Texas. Mustered into Confederate service on November 3, 1861.

OFFICERS

HENRY E. BRADFORD, Captain, 27 (Served in Trans-Mississippi Department from ?)

BENJAMIN F. CHURCH, First Lieutenant, 34 (5'7½", hazel eyes, dark hair, fair complexion; taken prisoner at Arkansas Post, Arkansas, on January 11, 1863; transferred to Trans-Mississippi Department on September 3, 1863)

LEVI T. METHVIN, Second Lieutenant, 32 (5'10", black eyes, black hair, dark complexion; taken prisoner at Arkansas Post, Arkansas, on January 11, 1863; served in Trans-Mississippi Department from ?)

MARK A. KELTON, Junior Second Lieutenant, 21, (5'4½" or 5'9½", dark eyes, dark hair, dark complexion; taken prisoner at Arkansas Post, Arkansas, on January 11, 1863; WIA near Atlanta, Georgia, on July 21, 1864; WIA near Jonesboro, Georgia, on September 1, 1864; present at final surrender at Greensboro, North Carolina, on April 26, 1865)

NON-COMMISSIONED OFFICERS

COLLINS L. KINNAN, First Sergeant, 24 (5'8", blue eyes, light hair, born in Ohio; taken prisoner at Arkansas Post, Arkansas, on January 11, 1863; took oath of allegiance to the U.S.A. at Camp Butler, Illinois, on February 19, 1863)

PORTER L. ELLIS, Second Sergeant, 22 (Taken prisoner at Arkansas Post, Arkansas, on January 11, 1863; escaped from Camp Butler, Illinois, on February 15, 1863)

GARRETT W. SEAY, Third Sergeant, 24 (Died in Sabine County, Arkansas, on August 19, 1862)

JOHN B. B. SUPPLE, Fourth Sergeant, 35 (Reduced to ranks and transferred to Company A, Sixteenth Texas Infantry regiment on October 20, 1862)

A. S. HOLMES, Sergeant (5'9", hazel eyes, brown hair, light complexion; deserted at Starks Landing, Louisiana, on March 23 or 25, 1865; took oath of allegiance to the U.S.A. at New Orleans, Louisiana, on April 2, 1865)

WILLIAM H. MEREDITH, First Corporal, 29 (6'0", blue eyes, dark hair, dark complexion, born in Matison County, Mississippi, occupation a school teacher; reduced to ranks on February 21, 1862; received a disability discharge on March 10 or 21, 1862)

THOMAS B. SHELTON, Second Corporal, 24 (Promoted first corporal on ?, 1862; reduced to ranks on ?, 1862; taken prisoner at Arkansas Post, Arkansas, on January 11, 1863; died at Camp Butler, Illinois, on February 25, 1863)

WILLIAM T. J. HARTRICK, Third Corporal, 24 (Promoted second corporal on ?, 1862; reduced to ranks on ?, 1862; taken prisoner at Arkansas Post, Arkansas, on January 11, 1863; escaped from Camp Butler, Illinois, on February 17, 1863)

JAMES E. PETTY, Fourth Corporal, 17 or 18 (5'3", blue eyes, dark hair, dark complexion, born in Arkansas; promoted third corporal on ?; received a disability discharge on September 2, 1862)

S. R. POTTE, Corporal (Taken prisoner at Arkansas Post, Arkansas, on January 11, 1863)

JAMES P. ASHFORD, Musician, 24 (Taken prisoner at Arkansas Post, Arkansas, on January 11, 1863; escaped from Arkansas Post, Arkansas, on January 11, 1863; served in Trans-Mississippi Department from ?)

JAMES M. CHAMBERS, Musician, 29 (5'11", dark eyes, dark hair, born in Tennessee; received a disability discharge on August 4, 1862)

PRIVATES

AIKEN, BARTLEY, 26 (Taken prisoner at Arkansas Post, Arkansas, on January 11, 1863; KIA at Jonesboro, Georgia, on September 1, 1864)

ANDERSON, JAMES, 27 (Taken prisoner at Arkansas Post, Arkansas, on January 11, 1863; died at Camp Butler, Illinois, on March 28, 1863)

ANDERSON, MICHAEL, 21 (5'8", dark eyes, dark hair, light complexion, born in Polk County, Arkansas, occupation a farmer; taken prisoner at Arkansas Post, Arkansas, on January 11, 1863; received a disability discharge on October 26, 1863)

ATWOOD, CORNELIUS M., 20 (Promoted second corporal on October 28, 1862; promoted first corporal on ?; taken prisoner at Arkansas Post, Arkansas, on January 11, 1863; WIA at Missionary Ridge, Tennessee, on November 25, 1863; WIA at Franklin, Tennessee, on November 30, 1864; present at final surrender at Greensboro, North Carolina, on April 26, 1865)

BAKER, JACKSON, 34 (Taken prisoner at Arkansas Post, Arkansas, on January 11, 1863; escaped from Camp Butler, Illinois, on March 10, 1863; served in Trans-Mississippi Department from ?)

BAWCOM, WILLIAM H., 21 (Taken prisoner at Arkansas Post, Arkansas, on January 11, 1863; died at Camp Butler, Illinois, on February 1, 1863)

BERRY, CHRISTOPHER A., 25 (Taken prisoner at Arkansas Post, Arkansas, on January 11, 1863; died at Tullahoma, Tennessee, on May 31, 1863)

BIGHAM, SAMUEL W., 50 or 51 (Taken prisoner at Arkansas Post, Arkansas, on January 11, 1863)

BIRCH, BENJAMIN J., 35 (5'6", blue eyes, dark hair, fair complexion, born in Kentucky; received a disability discharge on October 3, 1862)

BLACKBURN, RICHARD T., 20 (Promoted fourth corporal on September 7, 1862; taken prisoner at Arkansas Post, Arkansas, on January 11, 1863; promoted third corporal on ?, 1863; promoted second corporal on ?, 1863; WIA at Missionary Ridge, Tennessee, on November 25, 1863; returned to ranks on ?, 1864; KIA near Atlanta, Georgia, on July 21, 1864)

BLODGET, JAMES, 21 (Taken prisoner at Arkansas Post, Arkansas, on January 11, 1863; died at Camp Butler, Illinois, on February 10, 1863)

BOND, FRANCIS E., 23 (Served in Trans-Mississippi Department from ?)

BONNER, GEORGE A., 17 (Taken prisoner at Arkansas Post, Arkansas, on January 11, 1863; died at Camp Butler, Illinois, on March 27, 1863)

BOYD, ROLAND R., 20 or 21 (Taken prisoner at Arkansas Post, Arkansas, on January 11, 1863; died at Petersburg, Virginia, on May 9, 1863)

BOYD, WILLIS W., 23 (Taken prisoner at Arkansas Post, Arkansas, on January 11, 1863; taken prisoner at ?, Georgia, on April ?, 1865)

BROWN, JOHN W., 17 (Taken prisoner at Arkansas Post, Arkansas, on January 11, 1863)

BURLEY, SYLVESTER, 25 (Transferred from Company A on April 11, 1862; promoted fourth sergeant on September 18, 1862; taken prisoner at Arkansas Post, Arkansas, on January 11, 1863; present at final surrender at Greensboro, North Carolina, on April 26, 1865)

CEARNEL, HENRY S., 20 or 21 (Taken prisoner at Arkansas Post, Arkansas, on January 11, 1863; escaped from Camp Butler, Illinois, on February 15, 1863)

CEARNEL, W. P., 16 (5'5", blue eyes, brown hair, born in Missouri; transferred from Company A, Sixteenth Texas Infantry Regiment on October 20, 1862; taken prisoner at Arkansas Post, Arkansas, on January 11, 1863; took oath of allegiance to the U.S.A. at Camp Butler, Illinois, on March 30, 1863)

CHALK, ROBERT L., 20 (Promoted second corporal on August 17, 1862; promoted fifth sergeant on October 27, 1862; taken prisoner at Arkansas Post, Arkansas, on January 11, 1863; escaped from Camp Butler, Illinois, on February 17, 1863)

CHAPMAN, JOHN D., 24 (Escaped from Arkansas Post, Arkansas, on January 11 or 12, 1863; served in Trans-Mississippi Department from ?)

COWAN, JAMES W., 21 (Taken prisoner at Arkansas Post, Arkansas, on January 11, 1863)

CROW, REUBEN, 33 (Taken prisoner at Arkansas Post, Arkansas, on January 11, 1863; died at Camp Butler, Illinois, on February 17, 1863)

DAVIS, JOHN B., 36 (Taken prisoner at Arkansas Post, Arkansas, on January 11, 1863; transferred to Engineer Corps on ?, 1863; took oath of allegiance to the U.S.A. at Greensboro, North Carolina, on April 10, 1865)

DENTON, WILLIAM B., 40 (5'9" or 5'10½", blue eyes, dark hair, dark complexion, born in Perry County, Tennessee, occupation a farmer; received a disability discharge on March 23, 1862)

DODSON, WILLIAM T., 22 (Taken prisoner at Arkansas Post, Arkansas, on January 11, 1863; served in Trans-Mississippi Department from ?)

DOLLAR, D. W., 30 (Died at Navasota, Texas, on June 15, 1862)

DOSS, CHRISTOPHER C., 25 (Absent on surgeon's certificate from June 13, 1862)

DOSS, HARMON W., 20 (Absent from company from June 13, 1862)

DRAKE, FRANCIS M., 24 (Served in Trans-Mississippi Department from ?)

ELMS, HENRY, 18 (Taken prisoner at Arkansas Post, Arkansas, on January 11, 1863)

EVERETT, WILLIAM R., 25 (Taken prisoner at Arkansas Post, Arkansas, on January 11, 1863; died at LaGrange, Georgia, on June 16, 1864)

EVETTS, WILLIAM C., 20 (Taken prisoner at Arkansas Post, Arkansas, on January 11, 1863; served in Trans-Mississippi Department from ?)

FEWEL, LOUIS L., 18 (Deserted on November 5, 1862)

FLEMING, CHARLES, 18 (Taken prisoner at Arkansas Post, Arkansas, on January 11, 1863; present at final surrender at Greensboro, North Carolina, on April 26, 1865; POW records state that he died at Camp Butler, Illinois, on February 22, 1863)

FRANCESCO, JUAN, 22 (5'6½", black eyes, black hair, dark complexion, born in Texas, occupation a farmer; received a disability discharge on June 8, 1862)

GLOWNER, DAVID, 28 (Taken prisoner at Arkansas Post, Arkansas, on January 11, 1863; died at Camp Butler, Illinois, on March 31, 1863)

GRIFFITH, AMOS B., 22 (Taken prisoner at Arkansas Post, Arkansas, on January 11, 1863; KIA at Franklin, Tennessee, on November 30, 1864; POW records state that he died at Camp Butler, Illinois, on February 10, 1863)

HAGGERTON, CHARLES, 19 (Taken prisoner at Arkansas Post, Arkansas, on January 11, 1863)

HALL, JOSIAH A., 18 (Taken prisoner at Arkansas Post, Arkansas, on January 11, 1863; died at Camp Butler, Illinois, on April 1, 1863)

HAMILTON, WOODIE T., 24 (KIA at Arkansas Post, Arkansas, on January 11, 1863)

HAMPTON, WADE W., 22 or 24 (5'11", black eyes, dark hair, fair complexion, born in Louisiana; promoted first corporal on August 17, 1862; WIA at Arkansas Post, Arkansas, on January 11,

1863; taken prisoner at Arkansas Post, Arkansas, on January 11, 1863; received a disability discharge on July 9, 1863)

HANNON, ROBERT S., 20 (Taken prisoner at Arkansas Post, Arkansas, on January 11, 1863; died at Camp Butler, Illinois, on February 17, 1863)

HULSEY, GREEN E., 23 or 25 (Served in Trans-Mississippi Department from ?)

LEONARD, MARTIN (Taken prisoner at ? on April ?, 1863)

MAYES, DANIEL, 27 (6'0"; taken prisoner at Arkansas Post, Arkansas, on January 11, 1863; died at St. Louis, Missouri, on February 15, 1863)

McKENZIE, HARVEY, 41 (Taken prisoner at Arkansas Post, Arkansas, on January 11, 1863; escaped from Camp Butler, Illinois, on March 10, 1863)

McLAUGHLIN, ALONZO F., 21 (KIA at Arkansas Post, Arkansas, on January 11, 1863)

MERCHANT, DAVID B., 27 (Served in Trans-Mississippi Department from ?)

METHVIN, ALBERT, 20 (KIA at Arkansas Post, Arkansas, on January 11, 1863)

METHVIN, ALFORD, 20 (Taken prisoner at Arkansas Post, Arkansas, on January 11, 1863; WIA at New Hope Church, Georgia, on May 27, 1864; died of wounds at ? on June 12, 1864)

MURRAY, WILLIAM D., 25 or 26 or 28 (Taken prisoner at Arkansas Post, Arkansas, on January 11, 1863; escaped from a federal transport on January 30, 1863; served in Trans-Mississippi Department from ?)

OAKLEY, PLEASANT A., 24 (Taken prisoner at Arkansas Post, Arkansas, on January 11, 1863)

OLIPHANT, AARON E., 18 (Died at Arkansas Post, Arkansas, on December 4, 1862)

OLIPHANT, JAMES M., 47 (5'10½", dark eyes, gray hair, dark complexion, born in Green County, Georgia; received a disability discharge on December 29, 1862)

O'NEAL, STEPHEN, 23 (Taken prisoner at Arkansas Post, Arkansas, on January 11, 1863;; present at final surrender at Greensboro, North Carolina, on April 26, 1865)

PACE, JOSEPH A., 17 (Taken prisoner at Arkansas Post, Arkansas, on January 11, 1863; WIA at Chickamauga, Georgia, on September 20, 1863; KIA near Atlanta, Georgia, on July 20, 1864)

PARKS, HAMILTON, 18 or 19 (Taken prisoner at Arkansas Post, Arkansas, on January 11, 1863; WIA at Franklin, Tennessee, on November 30, 1864; taken prisoner at Franklin, Tennessee, on December 17 or 18, 1864)

PARKS, HENRY T., 24 (Taken prisoner at Arkansas Post, Arkansas, on January 11, 1863; taken prisoner at Franklin, Tennessee, on November 30, 1864)

PETTY, ISOM S., 16 (Taken prisoner at Arkansas Post, Arkansas, on January 11, 1863)

POLK, JOSIAH L., 19 (Promoted fourth corporal on August 17, 1862; taken prisoner at Arkansas Post, Arkansas, on January 11, 1863; WIA at Jonesboro, Georgia, on August 31, 1864; taken prisoner at Franklin, Tennessee, on November 30, 1864; died at Camp Douglas, Illinois, on January 21, 1865)

REED, WARREN, 25 (Taken prisoner at Arkansas Post, Arkansas, on January 11, 1863; present at final surrender at Greensboro, North Carolina, on April 26, 1865; POW records state that he died at Camp Butler, Illinois, on February 6, 1863)

ROYAL, JESSE, 49 (Taken prisoner at Arkansas Post, Arkansas, on January 11, 1863; died at Camp Butler, Illinois, on February 6, 1863)

SCOTT, JAMES B., 20 (Taken prisoner at Arkansas Post, Arkansas, on January 11, 1863; died at Petersburg, Virginia, on June 28, 1863)

SCOTT, JESSE G., 26 (Died at Benton, Arkansas, on August 23, 1862)

SHELTON, DRED D., 21 (Died at Arkansas Post, Arkansas, on November 16, 1862)

SHELTON, JAMES J., 26 (Taken prisoner at Arkansas Post, Arkansas, on January 11, 1863; died at Camp Butler, Illinois, on February 17, 1863)

SHELTON, JOHN, 28 (Promoted fourth corporal on February 21, 1862; promoted third sergeant on August 17, 1862; taken prisoner at Arkansas Post, Arkansas, on January 11, 1863; promoted first sergeant on March 4, 1864; WIA at Jonesboro, Georgia, on September 1, 1864; died of wounds at ? on ?)

SINCLAIR, JAMES A., 19 (Taken prisoner at Arkansas Post, Arkansas, on January 11, 1863; died at Camp Butler, Illinois, on April 4, 1863)

SINCLAIR, WILLIAM W., 18 (6'1", blue eyes, dark hair, born in Texas; received a disability discharge on September 2, 1862)

SMITH, GABRIEL W., 20 (Taken prisoner at Arkansas Post, Arkansas, on January 11, 1863; WIA near Atlanta, Georgia, on July 22, 1864)

SMITH, PETER (5'9", brown eyes, brown hair, born in Germany; taken prisoner at Arkansas Post, Arkansas on January 11, 1863; took oath of allegiance to the U.S.A. at Camp Butler, Illinois, on February 5, 1863)

SMITH, WILLIAM W., 21 (Served in Trans-Mississippi Department from ?)

SNODGRASS, JAMES A., 19 (WIA at Arkansas Post, Arkansas, on January 11, 1863; taken prisoner at Arkansas Post, Arkansas, on January 11, 1863)

STANDLEY, SIDNEY, 20 (Taken prisoner at Arkansas Post, Arkansas, on January 11, 1863)

ST. CLAIR, STEPHEN A., 25 (Died at Arkansas Post, Arkansas, on October 20 or 21, 1862)

STONE, JOHN A., 20 (KIA at Arkansas Post, Arkansas, on January 11, 1863)

SUTTON, ANDY, 23 (KIA at Arkansas Post, Arkansas, on January 11, 1863)

SUTTON, JESSE, 22 (Served in Trans-Mississippi Department from ?)

VAUGHN, NATHAN, 22 or 23 (Taken prisoner at Arkansas Post, Arkansas, on January 11, 1863; taken prisoner at Franklin, Tennessee, on November 30, 1864; enlisted into Company E, Sixth U.S. Volunteers on March 25, 1865)

WILLIAMSON, THOMAS T., 30 (Promoted color sergeant on August 20, 1862; taken prisoner at Arkansas Post, Arkansas, on January 11, 1863; served in Trans-Mississippi Department from ?)

COMPANY G — TRAVIS RIFLES — Composed of personnel recruited primarily in Travis County, Texas. Mustered into Confederate service on November 14, 1861.

OFFICERS

RHOADS FISHER, Captain, 28 (5'9" or 5'10", blue eyes, sandy or red hair, fair complexion, born in Matagorda, Texas; taken prisoner at Arkansas Post, Arkansas, on January 11, 1863; WIA near Atlanta, Georgia, on July 21, 1864; promoted major on November 2, 1864; taken prisoner at Franklin, Tennessee, on November 30, 1864)

GEORGE W. SAMPSON, First Lieutenant, 30 (Served in Trans-Mississippi Department from ?)

J. H. DINKINS, Second Lieutenant, 25 (Served in Trans-Mississippi Department from ?)

J. E. DOBBS, Second Lieutenant

DARIUS MARSH, Second Lieutenant, 28 (5'8", blue eyes, sandy hair, sandy complexion; taken prisoner at Arkansas Post, Arkansas, on January 11, 1863; transferred to Company E on May 24, 1863)

SEBRON G. SNEED, Third Lieutenant, 25 (5'7" or 5'8", blue eyes, dark hair, light or fair complexion; promoted junior second lieutenant on November 10, 1861; taken prisoner at Arkansas Post, Arkansas, on January 11, 1863; promoted second lieutenant on February 29, 1864; promoted regimental adjutant on June 18, 1864; WIA at Jonesboro, Georgia, on September 1, 1864)

NON-COMMISSIONED OFFICERS

DAVID M. WILSON, First Sergeant, 21 or 22 (5'8", gray eyes, auburn hair, fair complexion, born in Rutherford, Tennessee, occupation a farmer; taken prisoner at Arkansas Post, Arkansas, on January 11, 1863; served in Trans-Mississippi Department from ?)

JAMES TAYLOR, Second Sergeant, 38 (Reduced to ranks on ?, 1862; taken prisoner at Arkansas Post, Arkansas, on January 11, 1863; deserted on May 8, 1863)

JOSEPH A. COSTA, Third Sergeant, 21 (Promoted second sergeant on ?, 1862; served in Trans-Mississippi Department from ?)

PETER MURPHY, Fourth Sergeant, 22 (Deserted on April 21, 1862)

E. DEHORITY, First Corporal, 27 (Reduced to ranks on ?, 1862; taken prisoner at Arkansas Post, Arkansas, on January 11, 1863; promoted second corporal on March 1, 1864; WIA near Atlanta, Georgia, on July 22, 1864; present at final surrender at Greensboro, North Carolina, on April 26, 1865)

GEORGE W. STANLEY, Second Corporal, 21 (Taken prisoner at Arkansas Post, Arkansas, on January 11, 1863; died at Camp Butler, Illinois, on February 13, 1863)

J. T. STEPHENSON, Third Corporal, 25 (Escaped from Arkansas Post, Arkansas, on January 11, 1863; served in Trans-Mississippi Department from ?)

R. H. L. CROSTHWAIT, Fourth Corporal, 22 (WIA at Arkansas Post, Arkansas, on January 11,

1863; taken prisoner at Arkansas Post, Arkansas, on January 11, 1863; reduced to ranks on August 1, 1863; transferred to Engineer Corps on August 2, 1863)

ROSS B. MELLENGER, Bugler/Fifer, 17 (5'5", brown eyes, brown hair, born in Pennsylvania; taken prisoner at Arkansas Post, Arkansas, on January 11, 1863; took oath of allegiance to the U.S.A. at Camp Butler, Illinois, on March 5, 1863)

PRIVATES

ALEXANDER, NEWTON, 17 (5'6", gray eyes, brown hair, fair complexion, born in DeSoto Parish, Louisiana, occupation a farmer; received a disability discharge on June 4, 1862)

ALEXANDER, W. A., 14 (Taken prisoner at Arkansas Post, Arkansas, on January 11, 1863; took oath of allegiance to the U.S.A. at ? on May 8, 1863)

ALFORD, H. M., 30 (5'2", gray eyes, light hair, light complexion, born in New Madrid County, Missouri, occupation a clerk; taken prisoner at Arkansas Post, Arkansas, on January 11, 1863; received a disability discharge on November 17, 1864)

AMIDON, DWIGHT, 22 (Served in Trans-Mississippi Department from ?)

BALDWIN, JAME S., 27 (Transferred from Company C, Sixteenth Texas Infantry Regiment on June 7, 1862; taken prisoner at Arkansas Post, Arkansas, on January 11, 1863; taken prisoner at Franklin, Tennessee, on November 30, 1864)

BIRD, WILLIAM H., 18 (Transferred to Company C, Sixteenth Texas Infantry Regiment on June 7, 1862)

BROWN, JAMES F., 22 (Taken prisoner at Arkansas Post, Arkansas, on January 11, 1863; served in Trans-Mississippi Department from ?)

BURLESON, J. C., 18 (Taken prisoner at Arkansas Post, Arkansas, on January 11, 1863; WIA at Chickamauga, Georgia, on September 20, 1863)

BURLESON, JOHN T., 16 (Taken prisoner at Arkansas Post, Arkansas, on January 11, 1863; died at Camp Butler, Illinois, on March 15, 1863)

CARRINGTON, R. E., 16 (Transferred to Company ?, Sixteenth Texas Infantry Regiment on May 18, 1862)

CONDELL, ROBERT W., 21 (Taken prisoner at Arkansas Post, Arkansas, on January 11, 1863; transferred to C.S. Navy on April 10, 1864)

DAUGHERTY, JOHN S., 22 (Died at Arkansas Post, Arkansas, on September 29, 1862)

DUKES, JAMES, 19 (Taken prisoner at Arkansas Post, Arkansas, on January 11, 1863; WIA at Jonesboro, Georgia, on September 1, 1864; present at final surrender at Greensboro, North Carolina, on April 26, 1865)

DUNSON, WILLIAM M., 19 (Promoted third corporal on ?, 1862; taken prisoner at Arkansas Post, Arkansas, on January 11, 1863; promoted second corporal on ?, 1863; promoted first corporal on April ?, 1864; promoted junior second lieutenant on June 22, 1864; present at final surrender at Greensboro, North Carolina, on April 26, 1865)

GATLIN, N. M., 16 (Taken prisoner at Arkansas Post, Arkansas, on January 11, 1863; died at Camp Butler, Illinois, on April 2, 1863)

GILES, W. L., 28 (Taken prisoner at Arkansas Post, Arkansas, on January 11, 1863; served in Trans-Mississippi Department from March 1, 1864)

GLASSCOCK, FRANK, 18 (Received a disability discharge on September 28, 1862)

GLASSCOCK, L. P., 20 (Promoted second corporal on ?, 1862; taken prisoner at Arkansas Post, Arkansas, on January 11, 1863; promoted first corporal on ?, 1863; promoted third sergeant on April 16, 1864; WIA at Jonesboro, Georgia, on September 1, 1864; promoted ? sergeant on ?; present at final surrender at Greensboro, North Carolina, on April 26, 1865)

GRUMBLES, J. W., 24 (Served in Trans-Mississippi Department from ?)

GRUMBLES, SAMUEL, 20 (5'9" or 5'11", blue or hazel eyes, sandy or brown hair, fair or sandy complexion, born in Travis County, Texas, occupation a stock raiser; received a disability discharge on September 20, 1862)

GRUMBLES, T. A., 16 (Received a disability discharge on September 20, 1862)

HAMILTON, JAMES, 23 (Taken prisoner at Arkansas Post, Arkansas, on January 11, 1863; WIA at Chickamauga, Georgia, on September 20, 1863; WIA at New Hope Church, Georgia, on May 27, 1864; wounded at ? on November ? or December ?, 1864)

HILL, ABEL W., 19 (Escaped from Arkansas Post, Arkansas, on January 11, 1863; WIA near Atlanta, Georgia, on July 21 or 22, 1864)

HILL, E. B., 19 (Taken prisoner at Arkansas Post, Arkansas, on January 11, 1863; WIA near Atlanta, Georgia, on July 21, 1864; present at final surrender at Greensboro, North Carolina, on April 26, 1865)

HOLMAN, G. J., 33 (Taken prisoner at Arkansas Post, Arkansas, on January 11, 1863)

HUDSON, GREEN (Died at Victoria, Texas, on March 10, 1862)

JENKINS, S. L., 22 (Taken prisoner at Arkansas Post, Arkansas, on January 11, 1863; died at Dalton, Georgia, on ?)

JERNIGAN, ALBERT J., 25 (Promoted fourth sergeant on ?, 1862; taken prisoner at Arkansas Post, Arkansas, on January 11, 1863; promoted third sergeant on ?, 1863; WIA at Missionary Ridge, Tennessee, on November 25, 1863; promoted junior second lieutenant on March 9, 1864; resigned on August 20, 1864; received a disability discharge on ?)

JOHNSON, JOHN, 64 (5'8¾", gray eyes, gray hair, dark complexion, born in Kentucky, occupation a hunter; received a disability discharge on November 10, 1862)

JOURDAN, G. W., 28 (Taken prisoner at Arkansas Post, Arkansas, on January 11, 1863; POW records state that he died at Camp Butler, Illinois, on March 12, 1863)

JOURDAN, W. A., 21 (Taken prisoner at Arkansas Post, Arkansas, on January 11, 1863; died at Camp Butler, Illinois, on March 12 or 13, 1863; POW records state that G. W. Jourdan died at Camp Butler, Illinois)

KELLEY, JACOB, 17 (Taken prisoner at Arkansas Post, Arkansas, on January 11, 1863; WIA at Chickamauga, Georgia, on September 20, 1863; present at final surrender at Greensboro, North Carolina, on April 26, 1865)

KLINE, J. H., 17 (Taken prisoner at Arkansas Post, Arkansas, on January 11, 1863; died in transit on the Mississippi River on January 20, 1863)

LABENSKI, C. C., 17 (Taken prisoner at Arkansas Post, Arkansas, on January 11, 1863; present at final surrender at Greensboro, North Carolina, on April 26, 1865)

LOEVELL, D. W., 16 (Taken prisoner at Arkansas Post, Arkansas, on January 11, 1863; served in Trans-Mississippi Department from ?)

LOWREY, ALBERT M. (Transferred from Company A, of ?, on June 24, 1862; taken prisoner at Arkansas Post, Arkansas, on January 11, 1863; died at Camp Butler, Illinois, on March 7, 1863)

LOWREY, RANSOM, 19 (KIA at Arkansas Post, Arkansas, on January 11, 1863)

MALITZKY, L., 38 (Taken prisoner at Arkansas Post, Arkansas, on January 11, 1863; WIA at Franklin, Tennessee, on November 30, 1864; wounded at ? on February 13, 1865; present at final surrender at Greensboro, North Carolina, on April 26, 1865)

McCLURE, H. M., 20 (Taken prisoner at Arkansas Post, Arkansas, on January 11, 1863; WIA at Chickamauga, Georgia, on September 20, 1863)

MEEKS, M., 22 (Taken prisoner at Arkansas Post, Arkansas, on January 11, 1863; died at Camp Butler, Illinois, on March 23, 1863)

MEEKS, ROBERT, 21 (Taken prisoner at Arkansas Post, Arkansas, on January 11, 1863)

MILLETT, E. E., 19 (Taken prisoner at Arkansas Post, Arkansas, on January 11, 1863; deserted on a forged furlough on February 5, 1864)

MORRIS, S. W., 17 (Taken prisoner at Arkansas Post, Arkansas, on January 11, 1863; WIA near Atlanta, Georgia, on July 22, 1864; WIA at Franklin, Tennessee, on November 30, 1864)

OLDHAM, WILLIAM H., 18 (Taken prisoner at Arkansas Post, Arkansas, on January 11, 1863)

OLIPHANT, WILLIAM J., 16 (Taken prisoner at Arkansas Post, Arkansas, on January 11, 1863; WIA at Chickamauga, Georgia, on September 20, 1863; WIA at New Hope Church, Georgia, on May 27, 1864; WIA near Atlanta, Georgia, on July 22, 1864; taken prisoner near Atlanta, Georgia, on July 22, 1864)

PATTERSON, ROBERT, 16 (Taken prisoner at Arkansas Post, Arkansas, on January 11, 1863; died at Camp Butler, Illinois, on March 10, 1863)

PECK, S. R., 24 (Served in Trans-Mississippi Department from ?)

PEEL, WESLEY, 19 (Taken prisoner at Arkansas Post, Arkansas, on January 11, 1863; died at Petersburg, Virginia, on April 20, 1863)

PICKENS, ISRAEL, 33 (Died at Benton, Arkansas, on August 31, 1862)

PIPER, B. F., 19 (Taken prisoner at Arkansas Post, Arkansas, on January 11, 1863; WIA at Jonesboro, Georgia, on September 1, 1864; died of wounds at ? on ?)

RALSTEN, JAMES, 22 (Taken prisoner at Arkansas Post, Arkansas, on January 11, 1863; present at final surrender at Greensboro, North Carolina, on April 26, 1865)

ROBERTSON, BENONI, 17 (Taken prisoner at Arkansas Post, Arkansas, on January 11, 1863; KIA at Chickamauga, Georgia, on September 20, 1863)

ROUNDTREE, H. C., 20 (Taken prisoner at Arkansas Post, Arkansas, on January 11, 1863; promoted third corporal on March 1, 1864; WIA at Jonesboro, Georgia, on September 1, 1864)

RUTLEDGE, W. P., 19 (Taken prisoner at Arkansas Post, Arkansas, on January 11, 1863; died at Camp Butler, Illinois, on May 3, 1863)

SEVER, JEFFERSON, 20 (Taken prisoner at Arkansas Post, Arkansas, on January 11, 1863; WIA at New Hope Church, Georgia, on May 27, 1864; taken prisoner at New Hope Church, Georgia, on May 27, 1864; died of wounds at ? on ?)

SIMMS, F. M., 17 (5'6", black eyes, brown hair, born in Kentucky; promoted drummer on ?, 1862; taken prisoner at Arkansas Post, Arkansas, on January 11, 1863; took oath of allegiance to the U.S.A. at Camp Butler, Illinois, on February 19, 1863)

SIMMS, JAMES, 39 (5'6", gray eyes, black hair, red complexion, born in Dublin, Ireland; received a disability discharge on June 4, 1862)

SMITH, JAMES W., 22 (Taken prisoner at Arkansas Post, Arkansas, on January 11, 1863; present at final surrender at Greensboro, North Carolina, on April 26, 1865)

SNEED, WILLIAM J., 17 (Taken prisoner at Arkansas Post, Arkansas, on January 11, 1863; WIA at Missionary Ridge, Tennessee, on November 25, 1863)

STEPHENSON, A. B., 21 (Taken prisoner at Arkansas Post, Arkansas, on January 11, 1863; WIA near Atlanta, Georgia, on July 22, 1864; present at final surrender at Greensboro, North Carolina, on April 26, 1865)

SWEEM, J. M., 20 (Taken prisoner at Arkansas Post, Arkansas, on January 11, 1863; died in transit on the Mississippi River on January 22, 1863)

TEAFF, N. F., 21 (Died in Travis County, Texas, on October 9, 1862)

TEAGUE, G. M., 20 (Taken prisoner at Arkansas Post, Arkansas, on January 11, 1863; died at Camp Butler, Illinois, on March 12, 1863)

TERRELL, C. D., 22 (Taken prisoner at Arkansas Post, Arkansas, on January 11, 1863)

TINNIN, WILLIAM, 21 (Taken prisoner at Arkansas Post, Arkansas, on January 11, 1863)

TUCKER, J. T., 22 (Promoted fifth sergeant on October ?, 1862; taken prisoner at Arkansas Post, Arkansas, on January 11, 1863; promoted fourth sergeant on ?, 1863; promoted first sergeant on April ?, 1864; died at ? on ?, 1864)

TURNER, J. M., 18 (Taken prisoner at Arkansas Post, Arkansas, on January 11, 1863; taken prisoner at Franklin, Tennessee, on November 30, 1864)

TURNER, J. M. V., 23 (Taken prisoner at Arkansas Post, Arkansas, on January 11, 1863; died at Camp Butler, Illinois, on April 10, 1863)

WALKER, BENJAMIN F. (Taken prisoner at Franklin, Tennessee, on November 30, 1864)

WALKER, J. M., 18 (5'6", brown eyes, brown hair, born in Texas; taken prisoner at Arkansas Post, Arkansas, on January 11, 1863; took oath of allegiance to the U.S.A. at Camp Butler, Illinois, on ?, 1863)

WILKS, BENJAMIN F., 20 (Taken prisoner at Arkansas Post, Arkansas, on January 11, 1863; promoted fourth corporal on April 16, 1864; WIA at New Hope Church, Georgia, on May 27, 1864; taken prisoner at Franklin, Tennessee, on November 30, 1864)

WILLIAMS, SAMUEL, 17 (Died at Arkansas Post, Arkansas, on ?)

WILSON, A. J., 21 (Taken prisoner at Arkansas Post, Arkansas, on January 11, 1863; died at ? on ?, 1864)

WILSON, DON W., 17 (Received a disability discharge on August 1, 1862)

WILSON, MERIT D., 25 (5'2½", blue eyes, light hair, fair complexion, born in Louisiana, occupation a teamster; received a disability discharge on April 17, 1862)

WOODWARD, J. P., 18 (5'8½", gray eyes, light hair, fair complexion; taken prisoner at Arkansas Post, Arkansas, on January 11, 1863; present at final surrender at Greensboro, North Carolina, on April 26, 1865)

YATES, HENRY W., 18 (Deserted at Navasota, Texas, on June 8, 1862)

COMPANY H — Composed of personnel recruited primarily in Calhoun and Victoria Counties, Texas. Mustered into Confederate service on March 27, 1862.

OFFICERS

GEORGE P. FINLAY, Captain, 32 (6'4", gray eyes, brown hair, dark complexion; taken prisoner at Arkansas Post, Arkansas, on January 11, 1863; served in Trans-Mississippi Department from ?)

ROBERT B. HARVEY, First Lieutenant, 33 (6'0", blue eyes, dark hair, light complexion; taken prisoner at Arkansas Post, Arkansas, on January 11, 1863; KIA at Chickamauga, Georgia, on September 20, 1863)

JAMES A. McCORD, First Lieutenant, 27 (5'8", blue eyes, light hair, light complexion; WIA at Franklin, Tennessee, on November 30, 1864; taken prisoner at Columbia, Tennessee, on December 25, 1864)

NON-COMMISSIONED OFFICERS

JOHN P. PETTUS, First Sergeant, 27 or 28 (Demoted second sergeant on August 1, 1862; taken prisoner at Arkansas Post, Arkansas, on January 11, 1863; died at Ringgold, Georgia, on August 2, 1863)

WILLIAM J. ATCHESON, Third Sergeant, 32 (Promoted first sergeant on August 1, 1862; taken prisoner at Arkansas Post, Arkansas, on January 11, 1863; taken prisoner at ? on ?; died at Camp Chase, Ohio, on January 19, 1865)

HENRY H. SIMS, Drummer, 21 or 26 (Transferred from Company A on April 11, 1862; taken prisoner at Arkansas Post, Arkansas, on January 11, 1863; took oath of allegiance to the U.S.A. at City Point, Virginia, on April 14, 1863)

PRIVATES

ANDREWS, LAFAYETTE, 31 (Taken prisoner at Arkansas Post, Arkansas, on January 11, 1863; died at St. Louis, Missouri, on January 30, 1863)

ATWELL, JAMES, 51 (Taken prisoner at Arkansas Post, Arkansas, on January 11, 1863; KIA at Jonesboro, Georgia, on September 1, 1864)

BARWOLD, EDWARD, 25 (Taken prisoner at Arkansas Post, Arkansas, on January 11, 1863; promoted third sergeant on March 1, 1864; POW? near Atlanta, Georgia, on July 22, 1864)

BINDRICK, GEORGE (WIA near Atlanta, Georgia, on October ?, 1864; taken prisoner near Atlanta, Georgia, on ?, 1864; died at ? on October 18 or 22, 1864)

BLACK, AUGUSTUS, 23 (Taken prisoner at Arkansas Post, Arkansas, on January 11, 1863; taken prisoner near Atlanta, Georgia, on July 10, 1864)

BRIGHTWELL, CHARLES R., 35 (WIA at Arkansas Post, Arkansas, on January 11, 1863; taken prisoner at Arkansas Post, Arkansas, on January 11, 1863; served in Trans-Mississippi Department from ?)

BRIGHTWELL, JOHN A., 32 (Promoted third corporal on ?, 1862; taken prisoner at Arkansas Post, Arkansas, on January 11, 1863; promoted second corporal on ?, 1863; WIA at Franklin, Tennessee, on November 30, 1864; present at final surrender at Greensboro, North Carolina, on April 26, 1865)

BURNS, JOHN, 20 (Taken prisoner at Arkansas Post, Arkansas, on January 11, 1863; WIA at Chickamauga, Georgia, on September 20, 1863; taken prisoner at Franklin, Tennessee, on November 30, 1864; enlisted into the Fifth U.S. Volunteers at Camp Douglas, Illinois, on April 14, 1865)

CARDEN, JOSEPH W., 23 (Deserted on January 9, 1863)

CHICHESTER, WILLIAM G. (Taken prisoner at Arkansas Post, Arkansas, on January 11, 1863; died at Camp Butler, Illinois, on March 12, 1863; POW records state that he died at Camp Butler, Illinois, on February 1 or March 12, 1863)

COCKE, S. F., 18 (Taken prisoner at Arkansas Post, Arkansas, on January 11, 1863; WIA at Chickamauga, Georgia, on September 20, 1863; promoted second lieutenant on ?, 1863; promoted first lieutenant on April 18, 1864; KIA near Atlanta, Georgia, on June 22, 1864)

COLLER, FRANK, 27 (Taken prisoner at Arkansas Post, Arkansas, on January 11, 1863; KIA at Chickamauga, Georgia, on September 20, 1863)

COX, CHARLES W., 30 (Taken prisoner at Arkansas Post, Arkansas, on January 11, 1863)

COX, HARVEY H., 25 (Taken prisoner at Arkansas Post, Arkansas, on January 11, 1863)

COX, JOHN, 25 (Transferred from Company A on April 11, 1862; promoted first corporal on April 11, 1862; taken prisoner at Arkansas Post, Arkansas, on January 11, 1863; taken prisoner near Atlanta, Georgia, on August 22, 1864)

COX, JOSEPH H., 22 (Taken prisoner at Arkansas Post, Arkansas, on January 11, 1863; POW? near Atlanta, Georgia, on July 22, 1864)

CRENSHAW, MOSES, 48 (5'6", blue eyes, brown hair, born in England; taken prisoner at Arkansas Post, Arkansas, on January 11, 1863; took oath of allegiance to the U.S.A. at Camp Butler, Illinois, on March 30, 1863)

CROMWELL, ALEX G., 17 (Taken prisoner at Arkansas Post, Arkansas, on January 11, 1863; WIA at Chickamauga, Georgia, on September 20, 1863)

DELANEY, PHILIP, 45 (Taken prisoner at Arkansas Post, Arkansas, on January 11, 1863; deserted on January 18, 1863)

FAGAN, JOSEPH, 29 (Died at Arkansas Post, Arkansas, on November 5, 1862)

FRENCH, JAMES, 33 (Taken prisoner at Arkansas Post, Arkansas, on January 11, 1863; served in Trans-Mississippi Department from ?, 1863)

GAYLORD, EDWARD H. (Served in Trans-Mississippi Department from ?, 1863)

GISLER, JACOB, 22 (Transferred from Company A on April 11, 1862; taken prisoner at Arkansas Post, Arkansas, on January 11, 1863; taken prisoner at Franklin, Tennessee, on November 30, 1864)

HARVEY, HENRY B., 31 (5'8¾", hazel eyes, brown hair, dark complexion; promoted second lieutenant on March 30, 1862; taken prisoner at Arkansas Post, Arkansas, on January 11, 1863; promoted captain on October 19, 1863; cited for gallantry at Chickamauga; dropped from roll as captain on April 18, 1864)

HENSOLDT, ARNO, 31 (5'8", dark eyes, dark hair, dark complexion; transferred to Company I on September 23, 1862)

HIERSHERY, AUGUST, 34 (Taken prisoner at Arkansas Post, Arkansas, on January 11, 1863; taken prisoner at Chattanooga, Tennessee, on November 26, 1863; enlisted into the U.S. Navy on May 23, 1864)

HOGAN, GRANVILLE, 17 (6'0", blue eyes, light hair, dark complexion; taken prisoner at Arkansas Post, Arkansas, on January 11, 1863; taken prisoner at Raleigh, North Carolina, on April 18, 1865)

HOGAN, J. F., 20 (5'6¾", gray eyes, light hair, saffron complexion, born in Burleson County, Texas, occupation a stock raiser; received a disability discharge on September 3, 1862)

HOGAN, ROBERT, 26 (Received a ? discharge on July 22, 1862)

HUGHES, JAMES, 26 (6'2", brown eyes, dark hair, light complexion, born in Nacadoches, Texas, occupation a stock tender; received a disability discharge on June 5, 1862)

INGRAM, JASPER, 21 (Died at Arkansas Post, Arkansas, on January 10, 1863)

JOHNSON, GEORGE, 29 (Transferred from Company A on April 11, 1862; promoted fifth sergeant on September 23, 1862; promoted fourth sergeant on September 30, 1862; WIA at Arkansas Post, Arkansas, on ?, 1863; taken prisoner at Arkansas Post, Arkansas, on January 11, 1863; KIA at Missionary Ridge, Tennessee, on November 25, 1863)

KAY, JOHN W., 35 (5'7", blue eyes, black hair, born in South Carolina; promoted second corporal on ?, 1862; taken prisoner at Arkansas Post, Arkansas, on January 11, 1863; took oath of allegiance to the U.S.A. at Camp Butler, Illinois, on March 13, 1863; returned to company on ?, 1863; WIA at Chickamauga, Georgia, on September 20, 1863; present at final surrender at Greensboro, North Carolina, on April 26, 1865)

KINSELLA, EDWARD, 48 (Taken prisoner at Arkansas Post, Arkansas, on January 11, 1863; WIA at ? on ?, 1863)

KUHLENTHAL, ED., 23 (Transferred from Company A on April 11, 1862; taken prisoner at Arkansas Post, Arkansas, on January 11, 1863; promoted junior second lieutenant on March 9, 1864; promoted first lieutenant on June 22, 1864; WIA near Atlanta, Georgia, on July 5, 1864)

LINKENHOKER, WILLIAM P., 26 (6'0", brown eyes, dark hair, dark complexion; taken prisoner at Arkansas Post, Arkansas, on January 11, 1863; WIA at Chickamauga, Georgia, on September 20, 1863; taken prisoner at Spring Hill, Tennessee, on December 18, 1864)

LONGNECKER, ALBERT, 24 (Taken prisoner at Arkansas Post, Arkansas, on January 11, 1863; WIA near Resaca, Georgia, on May 14, 1864; taken prisoner near Atlanta, Georgia, on July 22, 1864)

MANES, JOHN, 18 (Taken prisoner at Arkansas Post, Arkansas, on January 11, 1863; WIA at Chickamauga, Georgia, on September 20, 1863; present at final surrender at Greensboro, North Carolina, on April 26, 1865)

McLEOD, ALEXANDER, 24 (WIA at Arkansas Post, Arkansas, on January 11, 1863; taken prisoner at Arkansas Post, Arkansas, on January 11, 1863; died at St. Louis, Missouri, on ?, 1863)

McLEOD, ANGUISH, 23 (Taken prisoner at Arkansas Post, Arkansas, on January 11, 1863; died at ? on April 10, 1864)

McLEOD, MURDOCK, 20 (Taken prisoner at Arkansas Post, Arkansas, on January 11, 1863; taken prisoner at Franklin, Tennessee, on November 30, 1864)

McLOUD, MALCOLM, 17 (Died at Benton, Saline County, Arkansas, on August 4, 1862)

McNAMARA, WILLIAM, 26 (6'1", blue eyes, brown hair, born in Ireland; transferred from Company A on April 11, 1862; taken prisoner at Arkansas Post, Arkansas, on January 11, 1863; took oath of allegiance to the U.S.A. at Camp Butler, Illinois, on March 10, 1863)

MOORE, SAMUEL, Jr. (Taken prisoner at ? on ?; died at Nashville, Tennessee, on ?)

MOSES, E. M., 20 (WIA at Arkansas Post, Arkansas, on ?, 1863; taken prisoner at Arkansas Post, Arkansas, on January 11, 1863; took oath of allegiance to the U.S.A. at ? on January ?, 1863)

MUCKEY, BILL, 28 (Taken prisoner at Arkansas Post, Arkansas, on January 11, 1863; KIA at Franklin, Tennessee, on November 30, 1864)

NEAL, JAMES H., 22 (6'1/2", hazel eyes, brown hair, dark complexion; taken prisoner at Arkansas Post, Arkansas, on January 11, 1863; deserted on October 12, 1864; took oath of allegiance to the U.S.A. at Louisville, Kentucky, on March 29, 1865)

NEWPORT, JAMES A., 25 (Transferred from Company A on April 11, 1862; taken prisoner at Arkansas Post, Arkansas, on January 11, 1863; promoted second lieutenant on August 13, 1863)

NIMMO, JOSEPH W., 26 or 27 (5'5", blue eyes, fair hair, light complexion, born in Homby County, Mississippi, occupation a painter; transferred from Company A on April 14, 1862; taken prisoner at Arkansas Post, Arkansas, on January 11, 1863; present at final surrender at Greensboro, North Carolina, on April 26, 1865)

O'RILEY, EDWARD, 25 (Taken prisoner at Arkansas Post, Arkansas, on January 11, 1863; WIA at Jonesboro, Georgia, on September 1, 1864; taken prisoner at Franklin, Tennessee, on November 30, 1864)

PATTON, JOHN, 26 (5'9", blue eyes, light hair, light complexion, born in Claiborne County, Mississippi, occupation a farmer; received a disability discharge on June 4, 1862)

POWER, JOHN, 25 (Transferred from Company A on April 11, 1862; promoted fourth corporal on August 1, 1862; promoted fifth sergeant on November 1, 1862; taken prisoner at Arkansas Post, Arkansas, on January 11, 1863; promoted second sergeant on ?, 1863)

RAY, WILLIAM L., 32 (Taken prisoner at Arkansas Post, Arkansas, on January 11, 1863; WIA near Atlanta, Georgia, on August 15, 1864; died of wounds at ? on ?)

RICE, STEPHEN E., 24 (6'0", blue eyes, brown hair, light complexion; promoted fifth sergeant on August 1, 1862; promoted junior second lieutenant on ?, 1862; taken prisoner at Arkansas Post, Arkansas, on January 11, 1863; promoted second lieutenant on ?, 1863; promoted first lieutenant on October 19, 1863; promoted captain on April 18, 1864; taken prisoner near Atlanta, Georgia, on July 22, 1864; WIA at Franklin, Tennessee, on November 30, 1864)

ROMERO, LOUIS, 22 or 25 (5'4", black eyes, black hair, born in Mexico; taken prisoner at Arkansas Post, Arkansas, on January 11, 1863; took oath of allegiance to the U.S.A. at Camp Butler, Illinois, on March ?, 1863; returned to company on ?; present at final surrender at Greensboro, North Carolina, on April 26, 1865)

ROOVY, JOHN (Died at Nashville, Tennessee, on ?)

ROSS, W. J. M. (Died at Nashville, Tennessee, on March ?, 1863)

ROWLAND, J. G., 40 (Received a disability discharge on September 4, 1862)

SAMPSON, JAMES A., 16 (Taken prisoner at Arkansas Post, Arkansas, on January 11, 1863; promoted fourth sergeant on March 1, 1864; WIA near Marietta, Georgia, on June 23, 1864; died of wounds at ? on ?)

SANCHEZ, MARION, 17 (Taken prisoner at Arkansas Post, Arkansas, on January 11, 1863; WIA at Spring Hill, Tennessee, on November 29, 1864)

SEAMAN, CHARLES, 37 or 38 (5'7¼", gray eyes, dark hair, dark complexion, born in New York; transferred from Company A on April 11, 1862; received a disability discharge on October 3, 1862)

SESSIONS, HENRI W., 25 (Taken prisoner at Arkansas Post, Arkansas, on January 11, 1863; WIA at Chickamauga, Georgia, on September 20, 1863; taken prisoner near Atlanta, Georgia, on July 22, 1864)

SIMS, JOHN M., 52 (5'10½", blue eyes, gray hair, ruddy red complexion, occupation a carpenter; promoted third sergeant on August 1, 1862; promoted second sergeant on ?, 1862; received a disability discharge on November 11, 1862)

SPENCER, WILLIAM N. (WIA near Marietta, Georgia, on June 21, 1864; present at final surrender at Greensboro, North Carolina, on April 26, 1865)

STAPP, HUGH S., 42 (Served in Trans-Mississippi Department from ?)

TANNER, JOHN, 25 (Taken prisoner at Arkansas Post, Arkansas, on January 11, 1863; died at Camp Butler, Illinois, on March 12, 1863)

TRAYLOR, PASCAL M., 17 (Taken prisoner at Arkansas Post, Arkansas, on January 11, 1863; KIA near Atlanta, Georgia, on July 22, 1864)

VENABLE, WILLIAM L., 27 (6'½", blue eyes, brown hair, fair complexion, occupation a farmer; taken prisoner at Arkansas Post, Arkansas, on January 11, 1863; died at Camp Butler, Illinois, on March 15, 1863)

WETHERELL, JAMES E., 26 (Transferred from Company A on April 11, 1862; promoted fourth sergeant on ?, 1862; promoted third sergeant on ?, 1862; taken prisoner at Arkansas Post, Arkansas, on January 11, 1863; transferred to Engineer Corps on ?, 1863)

WILBORN, GEORGE M., 22 (Taken prisoner at Arkansas Post, Arkansas, on January 11, 1863)

COMPANY I—Composed of personnel recruited primarily in DeWitt County, Texas. Mustered into Confederate service on April 11, 1862.

OFFICERS

C. P. NAUNHEIM, Captain, 28 (5'11", dark eyes, dark hair, dark complexion; taken prisoner at Arkansas Post, Arkansas, on January 11, 1863; resigned on May 9, 1863)

G. POETTER, First Lieutenant, 41 (Resigned on May 21, 1862)

L. ZUCH, Second Lieutenant, 36 (Resigned on May 20 or 21, 1862)

NON-COMMISSIONED OFFICERS

M. ARNOLD, First Sergeant, 27 (Resigned and returned to ranks on October 1, 1862)

FRANCIS SHERIDAN, First Sergeant (Taken prisoner near Nashville, Tennessee, on December 16, 1864)

JOHN WARZECHA, Second Sergeant, 36 (Received a disability discharge on September 3, 1862)

G. VOLST, Third Sergeant, 33 (5'9", brown eyes, brown hair, born in Prussia; promoted second sergeant on ?; resigned and returned to ranks on October 1, 1862; taken prisoner at Arkansas Post, Arkansas, on January 11, 1863; took oath of allegiance to the U.S.A. at Camp Butler, Illinois, on March ?, 1863)

A. STRIEBER, First Corporal, 22 (5'7", blue eyes, light hair, born in Germany; promoted first sergeant on October 1, 1862; taken prisoner at Arkansas Post, Arkansas, on January 11, 1863; took oath of allegiance to the U.S.A. at Camp Butler, Illinois, on March ?, 1863)

V. ZIMON, Third Corporal, 46 (5'5", blue eyes, brown hair, born in Germany; resigned and returned to ranks on October 1, 1862; taken prisoner at Arkansas Post, Arkansas, on January 11, 1863; took oath of allegiance to the U.S.A. at Camp Butler, Illinois, on March ?, 1863)

CHRIS BAYER, Corporal, 38 (5'6", blue eyes, light hair, fair complexion, born in Germany, occupation a shoemaker; received a disability discharge on September 3, 1862)

M. RIEDEL, Musician, 30 (5'6", blue eyes, light hair, born in Germany; taken prisoner at Arkansas Post, Arkansas, on January 11, 1863; took oath of allegiance to the U.S.A. at Camp Butler, Illinois, on March 13, 1863)

BARTON, O. P.

BISHOP, WILLIAM

BRYSH, ANTON, 24 (5'5", black eyes, sandy hair, dark complexion, born in Poland; received a disability discharge on May 15, 1863)

BURKHARD, J., 38 (Born in Germany; taken prisoner at Arkansas Post, Arkansas, on January 11, 1863; took oath of allegiance to the U.S.A. at Camp Butler, Illinois, on April 6, 1863)

CRILL, JOSEPH, 18 (Transferred from Company D on August 1, 1862; taken prisoner at Arkansas Post, Arkansas, on January 11, 1863)

DLUGOSH, JOSEPH, 24 (5'7", hazel eyes, brown hair, born in Prussia; taken prisoner at Arkansas Post, Arkansas, on January 11, 1863; took oath of allegiance to the U.S.A. at Camp Butler, Illinois, on March ?, 1863)

FREY, A., 20 (5'5", blue eyes, brown hair, born in Germany; promoted second sergeant on October 1, 1862; taken prisoner at Arkansas Post, Arkansas, on January 11, 1863; took oath of allegiance to the U.S.A. at Camp Butler, Illinois, on March ?, 1863)

GIBS, F., 32 (Deserted on April 25, 1862)

GOHLKI, JOHN, 28 (5'8", blue eyes, light hair, born in Germany; taken prisoner at Arkansas Post, Arkansas, on January 11, 1863; took oath of allegiance to the U.S.A. at Camp Butler, Illinois, on March ?, 1863)

GOLLA, JOHN, 24 (5'9", brown eyes, brown hair, born in Germany; promoted second corporal on October 1, 1862; taken prisoner at Arkansas Post, Arkansas, on January 11, 1863; took oath of allegiance to the U.S.A. at Camp Butler, Illinois, on March ?, 1863)

GOMERT, WILLIAM, 27 (5'6", brown eyes, black hair, born in Germany; taken prisoner at Arkansas Post, Arkansas, on January 11, 1863; took oath of allegiance to the U.S.A. at Camp Butler, Illinois, on March ?, 1863)

GREGORZYCK, F., 39 (Served in Trans-Mississippi Department from ?)

HENSOLDT, ARNO, 31 (5'8", dark eyes, dark hair, dark complexion; transferred from Company H on September 23, 1862; promoted second lieutenant on September 23, 1862; taken prisoner at Arkansas Post, Arkansas, on January 11, 1863; resigned on May 9, 1863)

HUTTIG, G., 28 (5'7", blue eyes, light hair, born in Germany; taken prisoner at Arkansas Post, Arkansas, on January 11, 1863; took oath of allegiance to the U.S.A. at Camp Butler, Illinois, on March ?, 1863)

JOSKA, JOSEPH, 27 (5'7", blue eyes, light hair, born in Germany; taken prisoner at Arkansas Post, Arkansas, on January 11, 1863; took oath of allegiance to the U.S.A. at Camp Butler, Illinois, on March ?, 1863)

KATZMARK, J., 26 (5'9", blue eyes, light hair, born in Germany; taken prisoner at Arkansas Post, Arkansas, on January 11, 1863; took oath of allegiance to the U.S.A. at Camp Butler, Illinois, on March ?, 1863)

KIELBASA, J., 23 (5'8", brown eyes, brown hair, born in Prussia; promoted first corporal on October 1, 1862; taken prisoner at Arkansas Post, Arkansas, on January 11, 1863; took oath of allegiance to the U.S.A. at Camp Butler, Illinois, on March ?, 1863)

KOLOZEY, S., 38 (5'9", blue eyes, brown hair, born in Germany; taken prisoner at Arkansas Post, Arkansas, on January 11, 1863; took oath of allegiance to the U.S.A. at Camp Butler, Illinois, on March ?, 1863)

KOSIELSKY, A., 25 (5'5", brown eyes, brown hair, born in Poland; taken prisoner at Arkansas Post, Arkansas, on January 11, 1863; took oath of allegiance to the U.S.A. at Camp Butler, Illinois, on March ?, 1863)

KUHL, JULIUS, 36 (5'8", gray eyes, brown hair, born in Germany; taken prisoner at Arkansas Post, Arkansas, on January 11, 1863; took oath of allegiance to the U.S.A. at Camp Butler, Illinois, on March ?, 1863)

LESSE, ALBERT, 17 (5'5", black eyes, black hair, born in Mexico; taken prisoner at Arkansas Post, Arkansas, on January 11, 1863; took oath of allegiance to the U.S.A. at Camp Butler, Illinois, on March ?, 1863)

LUNZIN, G., 38 (5'3", hazel eyes, brown hair, born in Germany; taken prisoner at Arkansas Post, Arkansas, on January 11, 1863; took oath of allegiance to the U.S.A. at Camp Butler, Illinois, on March ?, 1863)

MERTENS, H., 39 (Deserted on April 19, 1862)

NOBIS, WILLIAM, 30 or 31 (5'8", blue eyes, brown hair, born in Germany; taken prisoner at Arkansas Post, Arkansas, on January 11, 1863; took oath of allegiance to the U.S.A. at Camp Butler, Illinois, on March ?, 1863)

OBSTEN, FRANCIS, 21 (5'9", blue eyes, brown hair, born in Germany; taken prisoner at Arkansas Post, Arkansas, on January 11, 1863; took oath of allegiance to the U.S.A. at Camp Butler, Illinois, on March ?, 1863)

OPIELLA, J., 21 (5'8", blue eyes, light hair, born in Germany; taken prisoner at Arkansas Post, Arkansas, on January 11, 1863; took oath of allegiance to the U.S.A. at Camp Butler, Illinois, on March ?, 1863)

PALTER, J. W.

POTTER, HENRY, 36 (5'3", gray eyes, brown hair, born in Germany; taken prisoner at Arkansas Post, Arkansas, on January 11, 1863; took oath of allegiance to the U.S.A. at Camp Butler, Illinois, on March ?, 1863)

PRUTZ, WILLIAM, 30 (5'7", hazel eyes, brown hair, born in Germany; taken prisoner at Arkansas Post, Arkansas, on January 11, 1863; took oath of allegiance to the U.S.A. at Camp Butler, Illinois, on March ?, 1863)

REID, PATRICK, 25 (5'5", blue eyes, black hair, born in Ireland; taken prisoner at Arkansas Post, Arkansas, on January 11, 1863; took oath of allegiance to the U.S.A. at Camp Butler, Illinois, on March ?, 1863)

REIS, G., 26 (5'7", blue or black eyes, black hair, born in Germany; taken prisoner at Arkansas Post, Arkansas, on January 11, 1863; took oath of allegiance to the U.S.A. at Camp Butler, Illinois, on March ?, 1863)

REUSER, LOUIS, 19 (5'6", gray eyes, brown hair, born in Germany; taken prisoner at Arkansas Post, Arkansas, on January 11, 1863; took oath of allegiance to the U.S.A. at Camp Butler, Illinois, on March ?, 1863)

RIEDEL, C., 27 (Deserted on April 25, 1862)

RIEDEL, E., 19 (5'9", blue eyes, flaxen hair, born in Germany; taken prisoner at Arkansas Post, Arkansas, on January 11, 1863; took oath of allegiance to the U.S.A. at Camp Butler, Illinois, on March ?, 1863)

RIEDEL, F., 21 (Deserted on April 25, 1862)

RUMMEL, F., 18 (Taken prisoner at Arkansas Post, Arkansas, on January 11, 1863; remained at Camp Butler, Illinois, after exchange)

SAUERMILCH, C., 18 (Taken prisoner at Arkansas Post, Arkansas, on January 11, 1863; took oath of allegiance to the U.S.A. at Camp Butler, Illinois, on ?, 1863)

SCHROEDER, F., 25 (5'9", brown eyes, brown hair, born in Germany; taken prisoner at Arkansas Post, Arkansas, on January 11, 1863; took oath of allegiance to the U.S.A. at Camp Butler, Illinois, on ?, 1863)

SCHROEDER, G., 17 (5'10", brown eyes, black hair, born in Prussia; taken prisoner at Arkansas Post, Arkansas, on January 11, 1863; took oath of allegiance to the U.S.A. at Camp Butler, Illinois, on ?, 1863)

SHEFSKY, H., 36 (Transferred from Company C on August 1, 1862; served in Trans-Mississippi Department from ?)

SHEPPA, J., 21 or 22 (5'6", blue eyes, brown hair, born in Germany; taken prisoner at Arkansas Post, Arkansas, on January 11, 1863; took oath of allegiance to the U.S.A. at Camp Butler, Illinois, on March ?, 1863)

SHWURZ, THOMAS, 38 (Received a ? discharge on July 17, 1862)

SMUNDER, MARTIN, 38 (5'6", blue eyes, brown hair, born in Germany; taken prisoner at Arkansas Post, Arkansas, on January 11, 1863; took oath of allegiance to the U.S.A. at Camp Butler, Illinois, on March ?, 1863)

SPREMBERG, R., 26 (5'7", brown eyes, black hair, born in Germany; taken prisoner at Arkansas Post, Arkansas, on January 11, 1863; took oath of allegiance to the U.S.A. at Camp Butler, Illinois, on March ?, 1863)

STEPHAN, C., 21 (5'10", blue eyes, red hair, born in Prussia; taken prisoner at Arkansas Post, Arkansas, on January 11, 1863; took oath of allegiance to the U.S.A. at Camp Butler, Illinois, on March ?, 1863)

STURMER, G., 33 (5'5", brown eyes, brown hair, born in Germany; taken prisoner at Arkansas Post, Arkansas, on January 11, 1863; took oath of allegiance to the U.S.A. at Camp Butler, Illinois, on March ?, 1863)

THEA, JOHN, 21 (5'10", brown eyes, brown hair, born in Germany; taken prisoner at Arkansas Post, Arkansas, on January 11, 1863; took oath of allegiance to the U.S.A. at Camp Butler, Illinois, on March ?, 1863)

WILKINSON, W., 22 (5'5", blue eyes, brown hair, born in Germany; taken prisoner at Arkansas Post, Arkansas, on January 11, 1863; took oath of allegiance to the U.S.A. at Camp Butler, Illinois, on March ?, 1863)

ZOWADA, V., 24 (5'10", black eyes, black hair, born in Prussia; taken prisoner at Arkansas Post, Arkansas, on January 11, 1863; took oath of allegiance to the U.S.A. at Camp Butler, Illinois, on March ?, 1863)

COMPANY K — ALAMO RIFLES or ALAMO GUARDS — Composed of personnel recruited primarily in Bexar County, Texas. Mustered into Confederate service on March 31, 1862.

OFFICERS

SAMUEL W. McALLISTER, Captain, 31 (Served in Trans-Mississippi Department from ?, 1863; dropped from roll as captain on November 28, 1863)

HENRY BURNS, First Lieutenant, 46 (5'8", black eyes, dark hair, fallow complexion; taken prisoner at Arkansas Post, Arkansas, on January 11, 1863; displaced temporarily on May 24, 1863; served in Trans-Mississippi Department from ?, 1863)

EDWARD BRADEN, Second Lieutenant, 33 (5'8", gray eyes, light hair, fallow complexion; taken prisoner at Arkansas Post, Arkansas, on January 11, 1863; resigned on March 17, 1863)

JOSEPH R. GARZA, Junior Second Lieutenant, 23 (Promoted second lieutenant on March 17, 1863; promoted first lieutenant on ?; served in Trans-Mississippi Department from ?; KIA at ? on April 8, 1864)

NON-COMMISSIONED OFFICERS

MORTIMER O'DONOGHUE, First Sergeant, 37 (Taken prisoner at Arkansas Post, Arkansas, on January 11, 1863; promoted regimental sergeant major on May 14, 1863)

THOMAS COPELAND, Second Sergeant, 30 (5'7", hazel eyes, dark hair, dark complexion; taken prisoner at Arkansas Post, Arkansas, on January 11, 1863; promoted first sergeant on May 14, 1863; promoted junior second lieutenant on March 9, 1864; taken prisoner near Atlanta, Georgia, on July 21, 1864)

HENRY DERR, Third Sergeant, 46 (5'9", gray eyes, light hair, dark complexion, born in Bavaria; reduced to ranks on December 11 or 12, 1862; received a disability discharge on January 10, 1863)

ANDREW E. COTTON, Fourth Sergeant, 24 (Served in Trans-Mississippi Department from ?)

MANUEL DE YTURRI, First Corporal, 24 (Transferred to Company A, Thirty-third Texas Cavalry Regiment on May 26, 1862; reduced to ranks on September 1, 1862)

WILLIAM FOGA, Corporal (Taken prisoner at Arkansas Post, Arkansas, on January 11, 1863)

CHARLES MAINZE, Corporal, 26 (Promoted second sergeant on December 14, 1862; taken prisoner at Arkansas Post, Arkansas, on January 11, 1863; promoted first sergeant on April 1, 1864; taken prisoner near Atlanta, Georgia, on July 21, 1864)

EUGENE NAVARRO, Corporal, 22 (5'5", dark eyes, dark hair, dark complexion; taken prisoner at Arkansas Post, Arkansas, on January 11, 1863; promoted second lieutenant on March 9, 1864; promoted first lieutenant on April 8, 1864; taken prisoner at Franklin, Tennessee, on November 30, 1864)

GUSTAV SCHMIDT, Corporal, 44 (5'6½", black eyes, light hair, light complexion, born in Germany, occupation a merchant; served in Trans-Mississippi Department from ?; received a disability discharge on May 27, 1863)

JAMES MUSIOL, Drummer, 17 (Taken prisoner at Arkansas Post, Arkansas, on January 11, 1863; took oath of allegiance to the U.S.A. at Camp Butler, Illinois, on February 7, 1863)

ANDREWS, ———— (AWOL since date of enlistment)

BRADEN, ADAM, 20 (Taken prisoner at Arkansas Post, Arkansas, on January 11, 1863; WIA at Chickamauga, Georgia, on September 20, 1863; taken prisoner at Franklin, Tennessee, on November 30, 1864)

BRADEN, MARTIN, 20 (Taken prisoner at Arkansas Post, Arkansas, on January 11, 1863; promoted corporal on April 1 or 7, 1864; WIA near Marietta, Georgia, on June 24, 1864; died of wounds at ? on ?)

BURTSCHELL, HENRY, 21 or 22 (5'5", blue eyes, brown hair, born in Germany; taken prisoner at Arkansas Post, Arkansas, on January 11, 1863; took oath of allegiance to the U.S.A. at Camp Butler, Illinois, on March 2, 1863)

BUSTILLOS, ANTONIO, 22 (Taken prisoner at Arkansas Post, Arkansas, on January 11, 1863; WIA at Jonesboro, Georgia, on September 1, 1864; present at final surrender at Greensboro, North Carolina, on April 26, 1865)

CANNON, JAMES, 37 (5'4", blue eyes, brown hair, born in Pennsylvania; taken prisoner at Arkansas Post, Arkansas, on January 11, 1863; took oath of allegiance to the U.S.A. at Camp Butler, Illinois, on February 19, 1863)

CARDENA, JOSEPH, 24 (Taken prisoner at Arkansas Post, Arkansas, on January 11, 1863; taken prisoner near Nashville, Tennessee, on December 15, 1864; enlisted into the U.S. Army on April 22, 1865)

CHRISTLESS, MICHAEL, 21 (Taken prisoner at Arkansas Post, Arkansas, on January 11, 1863; transferred to Engineer Corps on August 2, 1863)

CRAFT, JOHN M., 24 (5'4", blue eyes, light hair, light complexion, born in Bavaria; received a disability discharge on November 10, 1862)

DESPRES, JOHN M., 50 (Taken prisoner at Arkansas Post, Arkansas, on January 11, 1863; died at Camp Butler, Illinois, on February 17, 1863)

DIGNOWITY, ALBERT W., 15½ (Recruit rejected by regimental doctor)

DILMAN, CHARLES (Taken prisoner at Arkansas Post, Arkansas, on January 11, 1863)

DIRR, JOHN (Taken prisoner near Franklin, Tennessee, on December 17, 1864; enlisted into the U.S. Army on March 25, 1865)

DOYLE, THOMAS L., 25 (5'4", gray eyes, light hair, light complexion; taken prisoner at Arkansas Post, Arkansas, on January 11, 1863; MIA at Chickamauga, Georgia, on September 20, 1863)

DUBY, ALEXANDER, 33 (5'6½", blue eyes, light hair, light complexion; taken prisoner at Arkansas Post, Arkansas, on January 11, 1863; MIA at Chickamauga, Georgia, on September 20, 1863)

FOOKE, WILLIAM, 35 (Promoted corporal on December 14, 1862; taken prisoner at Arkansas Post, Arkansas, on January 11, 1863; took oath of allegiance to the U.S.A. at Camp Butler, Illinois, on February 25, 1863)

FREMON, LEON A., 16 (Taken prisoner at Arkansas Post, Arkansas, on January 11, 1863; taken prisoner near Atlanta, Georgia, on July 21, 1864)

FRICK, CLAUS HENRY, 16 (Received a disability discharge on September 23, 1862)

GARNER, W. S., 38 (5'7½", hazel eyes, light hair, fair complexion, born in Philadelphia, Pennsylvania, occupation a butcher; received a disability discharge on June 4, 1862)

GARZA, SIMON, 39 (Taken prisoner at Arkansas Post, Arkansas, on January 11, 1863; WIA at Franklin, Tennessee, on November 30, 1864)

GORDON, JERRE, 31 (Served in Trans-Mississippi Department from ?)

GRELL, JOHN OTTO, 32 (Taken prisoner at Arkansas Post, Arkansas, on January 11, 1863; transferred to Engineer Corps on August 2, 1863)

GRIFFIN, CHARLES, 20 (5'8", black eyes, black hair, born in Michigan; taken prisoner at Arkansas Post, Arkansas, on January 11, 1863; took oath of allegiance to the U.S.A. at Camp Butler, Illinois, on March ?, 1863)

HAWKINS, AMBROSE, 16 (Taken prisoner at Arkansas Post, Arkansas, on January 11, 1863; WIA near Atlanta, Georgia, on July 20, 1864; present at final surrender at Greensboro, North Carolina, on April 26, 1865)

HESSLER, ERNEST, 35 (Received a disability discharge on ?, 1862)

HOEVER, CHARLES, 18 (Taken prisoner at Arkansas Post, Arkansas, on January 11, 1863; taken prisoner near Nashville, Tennessee, on December 15, 1864; enlisted into the U.S. Army on April 22, 1865)

HOEVER, FREDERICK, 17 (5'7", hazel eyes, dark hair, dark complexion; taken prisoner at Arkansas Post, Arkansas, on January 11, 1863; WIA near Atlanta, Georgia, on July 21, 1864; taken prisoner near Nashville, Tennessee, on December 15, 1864; enlisted into the U.S. Army on April 22, 1865)

HOGAN, ANDREW, 37 (Received a ? discharge on January 5, 1863)

HORL, GEORGE, 20 (Taken prisoner at Arkansas Post, Arkansas, on January 11, 1863; WIA near Atlanta, Georgia, on July 20, 1864; WIA at Jonesboro, Georgia, on September 1, 1864; taken prisoner at Raleigh, North Carolina, on April 17, 1865)

HUDSLER, HENRY (AWOL since date of enlistment)

MARQUERD, EDWARD, 19 (5'5", blue eyes, sandy hair, born in Germany; taken prisoner at Arkansas Post, Arkansas, on January 11, 1863; took oath of allegiance to the U.S.A. at Camp Butler, Illinois, on February 20, 1863)

MARQUERD, GUSTAV, 20 (5'4", brown eyes, sandy hair, born in Germany; taken prisoner at Arkansas Post, Arkansas, on January 11, 1863; took oath of allegiance to the U.S.A. at Camp Butler, Illinois, on ?, 1863)

MILLER, ARMSTED, 24 (Taken prisoner at Arkansas Post, Arkansas, on January 11, 1863; died at Camp Butler, Illinois, on February 12, 1863)

OSWALD, CARL, 21 (5'8", gray eyes, sandy hair, born in Germany; taken prisoner at Arkansas Post, Arkansas, on January 11, 1863; took oath of allegiance to the U.S.A. at Camp Butler, Illinois, on February 5, 1863)

PONSLEY, JOHN, 23 (Taken prisoner at Arkansas Post, Arkansas, on January 11, 1863; took oath of allegiance to the U.S.A. at Camp Butler, Illinois, on February 7, 1863)

RILEY, JAMES (5'9½", blue eyes, brown hair, light complexion; taken prisoner at ? on ?; took oath of allegiance to the U.S.A. at Old Capital Prison at Washington, D.C., on March 14, 1864)

SAN MIGUEL, ANDREW (Taken prisoner at Arkansas Post, Arkansas, on January 11, 1863; WIA at Franklin, Tennessee, on November 30, 1864; taken prisoner at Franklin, Tennessee, on December 17, 1864; enlisted into the U.S. Army on March 20, 1865)

SARATS, PETER V., 19 (Promoted fourth corporal on December 14, 1862; taken prisoner at Arkansas Post, Arkansas, on January 11, 1863; deserted on ?, 1864)

SCHMIDT, ALBERT, 21 (Taken prisoner at Arkansas Post, Arkansas, on January 11, 1863; promoted sergeant on April 1, 1864; WIA at Franklin, Tennessee, on November 30, 1864; taken prisoner near Franklin, Tennessee, on December 17, 1864)

SCHLUNZ, DEDLEF, 34 (Taken prisoner at Arkansas Post, Arkansas, on January 11, 1863; WIA at Chickamauga, Georgia, on September 20, 1863)

SCHOENEN, HENRY, 58 (5'7¾", blue eyes, gray hair, dark complexion, born in Prussia, occupation a tailor; received a disability discharge on November 10, 1862)

SCOFIELD, JOSEPH, 21 (Taken prisoner at Arkansas Post, Arkansas, on January 11, 1863; took oath of allegiance to the U.S.A. at Camp Butler, Illinois, on February 5, 1863)

SHEPPARD, WOODWORTH V., 24 (Received a disability discharge on ?, 1862)

SUNIGA, ANTONIO, 23 (Taken prisoner at Arkansas Post, Arkansas, on January 11, 1863; died at Camp Butler, Illinois, on May 8, 1863)

WILLIAMS, S. (Taken prisoner at Arkansas Post, Arkansas, on January 11, 1863)

MISCELLANEOUS NAMES LISTED ON THE
SIXTH TEXAS INFANTRY REGIMENTAL ROSTER

ANTONIA, S., Private (Taken prisoner at Arkansas Post, Arkansas, on January 11, 1863; took oath of allegiance to the U.S.A. at Camp Butler, Illinois, on ?, 1863)

FIDDLER, M., Laundress

HALLIBAITON, THOMAS, Private

HANSER, BENJAMIN D., Private

HANSER, WILLIE, Private

HARRIS, WILLIAM, Private

HASLEY, JAMES W., Private

HENDERSON, ISAAC E., Private
JONES, M., Hospital Matron
McNILL, O., Laundress (Received a ? discharge on May 22, 1862)
MILLER, GEORGE A., Musician
NAPIER, O., Hospital Matron
WELCH, W. P., Private

Notes

NOTES FOR PROLOGUE

1. S. Cooper to Earl Van Dorn, June 12, 1861, *War of the Rebellion: A Compilation of the Official Records of the Union and Confederate Armies,* 128 vols. (Washington, D.C.: Government Printing Office, 1880–1901), Series I, Vol. IV, 91–92 (hereafter cited as *O.R.*).

2. L. P. Walker to Edward Clark, June 30, 1861, *O.R.,* Series I, Vol. IV, 412.

3. General Order No. 1, September 18, 1861; H E. McCulloch to P. O. Hebert, September 20, 1861, *O.R.,* Series I, Vol. IV, 106–108.

4. H. E. McCulloch to P. O. Hebert, September 20, 1861, *O.R.,* Series I, Vol. IV, 107–108; Roy Grimes, ed., *300 Years in Victoria County* (Victoria: The Victoria Advocate Publishing Company, 1968), 259, 304; Benjamin C. Robertson to Mother, December 20, 1861, George Lee Robertson Papers (Eugene C. Barker Texas History Center, University of Texas, Austin; hereafter cited as BTHC); Victoria City Minutes, October 15, 1861.

5. Compiled Service Records, Sixth Texas Infantry Regiment, National Archives, Washington, D.C.

6. *Ibid.,* J. W. Petty, Jr., ed., *Victor Rose's History of Victoria* (Victoria: Book Mart, 1961), 178.

7. Compiled Service Records, Sixth Texas Infantry Regiment; "Gonzales County Elected Officials, 1839–1920" (Typescript; Gonzales Archives, County Courthouse, Gonzales).

8. *Ibid.;* John Columbus Marr, "The History of Matagorda County" (M.A. thesis, University of Texas, 1928), 146.

9. Compiled Service Records, 4th Texas Infantry Regiment; Walter Prescott Webb and H. Bailey Carroll, eds., *The Handbook of Texas,* 2 vols. (Austin: The Texas State Historical Association, 1952), Vol. II, 894.

10. Compiled Service Records, Sixth Texas Infantry Regiment; Petty, *Rose,* 97–98; Grimes, *300 Years,* 325, 466.

11. Compiled Service Records, Sixth Texas Infantry Regiment; Webb and Carroll, *Handbook,* Vol. I, 603.

12. Compiled Service Records, Sixth Texas Infantry Regiment; *Dallas Herald,* September 18, 1861; Francis B. Heitman, *Historical Register and Dictionary of the United States Army, From Its Organization, September 29, 1789 to March 2, 1903,* 2 vols., (Washington: Government Printing Office, 1903), Vol. I, 447.

13. Compiled Service Records, Sixth Texas Infantry Regiment; A. H. Phillips, Jr.,

to Cousin Mary, May 6, 1863, Lucille Pool Collection (Victoria College Library, Victoria).

14. By the Governor: Proclamation, *O.R.,* Series IV, Vol. I, 980–982.

15. Compiled Service Records, Sixth Texas Infantry Regiment.

16. Compiled Service Record of James W. Snodgrass, National Archives, Washington, D.C.; James M. McCaffrey, *This Band of Heroes: Granbury's Texas Brigade, C.S.A.* (Austin: Eakin Press, 1985), 5; Marr, "History of Matagorda," 148.

17. Victoria County Commissioners Court Minutes, 33, 44; Guadalupe County Commissioners Court Minutes, 526–527; Dayton Kelley, ed., "Jim Turner, Co. G., 6th Texas Infantry, C.S.A., From 1861 to 1865," *Texana,* Vol. XII (1974), 152; A. H. Phillips, Jr., to Cousin Mary, May 6, 1863, Pool Collection.

18. Sebron Sneed to Fannie, December 18, 1862, Sebron G. Sneed, Jr., Papers (BTHC); Benjamin C. Robertson to Sister, September 7, 1862, Robertson Papers (BTHC); Galveston *Tri-Weekly Telegraph,* September 3, 1862; Gilbert Cuthbertson, "Coller of the Sixth Texas," *Military History of Texas and the Southwest,* Vol. IX (1971), 130; P. O. Hebert to Samuel Cooper, *O.R.,* Series I, Vol. 53, 793–794.

19. Recollections of William J. Oliphant (MS, Austin Public Library, Austin), 32–33 (hereafter cited as Oliphant Recollections); A. H. Phillips, Jr., to Cousin Mary, May 6, 1863, Pool Collection.

20. R. R. Garland to Samuel Boyer Davis, *O.R.,* Series I, Vol. IV, 156–157; Benjamin C. Robertson to Pa, December 10, 1861; Benjamin C. Robertson to Mother, December 20, 1861, Robertson Papers (BTHC).

21. Kelley, "Turner," 152; Benjamin C. Robertson to Mother, December 20, 1861, Robertson Papers (BTHC).

22. Compiled Service Records, Sixth Texas Infantry Regiment.

23. *Ibid.;* Cuthbertson, "Coller," 131.

24. McCaffrey, *This Band,* 6.

25. *Ibid.;* Cuthbertson, "Coller," 131–132; Kelley, "Turner," 153.

26. Grimes, *300 Years,* 308.

27. William W. Phillips to Father, June 23, 1862, Lucille Pool Collection (Victoria College Library, Victoria); Cuthbertson, "Coller," 132; Benjamin C. Robertson to Father, August 6, 1862, Robertson Papers (BTHC); Benjamin C. Robertson to Sister, September 9, 1862, Robertson Papers (BTHC).

28. Edwin C. Bearss, "The Battle of the Post Arkansas," *The Arkansas Historical Quarterly,* Vol. XVIII (Autumn, 1959), 237.

29. *Ibid.,* 239–240; McCaffrey, *This Band,* 28; Norman D. Brown, ed., *One of Cleburne's Command* (Austin: The University of Texas Press, 1980), 3–4.

30. Special Order, No. 39, September 28, 1862, *O.R.,* Series I, Vol. XIII, 883–885.

31. Bearss, "Post Arkansas," 238–239; Sebron G. Sneed to Fannie, December 25, 1862, Sneed Papers (BTHC); Isaiah Harlan to E, December 3, 1862, Isaiah Harlan Papers (The Hill College History Complex, Hillsboro).

32. Sneed, *Ibid.;* A. H. Phillips, Jr., to Cousin Mary, May 6, 1863, Pool Collection; Isaiah Harlan to Brother, December 25, 1862, *Ibid.;* William W. Phillips to Father, November 9, 1862, Pool Collection.

33. Sneed, *Ibid.*

34. Bearss, "Post Arkansas," 243–246, 263.

35 T. J. Churchill to T. H. Holmes, May 6, 1863, *O.R.,* Series I, Vol. XVII, Pt. 1, 780; R. R. Garland to B. S. Johnson, April 1, 1863, *O.R.,* Series I, Vol. XVII, Pt. 1, 783.

36. Garland, *Ibid.*, 783–784.

37. A. H. Phillips, Jr., to Cousin Mary, May 6, 1863, Pool Collection.

38. *Ibid.;* James Deshler to B. S. Johnson, March 25, 1863, *O.R.*, Series I, Vol. XVII, Pt. 1, 793.

39. T. J. Churchill to T. H. Holmes, May 6, 1863, *O.R.*, Series I, Vol. XVII, Pt. 1, 781; R. R. Garland to B. S. Johnson, April 1, 1863, *O.R.*, Series I, Vol. XVII, Pt. 1, 784–785; R. R. Garland to S. Cooper, July 14, 1863, *O.R.*, Series I, Vol. XVII, Pt. 1, 786–787.

40. A. H. Phillips, Jr., to Cousin Mary, May 6, 1863, Pool Collection; W. W. Heartsill, *Fourteen Hundred and 91 Days in the Confederate Army* (Wilmington, North Carolina: Broadfoot Publishing Company, 1987), 100.

41. William J. Oliphant, "Arkansas Post," *Southern Bivouac*, I (New Series), 738; McCaffrey, *This Band*, 45.

42. Oliphant Recollections, 10–11; Harold B. Simpson, ed., *The Bugle Softly Blows: The Confederate Diary of Benjamin M. Seaton* (Waco: Texian Press, 1965), 31–32; Cuthbertson, "Coller," 135.

43. Cuthbertson, *Ibid.;* Oliphant Recollections, 11; Brown, *Cleburne's Command*, 30; Kelley, "Turner," 159; A. H. Phillips, Jr., to Cousin Mary, May 6, 1863, Pool Collections.

44. Helen Edith Sheppley, "Camp Butler in the Civil War Days," *Journal of the Illinois State Historical Society*, XXV (January, 1933), 310–311.

45. *Ibid.*, 311; Compiled Service Record of C. P. Naunheim, National Archives, Washington, D.C.; Galveston *Tri-Weekly Telegraph*, July 1, 1863.

46. William H. Krauss, *Story of Camp Chase* (Nashville: Publishing House of the Methodist Episcopal Church, South, 1906), 112; Joseph L. Eisendrath, Jr., "Chicago's Camp Douglas, 1861–1865," *Journal of the Illinois State Historical Society*, Vol. LIII (Spring, 1960), 45; Sheppley, "Camp Butler," 297; John L. Williams to Niece, July 18, 1862, John L. Williams Letters (BTHC); Brown, *Cleburne's Command*, 31; McCaffrey, *This Band*, 55.

47. Heartsill, *Fourteen Hundred*, 117; R. M. Collins, *Chapters From the Unwritten History of the War Between the States* (Dayton: Morningside House, Inc., 1988), 96–100.

48. Kelley, "Turner," 159; McCaffrey, *This Band*, 56–58.

49. Kelley, *Ibid.*, 159; Heartsill, *Fourteen Hundred*, 120; Collins, *Unwritten History*, 103–104; Brown, *Cleburne's Command*, 35.

50. Simpson, *Bugle Softly Blows*, 32; Heartsill, *Ibid.*, 122–125.

51. Mark Mayo Boatner, III, *The Civil War Dictionary*, Revised (New York: David McKay Company, Inc., 1988), 803; Kelley, "Turner," 160–161; Heartsill, *Ibid.*, 125–126.

52. Heartsill, *Ibid.*, 126; Kelley, *Ibid.*, 162; Benjamin C. Robertson to Father, May 16, 1863, Robertson Papers (BTHC).

53. Compiled Service Records, Sixth Texas Infantry Regiment.

54. *Ibid.;* Howell and Elizabeth Purdue, *Pat Cleburne: Confederate General* (Hillsboro: Hill Junior College Press, 1973), 190; Collins, *Unwritten History*, 130; Brown, *Cleburne's Command*, 43.

55. Simpson, *Bugle Softly Blows*, 34–35; Purdue, *Ibid.*, 192.

56. P. R. Cleburne to Archer Anderson, August 3, 1863, *O.R.*, Series I, Vol. XXIII, Pt. 1, 586–587.

57. Purdue, *Cleburne*, 194.

58. Collins, *Unwritten History*, 136; Simpson, *Bugle Softly Blows*, 35; Lucia Ruther-

ford Douglas, ed., *Douglas's Texas Battery, CSA* (Tyler: Smith County Historical Society, 1966), 70.

59. Thomas Lawrence Connelly, *Autumn of Glory: The Army of Tennessee, 1862–1865* (Baton Rouge: Louisiana State University Press, 1971), 132–133; Irving A. Buck, *Cleburne and His Command* (Dayton: Press of Morningside Bookshop, 1985), 133; Purdue, *Cleburne*, 195–196.

60. Simpson, *Bugle Softly Blows*, 37; Collins, *Unwritten History*, 143; McCaffrey, *This Band*, 65.

61. Purdue, *Cleburne*, 206; Brown, *Cleburne's Command*, 50.

62. Simpson, *Bugle Softly Blows*, 38–39.

63. Simpson, *Ibid.*, 39; Purdue, *Cleburne*, 208.

64. Simpson, *Ibid.*, 39; Buck, *Cleburne*, 135.

65. Glenn Tucker, *Chickamauga: Bloody Battle in the West* (Dayton: Press of Morningside Bookshop, 1984), 65, 70; Buck, *Ibid.*, 141; McCaffrey, *This Band*, 67–68.

66. Purdue, *Cleburne*, 216–217; Simpson, *Bugle Softly Blows*, 41.

67. Brown, *Cleburne's Command*, 52.

68. Purdue, *Cleburne's Command*, 218.

69. R. Q. Mills to Irving A. Buck, October 6, 1863, *O.R.*, Series I, Vol. XXX, Pt. 2, 188–189; Oliphant Recollections, 23–24; Collins, *Unwritten History*, 151–152.

70. Oliphant Recollections, 24; R. Q. Mills to Irving A. Buck, *Ibid.*, 188, 193; Purdue, *Cleburne*, 223.

71. Collins, *Unwritten History*, 158–159; R. Q. Mills to Irving A. Buck, *Ibid.*, 188–189.

72. R. Q. Mills to Irving A. Buck, *Ibid.*, 189–190, 193.

73. Purdue, *Cleburne*, 237–238; Compiled Service Records, Sixth Texas Infantry Regiment.

74. P. R. Cleburne to Kimloch Falconer, No Date, *O.R.*, Series I, XXXI, Pt. 2, 745–746.

75. *Ibid.*, 746–747.

76. *Ibid.;* Albert Jernigan to Parents, May 18, 1872, Albert Jernigan Letter (BTHC); Collins, *Unwritten History*, 177.

77. P. R. Cleburne to Kimloch Falconer, *Ibid.*, 749–750; Jernigan, *Ibid.*

78. P. R. Cleburne to Kimloch Falconer, *Ibid.*

79. *Ibid.*

80. *Ibid.*, 750–753; Albert Jernigan to Parents, May 18, 1872, Albert Jernigan Letter (BTHC); Collins, *Unwritten History*, 180–181.

81. Collins, *Ibid.*, 186.

82. James Lee McDonough, *Chattanooga: A Death Grip on the Confederacy* (Knoxville: The University of Tennessee Press, 1984), 209; Collins, *Ibid.*, 182–185.

83. McDonough, *Ibid.*, 209–211.

84. Buck, *Cleburne*, 176–177; Purdue, *Cleburne*, 254–255; Collins, *Unwritten History*, 188–189.

85. Buck, *Ibid.*, 179–181; Collins, *Ibid.*, 190.

86. H. B. Granbury to Irving A. Buck, December 3, 1863, *O.R.*, Series I, Vol. XXXI, Pt. 2, 773–775; Purdue, *Cleburne*, 260–263.

87. Oliphant Reminiscences, 28; Purdue, *Ibid.*, 267; McCaffrey, *This Band*, 97.

88. Purdue, *Ibid.*, 268; McCaffrey, *Ibid.*, 96.

89. Buck, *Cleburne*, 187.

90. Purdue, *Cleburne*, 291; Simpson, *Bugle Softly Blows*, 47–48; Collins, *Unwritten History*, 198–199.

91. Buck, *Cleburne*, 202–203.

92. Kelley, "Turner," 168.

93. *Ibid.*, 169; Collins, *Unwritten History*, 201; Buck, *Cleburne*, 203.

94. Kelley, *Ibid.*, 170; Collins, *Ibid.*, 200–201; Simpson, *Bugle Softly Blows*, 49; Buck, *Ibid.*, 203.

95. Kelley, *Ibid.*

96. Nathaniel Cheairs Hughes, Jr., *General William J. Hardee: Old Reliable* (Wilmington, North Carolina: Broadfoot Publishing Company, 1987), 197–198.

NOTES FOR DIARY

1. John Bell Hood's corps. consisted of Thomas C. Hindman's division, Carter L. Stevenson's division, Alexander P. Stewart's division and Robert G. Beckham's artillery.

Hood was born in Owingsville, Kentucky, on June 1, 1831. After graduating from the United States Military Academy in 1853, he served with the Second United States Cavalry Regiment. Hood resigned his commission in April 1861 and entered the Confederate army as a first lieutenant. His rise to the rank of lieutenant general in 1863 was spectacular and unequaled in the annals of Confederate military history. In September 1861, Hood was promoted colonel and placed in command of the Fourth Texas Infantry Regiment. By March 1862, he was a brigadier general and in command of the Texas Brigade, and in October 1862, Hood was promoted to major general. Meanwhile, he assumed command of a division which experienced considerable action at Gettysburg where Hood lost use of his left arm due to a shell fragment. During the Battle of Chickamauga, a minnie ball entered his right thigh which necessitated the amputation of his right leg. Afterwards, he was appointed lieutenant general and assigned to a corps in the Army of Tennessee. Later, Hood was assigned to command the Army of Tennessee and given the temporary rank of full general. In January 1865, after shattering the once proud Army of Tennessee in the Battles of Franklin and Nashville, he voluntarily relinquished his command. Hood died on August 30, 1873, at New Orleans of yellow fever. "The Opposing Forces in the Atlanta Campaign," *Battles and Leaders of the Civil War*, 4 vols., 2d ed. (New York: Thomas Yoseloff, 1956), IV, 290–291; Marcus J. Wright, (comp), *Texas In The War 1861–1865*, ed. by Harold B. Simpson (Hillsboro, Texas: The Hill Junior College Press, 1965), 82–83 (hereafter cited as Wright, *Texas*); Ezra J. Warner, *Generals in Gray* (Baton Rouge: Louisiana State University Press, 1959), 142–143 (hereafter cited as Warner, *Generals in Gray*).

2. William J. Hardee's corps was composed of Benjamin F. Cheatham's division, Patrick R. Cleburne's division, William H. T. Walker's division, William B. Bates division and Melanethon Smith's artillery.

Born in Georgia, William J. Hardee, nicknamed "Old Reliable," graduated from West Point in 1838. As a participant in the Mexican War he served with distinction. In 1856, Hardee became Commandant of the Corps of Cadets at West Point. The preceding year his two volume *Rifle and Light Infantry Tactics* was published. *Tactics* became the standard drill manual for the Union and Confederate army officers during the Civil War. In January 1861, he resigned from the regular army and in the following March accepted an appointment as a colonel in the Confederate army. Hardee rose to the rank of brigadier general in June 1861. Four months later, he was promoted a major general. By October 1862, Hardee was raised to the rank of lieutenant general and a corps commander in the Army of Tennessee. Warner, *Generals in Gray*, 124–125; Nathaniel Cheairs Hughes, Jr.,

General William J. Hardee, (Wilmington, North Carolina: Broadfoot Publishing Company, 1987), 47, 50, 55, 71 (hereafter cited as Hughes, *Hardee*).

3. When Joseph Johnston aligned the Confederate forces to block the Federal advance to Dalton, he underestimated the Union threat at Dug Gap on Rocky Face Mountain. Assigned to defend Dug Gap were the First and Second Arkansas (dismounted) Cavalry which were reinforced by J. Warren Grigsby's understrength Kentucky cavalry brigade. Before the Kentucky cavalrymen ascended the mountain, they dismounted and left their horses at the foot. As the fighting intensified, H. B. Granbury's and Mark P. Lowrey's brigades were sent as additional reenforcements. To get as many soldiers to the top of the mountain as fast as possible, Texas soldiers mounted and rode double on the horses left behind by Kentucky cavalrymen. However, most of the Texans, such as Leuschner, had to climb the mountain on foot. As Granbury's brigade raced up the mountain, the men threw their excess baggage aside. Later, after the area was secured, the Texans discovered that some of the soldiers they relieved stole "everything that was worth carrying away." Sebron Sneed, an officer in Company G of the Sixth Texas Infantry Regiment, wrote his wife that he considered their behavior as "thievish," but that "such acts are not uncommon . . . to tell you the plain fact there . . . [are] cowards in the Southern ranks as you will find any where else . . . Many are not only at war with the Federals but with the citizen." Thomas Lawrence Connelly, *Autumn of Glory* (Baton Rouge: Louisiana State University Press, 1971), 334–335 (hereafter cited as Connelly, *Autumn*); Howell and Elizabeth Purdue, *Pat Cleburne* (Hillsboro, Texas: Hill Jr. College Press, 1973), 302–303 (hereafter cited as Purdue, *Cleburne*); Sebron Sneed to Fannie, June 7, 1864, Sebron G. Sneed, Jr., Papers (Eugene C. Barker Texas History Center, University of Texas, Austin) (hereafter cited as Sneed [BTHC]).

4. A native Tennesseean, Nathan Bedford Forrest enlisted as a private in the Seventh Tennessee Cavalry Regiment. In October 1861, he was elected lieutenant colonel of a Tennessee cavalry battalion that he helped raise and organize. Prior to the Battle of Shiloh, he became colonel of the Third Tennessee, and in June 1862, he became a brigade commander in the Army of Tennessee. In August 1863, he assumed the command of the cavalry division in the Army of Tennessee and was promoted to brigadier general. In February 1865, he attained the rank of lieutenant general. Warner, *Generals in Gray*, 92.

5. Robert E. Lee's Army of Northern Virginia engaged Ulysses S. Grant's Army of the Potomac on May 5 and 6 in the bloody Battle of the Wilderness. In the two day engagement, Union casualties amounted to some 17,500 while the Confederates suffered losses of at least 7,000. James M. McPherson, *Battle Cry of Freedom,* (New York: Oxford University Press, 1988), 724–726.

6. Michael Schiewitz was born on December 7, 1842. He enlisted into the Confederate service in Victoria. After the Civil War, Schiewitz was employed at the Dutch Windmill Grist Mill at Moody and Santa Rosa streets, operated a freight line between Victoria and San Antonio, and engaged in stock raising. He died on May 16, 1915, and was buried in Ander Cemetery, Victoria County. Sidney R. Weisiger Collection (Victoria College Library, Victoria).

Harvey H. Cox was a member of Company H which was composed of volunteers from Calhoun and Victoria counties. He was twenty-five years of age when he mustered into Confederate service at Camp McCulloch in 1862. Compiled Service Record of Harvey H. Cox, National Archives, Washington, D.C.

7. The Battle of Resaca began on May 14 and was initiated by William T. Sherman who wanted to drive the Confederates from the bridges over the Oostanaula. Several unsuccessful attempts across open level ground were made by the Union troops. During the

fighting, a Yankee officer was heard encouraging his men by yelling, "You are the men who scaled Missionary Ridge, and you can carry this!" Perhaps, the officer was unaware that these particular Confederate troops had repulsed every assault on their position in that engagement and only withdrew when ordered to do so. The following day the Confederates, fearful of being flanked by the Union forces gave up their positions. Connelly, *Autumn*, 342; Irving A. Buck, *Cleburne And His Command* (Dayton: Morningside Bookshop, 1985), 211.

8. Andrew P. Cunningham was the son of J. A. Cunningham who migrated in 1845 to Victoria from Washington County. The elder Cunningham was elected as chief justice of Victoria County in 1864. After the war, Cunningham taught school. He died in 1867 during the Victoria yellow fever epidemic. J. W. Petty, Jr., ed., *Victor Rose's History of Victoria* (Victoria: Book Mart, 1961), 67, 107, 109.

9. Patrick Ronayne Cleburne was born in Ireland on March 17, 1828. He studied at Trinity College in Dublin and at the age of seventeen, ashamed of failing the language exam for Apothecaries' Hall, enlisted in the British Forty-first Regiment of Foot. After three years of service, Cleburne purchased a discharge and, in 1846 migrated to the United States with his brother, William, and his sister, Anne. He worked as a druggist's clerk in Cincinnati for six months before moving to Helena, Arkansas, where he was similarly employed. Within two years Cleburne became part owner of a drug store. Meanwhile, he studied law and was admitted to the bar in 1856. In 1860, he joined the Yell Rifles in Helena and participated in the seizure of the Little Rock Arsenal in January 1861. When Arkansas seceded, Cleburne enlisted in the Arkansas state service. In May 1861, he was chosen colonel of the Fifteenth Arkansas Regiment. The following March, Cleburne was promoted brigadier general and commanded a brigade at Shiloh. In December 1862, he was made a major general and became a divisional commander in Hardee's corps. Cleburne was killed at the Battle of Franklin on November 30, 1864. Buck, *Cleburne*, 19–22, 74–75; Warner, *Generals in Gray*, 53–54; Charles Edward Nash, *Biographical Sketches of Gen. Pat Cleburne and Gen. T. C. Hindman* (Dayton: Morningside Bookshop, 1977).

10. Joseph Eggleston Johnston was born in Virginia on February 3, 1807. After graduating from West Point in 1829, he participated in the Black Hawk, Second Seminole, and Mexican wars. In 1860, Johnston was appointed brigadier general. After Virginia seceded, he resigned his regular army commission and was commissioned a brigadier general in the Confederacy and placed in command at Harpers Ferry. Because of his performance at the Battle of First Manassas, Johnston was made a full general and given the command of the Army of Northern Virginia. A personal feud erupted between he and Jefferson Davis when the Confederate president ranked him below Samuel Cooper, Albert Sidney Johnston, and Robert E. Lee. Johnston contended that he should be the senior general since he outranked those above him when he resigned his regular army commission. Davis claimed, however, that Johnston's rank was a staff position rather than from the line. During the Peninsular Campaign, he was severely wounded at Seven Pines and his command was given to Lee. In November 1862, Johnston became commander of the Department of the West, a position he held until December 1863 when he was assigned to command the Army of Tennessee. Because his defensive strategy at Atlanta disturbed Davis, Johnston was replaced by John Bell Hood on July 14, 1864. In February 1865, he was again placed in command of the Army of Tennessee. Johnston surrendered to General William Sherman at Greensboro, North Carolina, on April 26, 1865. He died in Washington, D.C., on March 21, 1891. His death was attributed to a cold contracted while marching bareheaded in Sherman's funeral procession. Warner, *Generals in Gray*, 162; Norman D. Brown, ed., *One of Cleburne's Command* (Austin: University of Texas Press, 1980), 69–

70 (hereafter cited as Brown, _Cleburne's Command_); James M. McCaffrey, _This Band of Heroes_ (Austin: Eakin Press, 1985), 154 (hereafter cited as McCaffrey, _This Band_).

11. During the late afternoon, a reconnaissance party of Hood's came upon an entire Federal corps. Shortly thereafter, General Joseph Hooker's corps moved against Hood at New Hope Church. The attack, however, was stopped under the intense shelling by Major General A. P. Stewart's massed artillery. Connelly, _Autumn_, 355.

12. Unlike the Union army which was divided numerically, Confederate units, perhaps because of the Southern folk culture, were primarily referred to by the name of one of its commanders. The brigade was initially led by Brigadier General James Deshler, a native of Alabama and an 1854 graduate of West Point who entered the Confederate army as a captain of artillery in 1861. On July 28, 1863, he was appointed a brigadier general in Cleburne's division. When Deshler was killed in the Battle of Chickamauga on September 20, 1863, the brigade's command passed to Colonel Hiram Bronson Granbury of the Seventh Texas Infantry Regiment. Granbury was born and raised in Mississippi. In the early 1850s, he moved to Waco, Texas, where Granbury practiced law and elected chief justice of McLennan County. When Texas seceded, Granbury recruited the Waco Guards and was assigned to the Seventh Texas Infantry Regiment. Ultimately, he became the colonel of the regiment and on March 5, 1864, Granbury was promoted brigadier general to rank from February 29. He was killed at the Battle of Franklin on November 30, 1864. Warner, _Generals in Gray_, 71–72, 114–115; McCaffrey, _This Band_, 1.

In 1893, Granbury's sister, Mrs. Nautie Granberry Moss of Brownwood, Texas, told an interviewer that the family had always spelled their surname as Granberry, but Hiram for personal reasons insisted on spelling his name Granbury. Brown, _Cleburne's Command_, 74.

13. Daniel Cherilette Govan was born in North Carolina but reared in Mississippi. In 1849, he and Benjamin McCulloch, a relative, moved to California during the gold rush. Govan returned to Mississippi in 1852. Nine years later, he drifted to Arkansas. At the outbreak of the Civil War, Govan raised a company of Arkansas infantry which became a component of the Second Arkansas Infantry Regiment. Subsequently, Govan became the regiment's colonel. In 1863, he was promoted brigadier general and placed in command of the Arkansas brigade. During the Battle of Jonesboro on September 1, 1864, Govan was captured and held as a prisoner for a couple of weeks before being exchanged. Purdue, _Cleburne_, 380, 382; Warner, _Generals in Gray_, 112–113.

14. Joseph T. Hearne was originally an adjutant in the Tenth Texas Infantry Regiment. Prior to the fall of Arkansas Post, he was promoted to Deshler's staff. Buck, _Cleburne_, 220; McCaffrey, _This Band_, 189.

15. The Tenth Texas Infantry Regiment was organized by Colonel Allison Nelson, a resident of Bosque County who was a former member of the Texas Legislature and a delegate to the Secession Convention. In September 1862, Nelson was promoted to brigadier general and assigned a division under General Theophilis H. Holmes. He was replaced as regimental commander by Roger Q. Mills from Navarro County. After the Civil War, Mills was elected to the United States House of Representatives and Senate. The Tenth Texas was captured at Arkansas Post. After it was exchanged at City Point, Virginia, in 1863, the regiment was consolidated with the Sixth Texas Infantry and Fifteenth Texas Cavalry (dismounted) regiments. In March 1864, the Tenth Texas resumed its individual status.

The Seventh Texas Infantry Regiment was formed by John Gregg who moved to Texas from Alabama in the 1850s. Gregg was a member of the Texas Secession Convention and a Texas delegate to the Provisional Congress of the Confederacy at Montgomery, Alabama. When he was elevated to brigadier general, the command of the regiment passed to Granbury.

The Twenty-fourth Texas Cavalry Regiment and the Twenty-fifth Texas Cavalry Regiment were created in 1862. They initially were designated as the First and Second Texas Lancers, but there is no evidence that lances were ever issued to the units. Before their arrival at Arkansas Post in 1862, the regiments were dismounted and served as infantry. In May 1863, the two regiments were consolidated and placed under the command of Colonel Franklin C. Wilkes, a Methodist minister who helped raise the Twenty-fourth Texas Cavalry Regiment. Wright, *Texas,* 27, 82, 89, 113; McCaffrey, *This Band,* 8, 10, 61–62, 99.

16. Johnston deployed his army from Dallas to Pickett's Mill. W. B. Bate's and Benjamin F. Cheatham's divisions anchored the left at Dallas, Leonidas Polk's corps maintained the center, and Hood's corps was on the right at New Hope Church. Hood's section was extended to Pickett's Mill, a half mile from Little Pumpkinvine Creek, by Patrick Cleburne's division. In an effort to better protect themselves, the Confederates built a series of breastworks and trenches. The Texans, however, were assigned an area without breastworks. The Federal attack on Cleburne's division commenced at 5:00 P.M. Granbury's brigade was maneuvered to the extreme right of the division and received the full fury of the Federal advance. A Union soldier seeing the Texans were without breastworks was prompted to yell, "Ah! damn you, we have caught you without your logs now." To the chagrin of the attacking force, the natural terrain served Granbury's men with sufficient protection. Cleburne noted in his official battle report, the Texans "slaughtered them with deliberate aim." Sebron Sneed, an officer in the Sixth Texas, in a letter to his wife wrote that the Federals "came up bravely but our men kept such a shower of minnies in their faces that flesh and blood could not stand it . . . The balls flew as thick as hail and death stalked around . . . The enemy shot about a foot too high or they would have wounded or killed half the command." After the fighting subsided, Granbury counter-attacked, but encountered virtually no resistance. Connelly, *Autumn,* 354–356; McCaffrey, *This Band,* 108–109; Purdue, *Cleburne,* 323–326; Sneed Papers (BTHC); Recollections of William J. Oliphant (MS, Austin Public Library, Austin), 32–33 (hereafter cited as Oliphant Recollections).

17. Samuel T. Foster, a seasoned veteran of the brigade, recorded in his diary that he "counted 50 dead men in a circle of 30 ft. . . . I have seen many dead men, and seen them wounded and crippled in various ways . . . but I never saw anything before that made me sick . . . I do not believe that if a soldier could be made faint, that I would have fainted if I had not passed on and got out of that place as soon as I did." Another Texan when he saw the battlefield exclaimed that "hundreds upon hundreds, in every conceivable position; some with contorted features, showing the agony of death, others as if quietly sleeping. I noticed some soft, beardless faces, which ill comported the savage warfare in which they had been engaged." A third Texan stated that "the field looked as though a great blue carpet had been spread out over the ground. Dead men were every where, they lay in solid lines just as they fell and in many places were in heaps." Brown, *Cleburne's Command,* 88; Samuel Carter, III, *The Siege of Atlanta* (New York: Bonanza Books, 1973), 138.

18. Joseph Koger Dixon was a native of Noxubee County, Mississippi. He entered West Point in 1857 but left before graduation. When the Noxubee Rifles was formed, he was commissioned a third lieutenant. In January 1861, Dixon participated in an expedition to Pensacola. Afterwards, he was appointed a second lieutenant in the Confederate army and was captured at Fort Saint Philip while helping to defend New Orleans. When Dixon was exchanged during the summer of 1862, he was assigned to the Army of Ten-

nessee. On December 31, 1862, at the Battle of Murfreesboro, he was wounded. Upon his return to active duty, Dixon was promoted a major and given the responsibility of divisional inspector general. Braxton Bragg to H. W. Halleck, June 16, 1862, *War of the Rebellion: A Compilation of the Official Records of the Union and Confederate Armies*, 128 vols. (Washington, D.C.: Government Printing Office, 1880–1901), Series II, Vol. IV, 27 (hereafter cited as *O.R.*); Buck, *Cleburne*, 22, 28–29.

19. The skirmish fire that Leuschner heard was precipitated by a Confederate soldier shooting at a lightning bug. The ball passed over the head of a Yankee picket who thought he was the intended victim and returned the shot. Suddenly, both sides believed that an attack was imminent and began firing their muskets. Under the impression that a night attack was in progress, Federal artillery opened fire upon the Confederates. Purdue, *Cleburne*, 328–329.

20. Mark Perrin Lowrey was a native of Tennessee but moved to Mississippi in 1845 with his widowed mother. After service in the Mexican War, he became a Baptist minister. In 1862, Lowrey was appointed colonel of the Thirty-second Mississippi Infantry. The Mississippi regiment was assigned to Colonel S. A. M. Wood's Mississippi and Alabama Brigade. When Wood resigned his commission on October 17, 1863, Lowrey was promoted brigade commander. Purdue, *Cleburne*, 238; Warner, *Generals in Gray*, 195, 344.

21. Hardee stated that the troop movement was "the hardest march I have known troops to encounter . . . through mud, & rain and darkness." Hughes, *Hardee*, 208.

22. Lucius Eugene Polk was born at Salisbury, North Carolina, on July 10, 1833. At the age of two, his family moved to Tennessee. In 1851, after attending the University of Virginia, he settled near Helena, Arkansas. When the Yell Rifles were organized, he enlisted as a private. Ultimately, he became a junior officer in the Fifteenth Arkansas Infantry. After the Battle of Shiloh, he was promoted captain. In December 1862, Polk succeeded Cleburne as brigade commander. On June 17, 1864, he was shot in the leg, the fourth time he was wounded in battle. So severely was Polk injured, he was unable to perform further field duty. During the Atlanta Campaign, Polk's brigade was decimated in casualties to the point that it was disbanded. The survivors were distributed to other brigades. Warner, *Generals in Gray*, 243–244; Purdue, *Cleburne*, 331.

23. Leonidas Polk, an uncle of Lucius Eugene Polk, was born in Raliegh, North Carolina, on April 10, 1806. Not long after his graduation from West Point in 1827, he resigned his commission and entered the Episcopal ministry. Polk was appointed a major general in the Confederate army on June 25, 1861, and a lieutenant general in October 1862. He helped organize the Army of Mississippi which would later become part of the Army of Tennessee. On June 14, 1864, Polk while reconnoitering Federal positions near Marietta with Johnston, Hardee, and W. H. Jackson atop of Pine Mountain was fired upon. All the Confederate officers except Polk moved to safety. Consequently, he was struck and instantly killed by a shell from a Parrott gun. John L. Wakelyn, *Biographical Dictionary Of The Confederacy* (Westport, Connecticut: Greenwood Press, 1977), 349–350; Buck, *Cleburne*, 223; Hughes, *Hardee*, 209–210; Warner, *Generals in Gray*, 242–243.

24. Cleburne's division was located two and a half miles southeast of Gigal Church which was located east of Mud Creek. When Union artillery shelled the division, the Confederates returned the fire. The result was a furious cannonade between the two sides. Purdue, *Cleburne*, 330–331.

25. The Kennesaw Mountain line began two miles east of the Western & Atlantic Railroad, ran westward along the crest of the Kennesaw Mountain for seven miles, then curved to the southwestern base of the Little Kennesaw. At this point, the Confederate positions extended for three miles, crossed the Dallas Road and up a ridge which is now

known as Cheatham's Hill. The line ended north of a fork of Ward Creek. The person who was primarily responsible for establishing the Kennesaw Mountain line was the army's chief engineer, Colonel S. W. Presstman. Purdue, *Cleburne*, 331–332; Connelly, *Autumn*, 357.

26. During the afternoon, Hood launched an unsuccessful attack against well-entrenched Federal forces at Kolb's Farm. His men faced extreme artillery and rifle fire. A Confederate soldier who was wounded in the fight wrote that "shell and shot and miney balls flew thick as hale." In the engagement, Hood lost 1,000 men while the Federal loss was less than 300 men. James Lee McDonough and James Pickett Jones, *War So Terrible* (New York: W. W. Norton & Company, 1987), 180–181.

27. Edward O'Riley enlisted as a private in Company H on March 27, 1862. He was captured, along with his company, at Arkansas Post. O'Riley was captured again at the Battle of Franklin. For some reason, Leuschner inserted Ed O'Riley in his journal. It may have been that O'Riley was one of the skirmishers, and since he was from the Victoria area, Leuschner made note of O'Riley's participation. Compiled Service Record of Edward O'-Riley, National Archives, Washington, D.C.

28. Benjamin Franklin Cheatham was a native of Tennessee. During the Mexican War, he served as a colonel with the Tennessee volunteers. On July 9, 1861, Cheatham was appointed a brigadier general in the Provisional Army of the Confederacy. The following March, he was promoted to major general. When Hardee's request to be removed as corps commander was honored in September 1864, Cheatham was elevated to the vacancy created by Hardee. Hood recommended that he be made a lieutenant general, but in December 1864, withdrew the recommendation on the ground that Cheatham failed to carry out his assignment at Spring Hill, Tennessee, on November 29, 1864, by permitting Federal troops to establish defensive positions at Franklin from which they inflicted heavy losses on the Army of Tennessee. Buck, *Cleburne*, 52–53; Warner, *Generals in Gray*, 48–49.

29. The engagement Leuschner refers to was the Battle of Kennesaw Mountain. In the battle, artillery shells and gun wadding ignited the dry grass. The Federal wounded who laid before the Confederate entrenchments faced the possibility of being engulfed in the flames. Lieutenant Colonel William H. Martin of the First Arkansas Regiment offered the Yankees a truce, which was accepted, until the wounded could be removed. Confederate soldiers left their positions and aided their Union counterparts. As soon as the fallen Federals were removed from the battlefield, the fighting resumed. Buck, *Cleburne*, 224–225.

30. Because Johnston was concerned that the Federals might turn his flanks, he evacuated the Kennesaw Mountain line. Cleburne's division withdrew to Smyra Camp Ground, ten miles south of Marietta. Buck, *Cleburne*, 226.

31. During the engagement, a yankee officer shouted, "Forward, men! forward!" The Confederate soldiers responded by yelling, "Come on, boys! come on!" A German in gray added, "Trow away de knapsacks!" His compatriots, however, pleaded with the Union soldiers not to do so because they wanted them. "F. A. Blossman to Ma," July 8, 1864, *Confederate Veteran*, Vol. VII (1899), 221–222.

F. A. Shoup, chief of artillery, using slave labor constructed redoubts of heavy logs connected by a stockade of logs firmly established in the ground. So formidable were the fortifications that William T. Sherman selected to flank Johnston's army rather than run the possibility of heavy casualties with a frontal attack. McCaffrey, *This Band*, 113.

32. Cleburne was not entirely satisfied with the entrenchments that Sherman described the strongest he had ever seen. The Confederate general ordered his men to

strengthen the fortification by reenforcing the stockade of logs that were set in the ground with earth-covered timber. Purdue, *Cleburne,* 337.

33. To relieve Federal military pressure on Richmond, General Robert E. Lee sent Major General Jubal Early northward to threaten Washington. Early did not seize Harpers Ferry as Leuschner recorded. The raiders circumvented the community after they found it too strong to take. By July 11, Early's command reached the suburbs of the Federal capital. Because the defenses at Washington were strengthened with additional troops, Early thought it prudent to withdraw before his escape routes were severed. He remarked to one of his officers as the Confederates began their retreat, "Major, we haven't taken Washington, but we've scared Abe Lincoln like hell!" Frank E. Vandiver, *Jubals's Raid* (New York: McGraw-Hill Book Company, Inc., 1960), 82–86, 170–171.

34. Convinced that Johnston was not the person to stop the Federal advance in Georgia, President Jefferson Davis on July 17 ordered the more aggressive Hood to replace Johnston as commanding general of the Army of Tennessee. Hood, Hardee, and General A. P. Stewart sent a telegram to Davis requesting that the removal be suspended until the fate of Atlanta was determined. They were concerned that a change in command would require a general reorganization of the army, an unnecessary and, perhaps, detrimental burden at a critical juncture of the campaign. Davis rejected their plea.

The morale of the Confederate soldiers sagged, as Leuschner indicated, when they learned of Johnston's removal. Samuel T. Foster wrote, "For the first time, we hear men openly talk about going home." William Oliphant stated that the "men were astonished and for the first time appeared disheartened." Colonel J. C. Nisbet of the Georgia volunteers remarked that as his men marched past their former commander, "There was no cheering. We simply passed silently, with heads uncovered. Some of the officers broke ranks and grasped his hand, as the tears poured down their cheeks." Connelly, *Autumn,* 421–422; Brown, *Cleburne's Command,* 106; Oliphant Recollections, 38; Carter, *Seige,* 190–191.

35. Hood's first test as the new commander of the Army of Tennessee came at Peachtree Creek when the Federal Army of the Cumberland under George H. Thomas crossed the stream. The Confederate general ordered an attack. Although the Southern army was initially successful, the Confederates failed to dislodge the Union troops. Hood blamed Hardee for the defeat. The commanding general thought that Hardee was too timid in the assault and did not press Thomas. In the engagement, James B. McPherson's Union Army of Tennessee held the eastern wing of Thomas' forces and engaged Joseph Wheeler's cavalry and Cheatham's infantry. Cleburne's division, which was in reserve when the battle began, moved to Bald Hill to assist the cavalrymen. Hughes, *Hardee,* 223–224; Purdue, *Cleburne,* 346–347; Connelly, *Autumn,* 444.

36. The Seventeenth Texas Cavalry (dismounted) Regiment entered Confederate service on March 16, 1862, under the command of Colonel George F. Moore. The unit was assigned to Brigadier General Albert Rust in Arkansas. The regiment was dismounted in the summer of 1862, removed from Rust's command, and eventually sent to Arkansas Post. After its capture and exchange in 1863, the unit was consolidated with the Eighteenth, the Twenty-fourth, and the Twenty-fifth Texas Cavalry (dismounted) regiments. Wright, *Texas,* 117; McCaffrey, *This Band,* 16–17, 19; Warner, *Generals in Gray,* 266–267.

37. Frank Blossman was a member of Company A. Compiled Service Record of F. E. Blossman, National Archives, Washington, D.C.

38. When the Texans relieved the cavalry, they discovered that the entrenchments were inadequate. The cavalrymen unaccustomed to digging trenches were improperly

placed, and the entrenchments were not strong enough to withstand a severe bombardment. While Cleburne's men were trying to improve their defenses, Yankee riflemen and artillery inflicted heavy casualties on the Confederates. Union losses were also high. One Federal brigade lost forty percent of its men. Cleburne described the fighting as "the bitterest" of his life. Mortimer Leggett's division, supported by Giles A. Smith's division, assaulted the Confederate positions. During the engagement, elements of Cleburne's division were driven from Bald Hill, the remainder were replaced by another command. A company in the Eighteenth Texas Cavalry (dismounted) regiment, not the Seventeenth Texas, suffered the loss of its entire command when a twenty pound Parrott gun shell passed along a trench, beheading six men and severely wounding twelve. Purdue, *Cleburne,* 347–348; McDonough, *War,* 219; Buck, *Cleburne,* 233–234.

39. Major General James Birdseye McPherson, commander of the Union Army of Tennessee, and members of his staff ignored warnings that the Confederates held the woods that were in his immediate front on the road they were riding. The party came upon enemy skirmishers who challenged them. McPherson and his staff quickly wheeled their horses to escape. The Confederates fired a volley and killed the general. Another Union soldier was knocked from his horse, breaking and stopping his watch at 2:02 as he fled from the area and, thereby, established the time of death of McPherson. Grenville M. Dodge, *The Battle of Atlanta and Other Campaigns, Addresses, Etc.* (Denver: Sage Books, 1965), 43.

40. Hood ordered Hardee's corps to attack the rear of the Federal army. Hardee deployed his men from Cobb's Mill to Decatur. Cleburne's division was placed on the left on the McDonough Road. To the right of Cleburne, in the order they were positioned, were the divisions of W. H. T. Walker, William Bate, and George Maney. The Federals did not anticipate the Confederate movement and were caught by surprise. The Texans, yelling like Comanche Indians, rapidly passed through a gap between the Union defenses and extended themselves beyond their support. Because the battlefield was covered with dense underbrush and trees, the Lone Star State regiments became separated. When the order was given to retire, not all the units received the command and were stranded from the main body of Granbury's brigade. In the confusion, the Sixth Texas joined Govan's brigade for the remainder of the fighting and helped capture two Union battle flags. At nightfall, the fighting was terminated and the Confederates returned to their entrenchments. Granbury's brigade suffered an enormous amount of casualties. The temporary brigade commander, James A. Smith, was wounded as were all the brigade leaders, except one. The Seventeenth and Eighteenth Texas Consolidated Cavalry (dismounted) regiments were almost decimated. Overall, 312 men were either killed, wounded or reported missing from the brigade, a severe blow to an already understrength unit. Oliphant Recollections, 45; McCaffrey, *This Band,* 117– 121; Hughes, *Hardee,* 227–232; Connelly, *Autumn,* 447–450.

41. Schiewitz was hit with a minnie ball in the external region of his left thigh. Compiled Service Record of Michael Schiewitz, National Archives, Washington, D.C.

Pascal M. "Pack" Traylor was a private in Company H. He was the son of Winn Traylor, one of the first cattle barons in Victoria County. Leuschner wrote Traylor's name in pencil, which probably means that the comment was an afterthought. Although the official service records do not state that Traylor was killed in the war, local records indicate otherwise and Leuschner undoubtedly intended to place Traylor's death at the Battle of Atlanta. Compiled Service Records of Pascal M. Traylor, National Archives, Washington, D.C.; Petty, *History of Victoria,* 205.

42. Survivors of the Battle of Atlanta, many of whom were combat hardened veter-

ans, were visibly shaken at what they saw on the morning after the engagement. "The sight of the great number of Confederate dead in front of our lines was appalling," wrote Willard Warner, "and never to be forgotten by those who saw it." Andres West stated that "many times have I prayed that visions of those . . . who met death in one of the deadliest battles in the history of the world, might be blotted forever from my recollection." He added, "It was necessary in some places to climb over the heaps of the dead. The wonder seemed to be not that there were so many dead, but that any lived at all." Carter, *Seige*, 233–234.

43. The "Fort" Leuschner mentions was probably a stone house that Cleburne used as divisional headquarters. It was located on a knoll that was covered with a grove of large oaks and was in the direct line of fire of Union artillery which systematically lobbed shells at the Confederates every day at noon. Buck, *Cleburne*, 247.

44. Sebastian Meyer was mustered into the Confederate army with Leuschner at Victoria. He was captured at Nashville on December 17, 1864. Compiled Service Record of Sebastian Meyer, National Archives, Washington, D.C.

45. As Sherman shifted the Union Army of Tennessee to gain control of the rail junction at East Point, Hood sent the divisions of Stephen D. Lee and A. P. Stewart to attack the Federal army. The fighting occurred at Ezra Church and ended with a Union victory. Connelly, *Autumn*, 453–455.

46. On August 3, the Sixth Texas was moved southwest of Atlanta along the railroad to West Point. Union artillery shells were periodically fired into Atlanta, causing the non-combatants to be gravely concerned. One Atlanta resident wrote, "We have had a considerable taste of the beauties of bombardment today. The enemy have thrown a great many shells into the city and scared the women and children and *some* of the *men* pretty badly . . . This seems to me a very barbarous mode of carrying war, throwing shells among women and children." Molly Smith and her family had no sooner sat down for a breakfast meal when a shell fell upon their house, exploded in an adjoining room and flipped over a grand piano. No one in the family was injured, only frightened. McCaffrey, *This Band*, 122; Carter, *Seige*, 232–234.

47. Cleburne's division began to maneuver to the extreme left of the army to match a corresponding movement by the Union army. By August 9, the division was within two miles of East Point, and on August 16, pushed closer to the community. Buck, *Cleburne*, 249.

48. On August 25, an inspection report on Cleburne's division was written. The account remarked: "The material of which this command is composed [is] of the very best. Mostly Young & active men — the first to enter the Confed. Service." It further stated, "The military appearance of both officers & men, as well as their comfort would be greatly improved if *soap* could be *supplied*." No soap had been distributed to the men for nearly a month. Purdue, *Cleburne*, 370–371.

49. On August 26, Sherman began to deploy his troops for the purpose of severing the railroad between Jonesboro and Atlanta. His withdrawal from the trenches facing Atlanta was unexpected by the Confederates who found themselves speculating as to what the enemy planned to do. Cleburne's division was ordered on August 30 to Jonesboro, twenty-six miles south of Atlanta. When the Confederate force reached its destination on August 31, a battle line was formed with Granbury's brigade on the left, Lowrey's brigade in the center, and Mercer's brigade on the right. Govan's brigade was held in reserve. Hughes, *Hardee*, 234; Buck, *Cleburne*, 250–251.

50. Acting upon Hood's order to drive the Federals across the Flint River, Hardee's corps commanded by Cleburne, moved forward about 3:30 P.M. When Granbury's and

Lowrey's brigades were within 300 yards of the Union troops, they charged through an open field, driving the enemy from the rail barricades they were using for protection. A Texan who participated in the attack recorded in his diary that the Yankees "couldn't stand it but broke and ran like good fellows. They runing for life and we for fun, and the objects being so muck [much] in their favor that they out ran us by odds and got away (except the killed and wounded)." The Tenth Texas, ignoring orders not to pursue the Federals across the Flint River, crossed the river and chased a Union battery, which threatened the Texans, from the field. When the engagement ended, the Confederates established positions on the east side of the Flint. Purdue, *Cleburne*, 375–376; Brown, *Cleburne's Command*, 125–126.

51. At 2:00 A.M. on September 1, Hood withdrew S. D. Lee's corps from Jonesboro. To fill the void left by Lee, Cleburne's division was strung out in single rank. The new positions, as the men discovered, were inadequate. The entrenchments were too close to the enemy, incomplete, and were poorly located. In some instances, there were no entrenchments at all. While Cleburne's division tried to improve their defenses, it was harassed by Federal artillery and sharpshooters. Hughes, *Hardee*, 238–239.

52. William Henry Talbot Walker was born in Georgia. In 1837, he graduated from the United States Military Academy. Within a year after leaving West Point, Walker sustained a severe wound while fighting the Seminole Indians and resigned his commission. In 1840, he reentered the army and served with distinction in the Mexican War. During the conflict, he received near fatal wounds. In December 1860, Walker again resigned his commission. The following May, he accepted a Confederate brigadier generalship. In October 1861, Walker left the Confederate army and became a major general in the Georgia state troops. He later reentered the Confederate army as a brigadier general and on May 3, 1863, became a major general. In the Atlanta Campaign, Walker commanded a division in Hardee's corps. He was killed by Union pickets on July 22, 1864. Because of heavy personnel losses, including the death of Walker, and the need to strengthen the other divisions, Hardee distributed the three brigades of Walker's division throughout the corps. Hugh W. Mercer's brigade was placed in Cleburne's division. Leuschner apparently was referring to this brigade as Walker's division. Warner, *Generals in Gray*, 324–325; Hughes, *Hardee*, 232–233.

53. Before the Confederates could complete the breastworks, Govan's brigade at about 3:00 P.M. received the main Federal assault. The first charge was stopped, but the succeeding one broke the brigade's resistance. Govan and some 600 of his men were captured. In a series of hotly contested counterattacks, the Confederates regained most of the lost ground. When Govan's brigade was overrun, Granbury's brigade received enemy fire from that area. The Texans redeployed to meet an expected attack. However, they reoccupied their original positions when it was learned that reenforcements were nearby to aid them. The Union forces made repeated assaults upon Granbury's brigade, but they failed to break the line. At 11:00 P.M., the brigade was withdrawn to new positions. When the Texans redeployed, Hardee who was not aware of the reason behind the maneuver thought the brigade gave way and rode forward to rally the troops. He met Granbury who testily stated, "General, my men never fall back unless ordered back." Hughes, *Hardee*, 239–240; Buck, *Cleburne*, 255–256.

54. Leuschner was correct in his assessment of the battle. The Sixth and Fifteenth Consolidated Regiment suffered the greatest number of casualties, but they inflicted the heaviest damage to the Federals. Granbury's losses amounted to eighteen killed and eighty-nine wounded. McCaffrey, *This Band*, 125.

55. Edward Mehnert enlisted in Company B at Victoria on January 11, 1862. Louis

Couturier enlisted as a private in Company B at Victoria on September 30, 1861. He was promoted second sergeant on March 1, 1864. Compiled Service Records of Edward Mehnert and Louis Couturier, National Archives, Washington, D.C.

56. John Gibson joined Company B as a private on December 1, 1861. He was elected a junior second lieutenant on November 10, 1862, and was promoted a senior second lieutenant in September 1863. In the Battle of Missionary Ridge, Gibson received a slight finger wound. Benjamin M. Seaton, a member of the Tenth Texas was wounded in the Battle of Jonesboro and placed on the train to be transported to the hospital. He wrote in his diary that the wreck was "a perfect smashup with the train — 26 kiled and a grate many wounded." Compiled Service Records of John Gibson, National Archives, Washington, D.C.; *Tri Weekly-Telegraph* (Houston), February 1, 1864; Harold B. Simpson, ed., *The Bugle Softly Blows: The Confederate Diary of Benjamin M. Seaton* (Waco: Texian Press, 1965), 60.

57. Jacob Henry Fox was born in Cirnay, Alsace, Germany on July 27, 1841, to Jacob and Marianna Fox. He, along with the members of his family, migrated to Victoria in the mid-1840s. He was an original member of Company B. Fox was wounded several times during the Civil War. Prior to being shot at the Battle of Jonesboro, he was wounded in the Battle of Atlanta. Fox was also hit at the Battle of Franklin, resulting in his forefinger being amputated. After the war, he owned and operated a gin and grist mill that was located in present Riverside Park. Fox's Bend, a segment of the park, was named for him. Compiled Service Records of Jacob Fox, National Archives, Washington, D.C.; *Tri-Weekly Telegraph* (Houston), September 5, 1864 and March 3, 1865; Weisiger Collection.

58. Hardee concluded that his defenses were untenable and ordered a troop withdrawal about midnight. His corps reached Lovejoy's Station early the following morning and immediately began to construct breastworks. Meanwhile, Hood withdrew from Atlanta, conceding the city to Sherman. Before Hardee's entrenchments were completed, strong skirmishing occurred. The Confederates withstood two assaults but held their ground. Connelly, *Autumn*, 466–467.

59. Stewart's corps, Lee's corps, and the First Division Georgia militia.

60. On September 5, Sherman began pulling his troops back toward Atlanta to regroup and rest. The following day, he withdrew the remaining Federal units facing the Confederates at Lovejoy's Station. Buck, *Cleburne*, 258.

61. The already troubled personal relations between Hood and Hardee reached the breaking point after the Battle of Jonesboro. Before the engagement, Hardee asked President Davis to relieve him from his command, but Davis persuaded Hardee to stay. After Jonesboro, Hood openly criticized Hardee and asked Davis to replace the corps commander. Because of the discord between the two generals, the need to plot new military strategy, and the desire to boost the morale of the army, the Confederate president decided to visit Georgia. Included in the traveling entourage was Francis R. Lubbock, former governor of Texas. When Hood's army stood in formation to receive the dignitaries from Richmond, Lubbock stopped in front of a regiment composed primarily of Irishmen which he mistook as a Texas unit. He doffed his hat and said, "I am Governor Lubbock of Texas." Expecting to hear cheers, the former governor instead heard one of the soldiers say with a heavy Irish brogue, "An who the bloody H——l is governor Lubbock?" The embarrassed Texan, without muttering a word, rode off. Later, he addressed the Texas Brigade and advised them to stay east of the Mississippi which Lubbock declared was the best region for soldiering. Lubbock attempted to brighten the spirits of the Texans by painting a rosy picture of the condition in the Lone Star State. Hughes, *Hardee*, 245–248; Connelly, *Au-*

tumn, 470; Brown, *Cleburne's Command,* 133; Lucia Rutherford Douglas, *Douglas's Texas Battery, CSA* (Waco: Texian Press, 1966), 136–137.

62. Hood concluded that if his army remained static, Sherman would benefit militarily since Union forces could, without Confederate pressure, rest, resupply, or, perhaps, march into Alabama and destroy the Confederate munitions. He, therefore, decided to cut Sherman's communication line with Tennessee. On October 1, Hood's army crossed the Chattahoochee at Pumpkin Town and Phillip's Ferry. His troops stopped and rested eight miles north of Pray's Church. By October 2, Cleburne's division reached Powder Springs which was located twelve miles southwest of Marietta. Connelly, *Autumn,* 476–477; Buck, *Cleburne,* 262; Purdue, *Cleburne,* 388.

63. From October 2 to October 6, Confederate units destroyed positions of the Western and Atlantic Railroad between the Etowah and Chattahoochee. They also captured Union detachments at Big Shanty and Acworth. Connelly, *Autumn,* 480.

64. By the end of October, Hood decided to cross the Tennessee River, capture Nashville, and march into Kentucky where he would enlist new recruits. After modifying his initial marching route, he selected Tuscumbia, Alabama, as the place where the army would cross the Tennessee. At Decatur, forty miles east of Tuscumbia and fortified with Federal troops, Cleburne's and Bate's divisions engaged the enemy on October 27 and October 28. The skirmishing permitted the main body of the Confederate army to safely bypass the community. Purdue, *Cleburne,* 389–390.

65. On November 13, Hood established his headquarters at Florence, Alabama, and began moving the troops to that location. Not until November 15, however, did the entire command cross the Tennessee River. Nathan Bedford Forrest's cavalry division joined Hood's army on November 14. Buck, *Cleburne,* 263.

66. Before breaking camp, the regimental commanders addressed their men. The soldiers were told that Hood told them, "That we will have some hard marching and some fighting, but that he is *not going to risk a chance for a defeat in Tenn. That he will not fight in Tenn. unless he has an equal number of men and choice of the ground.*" The Texans always felt they could defeat an equal number of the enemy "with the choice of ground, and every man felt anxious to go under these promises from Genl Hood." Brown, *Cleburne's Command,* 145.

67. Forrest's cavalry was sent ahead of the infantry, and in a series of skirmishes with Federal cavalry drove the enemy from their positions. As the Confederate army advanced, the Union forces, led by John McAllister Schofield, under fire from Forrest, built entrenchments around Columbia, Tennessee. When Hood's infantry reached Columbia on November 27, Schofield relinquished the town to the Confederates and occupied a stronger position on the north side of the Duck River. James Lee McDonough and Thomas L. Connelly, *Five Tragic Hours: The Battle of Franklin* (Knoxville: The University of Tennessee Press, 1983), 31–34.

68. Cleburne, on November 28, assembled his command and presented what would turn out to be his last speech to his men. Purdue, *Cleburne,* 393.

69. Spring Hill was thirteen miles north of Columbia. At dawn on November 29, Confederate troops began a pontoon crossing of the Duck River above Schofield's position. Hood intended to flank the Federals, seize Spring Hill, and cut the Union army's route to Nashville. Meanwhile, Schofield, anticipating such a move, commenced a withdrawal. Forrest's cavalry reached Spring Hill first and engaged the well-entrenched Federals. Cleburne's division was instructed to take the Columbia Pike which ran south of the village. Uninformed as to the union strength and location, Cleburne was thwarted. He then turned his command toward Spring Hill, but because of confusing and contradicting orders by the

Confederate high command, no assault was made at Spring Hill. During the night, the Federal troops retreated to Franklin. The Confederates were not aware of the withdrawal until the morning of November 30. McDonough, *Five,* 45–53.

70. Ignoring the advice from his generals that a frontal attack on the strong Federal entrenchments would be suicidal, Hood ordered an assault. Granbury's brigade, situated on the Columbia Pike, formed the left wing of Cleburne's division when the Confederates charged the Union defenses. The attack began at 4:00 P.M. as the army band played "Dixie" and "The Bonnie Blue Flag." George Wagner's Union division was overrun without much difficulty. When the Federal outer defense collapsed, the Federal soldiers fled to the rear, closely pursued by the Confederate soldiers. In fact, some of the Southerners reached the enemy's main line as soon as the retreating Union soldiers did. Fighting became extremely heavy as Yankee fire cut enormous holes in the Confederate ranks. Meanwhile, the men in gray, who reached the entrenchments, fought hand-to-hand combat. The two sides continued the struggle until after 9:00 P.M. During the night, the Federal army withdrew toward Nashville.

The Confederate losses at Franklin were very severe. The Civil War was known for battles with high casualty figures, but for an engagement that lasted for only some five hours, the Battle of Franklin was almost without equal. Hood's losses were 1,750 killed, over 4,000 wounded, and 702 taken prisoner. Included among the Confederate dead were five generals, and a sixth would subsequently die from wounds received in the fight. McDonough, *Five,* 61–63, 130, 157, 161; Connelly, *Autumn,* 503–506.

71. Leuschner may have been referring to Bragg's capture of the Union fort at Munfordville, forty miles southwest of Bowling Green, on September 17, 1862. Munfordville was a strategic point where the Louisville and Nashville Railroad crossed. Thomas Lawrence Connelly, *Army of the Heartland,* (Baton Rouge: Louisiana State University Press, 1967), 229; James Lee McDonough, *Stones River: Bloody Winter in Tennessee* (Knoxville: The University of Tennessee Press, 1980), 26–27.

72. The celebration was probably the result of hearing the news that Hood was defeated at Nashville. After the Battle of Franklin, the Confederates pressed onward to Nashville. The Federals had occupied this city for a couple of years and built an elaborate defensive system. When Hood reached Nashville, he constructed a defensive line. He thought that sooner or later the Federal army would leave their entrenchments and attack his army, an alternative that was more acceptable than risking the destruction of the Confederate army with another frontal assault against a well-entrenched enemy. On December 15, Union troops attacked as Hood hoped they would. Fighting occurred throughout the day, eventually ending at sunset. The next day at daybreak the engagement resumed. By midafternoon, the numerically inferior Confederate army, faced with the prospect of annihilation, retreated to Alabama. McCaffrey, *This Band,* 141–147; Stanley F. Horn, *The Decisive Battle of Nashville* (Knoxville: University of Tennessee Press, 1956), 159.

73. At daybreak on April 2, Federal forces advanced against the Confederates at Petersburg. After a determined defense, the Southerners were driven from their trenches. Robert E. Lee sent a message to President Davis telling him that Richmond should be abandoned. The Confederate president received the communique while attending Sunday worship services at St. Paul's Church. Without uttering a word, he left the church and shortly thereafter vacated the city. The government documents that the officials could not take with them were burned. Mob rule swept Richmond, and the city was put to the torch. Order was restored and the flames subdued the following day when Federal troops entered Richmond. On April 4, United States President Abraham Lincoln arrived in the city and visited the former Confederate executive building. As Lincoln walked the streets

118

of Richmond, he was besieged by black people who affectionately reached out to touch him and shouted expressions of gratitude for freeing them from the bonds of slavery. McPherson, *Battle Cry*, 845–847.

74. Lincoln, his wife Mary, Clara Harris, and H. R. Rathbone attended a play, "Our American Cousin," at Ford's Theatre. While viewing the production, actor John Wilkes Booth, undetected, entered the presidential box shortly after 10:00 P.M. and shot the president in the back of the head. The unconscious Lincoln was rushed from the theatre to William Patterson's home, located across the street, and was placed in a bedroom where doctors treated him. The next day, April 15, at 7:22 A.M., Lincoln died. E. B. Long, *The Civil War Day by Day: An Almanac, 1861–1865* (Garden City: Doubleday & Company, Inc., 1971), 675–677.

75. This contraption was known as "Morgan's mule." The prison guards in a demonstration of sarcasm apparently named it for John H. Morgan, a Confederate general who conducted raids into Tennessee, Kentucky, Indiana, and Ohio. A former prisoner of Camp Douglas described the device as "a frame . . . of rough two by four scantling, such as we might call a horse . . . The trestle was made about ten feet high and twenty feet long." J. J. Moore, "Camp Douglas," *Confederate Veteran*, Vol. XI (1903), 270; Warner, *Generals in Gray*, 221.

76. Lee, outnumbered in soldiers by a margin of five or six to one and almost surrounded, surrendered to Ulysses S. Grant on April 9. The two commanding generals met in the home of William McLean at Appomattox. The terms of the capitulation were generous. Lee's troops were permitted to return home "not disturbed by U.S. authority so long as they observe their paroles and the laws in force where they may reside." Grant also allowed the Confederate soldiers who possessed horses to keep them so they could "put in a crop to carry themselves and their families through the next winter." McPherson, *Battle Cry*, 848–849.

77. Leuschner on one of the journal papers wrote Lick Skilled, Panola County, Texas.

78. At Shreveport, Leuschner and the other ex-Confederate soldiers broke up into small traveling parties. They thought it would be easier for them to acquire provisions. Leuschner's companion was a John Myers. (This may have actually been Sebastian Meyer who was captured at the Battle of Nashville and was imprisoned at Camp Douglas.) Myers purchased a mule in an East Texas community with money he apparently acquired while in prison from marketing of gutta-percha rings and some trinkets he had in his possession. After he and Leuschner strapped their blankets, knapsacks, and other items, including a loaded dragoon six-shooter, on the mule's back, Myers and the mule took the lead while Leuschner proceeded to walk behind the animal. No sooner had they taken a few steps, the mule began to buck. With its head between its forelegs, "humped his back into a grecian bend, and made a mad plunge seemingly to the front, rear, and both flanks simultaneously." The wild movement of the animal caused the revolver to fire. "Citizens fled the scene in dismay . . . as the mule turned a bend in the road some three hundred yards distant, the gun firing a salute as he passed from sight." Ultimately, Myers and Leuschner caught and subdued the animal. Petty, *History of Victoria*, 160.

79. After the Sixth Texas surrendered in North Carolina, the Texans divided into small groups and made their way to Greenville, Tennessee, where they boarded trains on May 22 for Nashville. From Nashville, they traveled by steamer to New Orleans. As the vessel pushed southward, Confederate veterans left the steamer whenever it was in the vi-

cinity of their homes. On June 1, the steamboat reached New Orleans. Here the men remained for about ten days before they caught a ship that transported them to Galveston. McCaffrey, *This Band*, 157.

NOTES FOR EPILOGUE

1. Thomas Lawrence Connelly, *Autumn of Glory: The Army of Tennessee, 1862–1865* (Baton Rouge: Louisiana State University Press, 1971), 511–512; John B. Hood, *Advance and Retreat* (Bloomington: Indiana University Press, 1969), 303.

2. Thomas Robson Hay, *Hood's Tennessee Campaign* (Dayton: Press of Morningside Bookshop, 1976), 172–174; James M. McCaffrey, *This Band of Heroes: Granbury's Texas Brigade, C.S.A.* (Austin: Eakin Press, 1985), 146; R. M. Collins, *Chapters From the Unwritten History of the War Between the States* (Dayton: Morningside House, Inc., 1988), 259–268.

3. Hay, *Hood*, 173–174.

4. McCaffrey, *This Band*, 148–149; William E. Stanton to Mary G. Moody, March 30, 1865, William E. Stanton Letters (Eugene C. Barker Texas History Center, University of Texas, Austin; hereafter cited as BTHC); Collins, *Unwritten History*, 274.

5. McCaffrey, *Ibid.*; William E. Stanton to Mary G. Moody, *Ibid.*

6. Connelly, *Autumn*, 517–520.

7. McCaffrey, *This Band*, 149–150; Collins, *Unwritten History*, 273–286.

8. Connelly, *Autumn*, 526–527.

9. Collins, *Unwritten History*, 291–292.

10. Collins, *Ibid.*, 530; Norman D. Brown, ed., *One of Cleburne's Command* (Austin: The University of Texas Press, 1980), 162; Compiled Service Records, Sixth Texas Infantry Regiment, National Archives, Washington, D.C.

11. Brown, *Cleburne's Command*, 163; Irving A. Buck, *Cleburne and His Command* (Dayton: Press of Morningside Bookshop, 1985), 306.

12. McCaffrey, *This Band*, 154; Brown, *Ibid.*, 167.

13. Brown, *Ibid.*, 168; McCaffrey, *Ibid.*, 154.

14. Joseph E. Johnston, *Narrative of Military Operations*, ed. by Frank Vandiver (Bloomington: Indiana University Press, 1959), 410; W. J. Hardee to Pierre G. T. Beauregard, April 18, 1865, *War of the Rebellion: A Compilation of the Official Records of the Union and Confederate Armies*, 128 vols. (Washington, D.C.: Government Printing Office, 1880–1901), Series I, Vol. XLVII, Pt. III, 809 (hereafter cited as *O.R.*).

15. William E. Stanton to Mary G. Moody, March 30, 1865, William E. Stanton Letters (BTHC); J. W. Green to J. E. Johnston, May 7, 1865, *O.R.*, *Ibid.*, 873; Z. B. Vance to Joseph E. Johnston, April 20, 1865, *O.R.*, *Ibid.*, 815.

16. Compiled Service Records, Sixth Texas Infantry Regiment.

Charles A. Leuschner when he was a candidate for county treasurer in 1882.
— Courtesy of Mr. and Mrs. David Bianchi

*Sophia Elizabeth Bischoff Leuschner, wife of Charles A. Leuschner,
circa 1870.*
— Courtesy of Mr. and Mrs. David Bianchi

Emilie Leuschner, mother of Charles A. Leuschner, circa 1870.
— Courtesy of Mr. and Mrs. David Bianchi

Home of Charles A. Leuschner, Victoria, Texas. Leuschner is sitting in chair on the front porch. Circa 1880.

— Courtesy of Robert Bianchi

August F. Leuschner, brother of Charles A. Leuschner, Emilie Leuschner, mother, and Charles A. Leuschner, January 1866.

— Courtesy of Mr. and Mrs. David Bianchi

W. Hasdorf, Charles A. Leuschner, V. Hardy, 1868.

— Courtesy of Robert Bianchi

Funeral procession of Charles A. Leuschner. August Wagner's Silver Coronet Band is in the foreground.

— Courtesy of Mrs. Lela Welder Cliburn

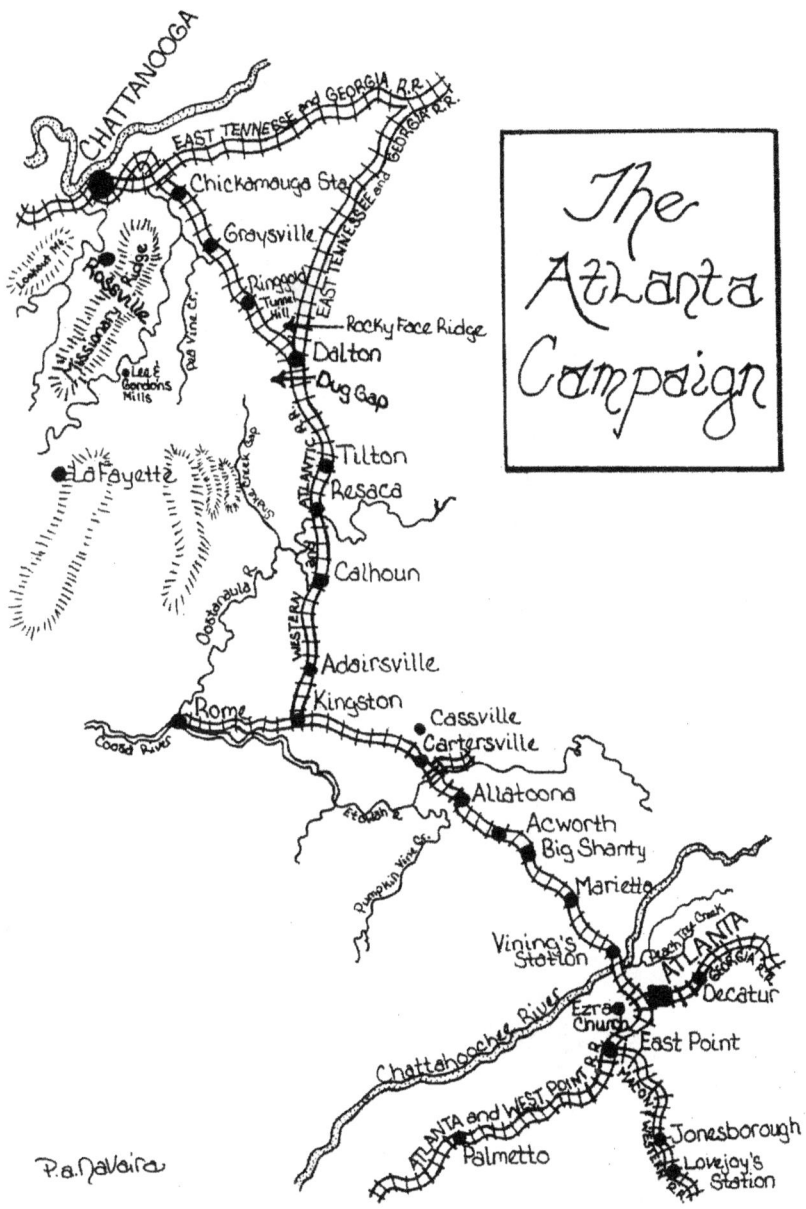

The Atlanta Campaign

CHATTANOOGA

EAST TENNESSE and GEORGIA R.R.

Chickamauga Sta.

Graysville

Ringold
Tunnel Hill

Rocky Face Ridge

Dalton

Dug Gap

Tilton

Resaca

Calhoun

Adairsville

Kingston

Rome

Cassville
Cartersville

Allatoona

Acworth
Big Shanty

Marietta

Vining's Station

ATLANTA

Decatur

Ezra Church

East Point

Jonesborough

Palmetto

Lovejoy's Station

Chattahoochee River

Coosa River

Oostanaula

LaFayette

Lookout Mt.

Rossville

Missionary Ridge

Lee & Gordons Mills

Pea Vine Cr.

EAST TENNESSEE and GEORGIA R.R.

WESTERN and ATLANTIC R.R.

ATLANTA and WEST POINT R.R.

Peach Tree Creek

P.a. Navaira

Entrenchment of Texas troops at Kennesaw Mountain, Georgia.

Entrenchment of Texas troops at Kennesaw Mountain, Georgia.

Ringgold Gap, Georgia.

*Site where Brig. Gen. James Deshler was killed during the
Battle of Chickamauga, Georgia.*

Entrenchment of Texas troops at Pickett's Mill, Georgia.

Entrenchment of Texas troops at Pickett's Mill, Georgia.

Entrenchment of Texas troops at Pickett's Mill, Georgia.

Site of Texas troops at Missionary Ridge, Tennessee.

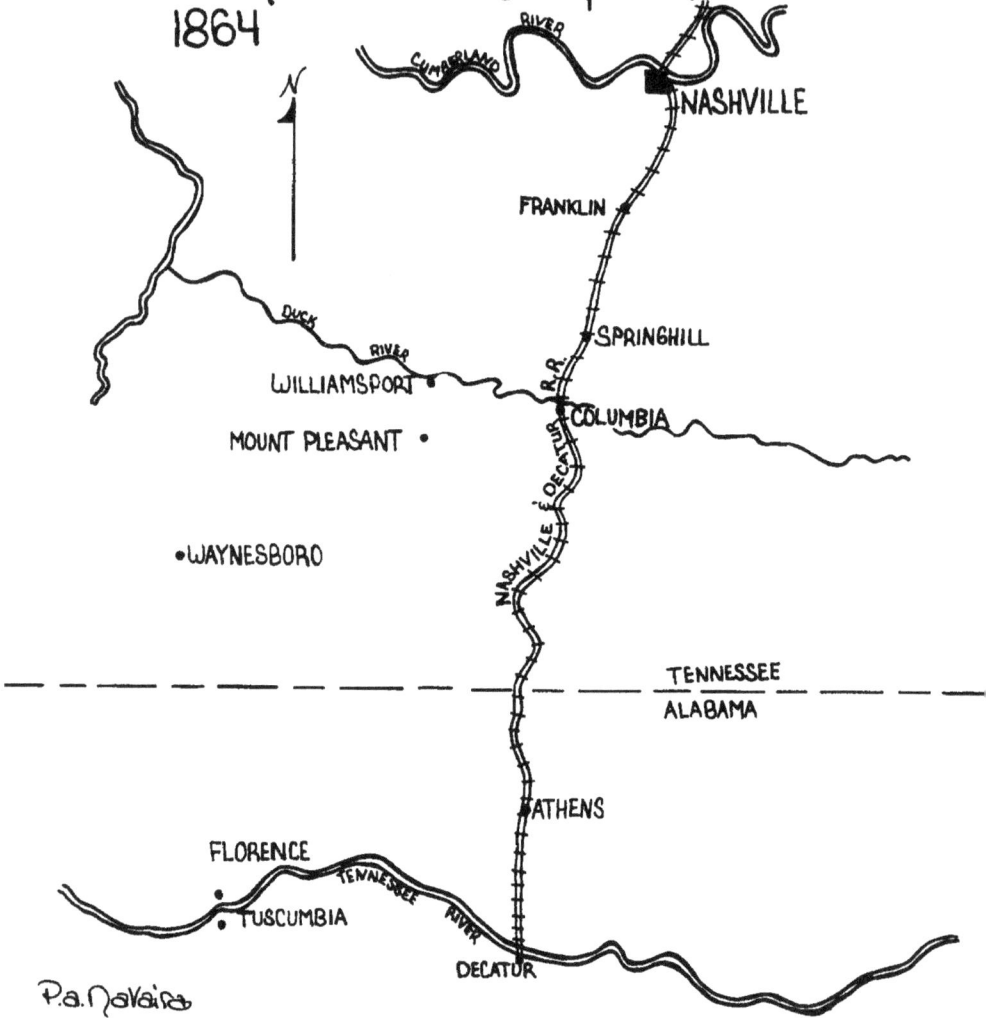

Hood's Nashville Campaign
1864

N

CUMBERLAND RIVER

NASHVILLE

FRANKLIN

DUCK RIVER

SPRINGHILL

WILLIAMSPORT

COLUMBIA

MOUNT PLEASANT

NASHVILLE & DECATUR R.R.

•WAYNESBORO

TENNESSEE
ALABAMA

ATHENS

FLORENCE

TENNESSEE RIVER

TUSCUMBIA

DECATUR

P.a. Navaira

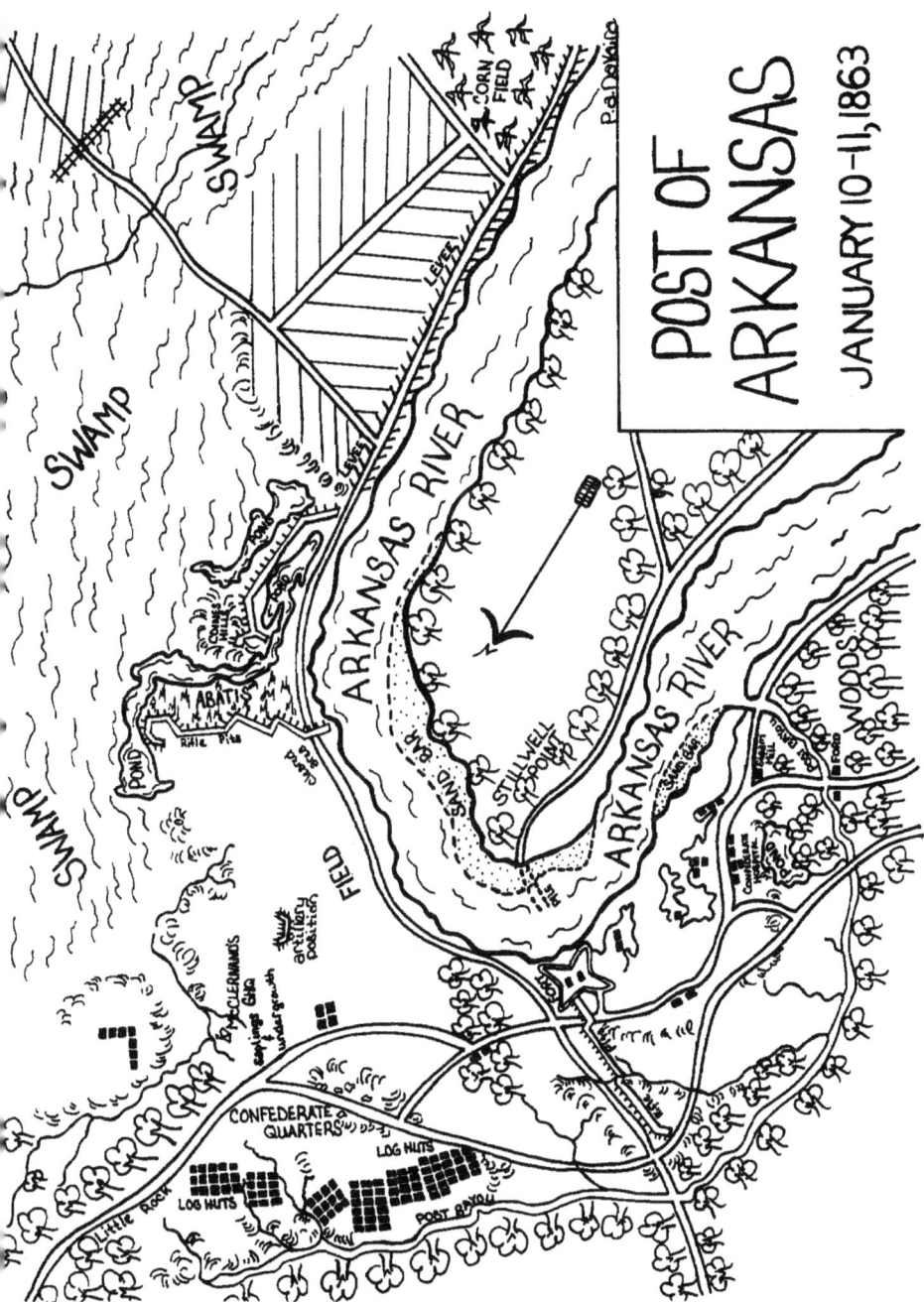

POST OF
ARKANSAS
JANUARY 10-11, 1863

www.ingramcontent.com/pod-product-compliance
Lightning Source LLC
Chambersburg PA
CBHW060436090426
42733CB00011B/2292